Tokyo

city guide

Chris Taylor

Tokyo – city guide
1st edition

Published by
  Lonely Planet Publications
  Head Office: PO Box 617, Hawthorn, Vic 3122, Australia
  Branches: PO Box 2001A, Berkeley, CA 94702, USA
       12 Barley Mow Passage, Chiswick W4 4PH, UK

Printed by
  Colorcraft Ltd, Hong Kong

Photographs by
  Richard I'Anson (RI'A), Robert Strauss (RS),
  Chris Taylor (CT), Tony Wheeler (TW)

  Front cover: Ginza cross walk (Peter Hendrie, The Image
  Bank)
  Front gate fold: Hie-jinja shrine, Akasaka (CT)
  Back cover: Souvenir stall, Asakusa shrine (RI'A)
  Back gate fold: Cherry blossoms (CT)

First Published
  March 1993

National Library of Australia Cataloguing In Publication Data
Taylor, Chris, 1961-
  Tokyo city guide

  1st ed.
  Includes index
  ISBN 0 86442 175 3
  1. Tokyo (Japan) - Guidebooks. I. Title. (Series: Lonely
  Planet city guide).

915.21350449
text & maps © Lonely Planet 1993
Tokyo Subway Network reproduced by kind permission of
Teito Rapid Transit Authority
photos © photographers as indicated 1993

Chris Taylor

Chris Taylor spent his early years in England. He emigrated to Australia with his family in the '70s, and has followed numerous occupations that found him variously on Great Keppel Island, in Mt Isa, London and Tokyo in between extended bouts of travel in Asia. After completing a degree in English Literature and Chinese, Chris joined the Lonely Planet team to work on our phrasebook series. More recently he has worked as a co-author of *Japan - a travel survival kit* and author of Lonely Planet's *Mandarin Chinese phrasebook*. He is currently based in Taiwan, where he works as a freelance writer and translator.

From the Author

Special thanks must go to Wen-Ying for accompanying me on part of my trip to Tokyo, helping me out with the research and keeping me going through the writing process with innumerable cups of coffee. Other special thanks are due to John 'I-love-Mongolia' Ravenscroft for his insider's tips on Tokyo, and Greg Star and Andrew Marshall of the *Tokyo Journal* team for their generosity with material accumulated by the *Tokyo Journal* over its many years of publication in Tokyo. Thank you, too, to Kibo of the Kimi Ryokan for all his help.

The following people deserve a mention for enliving my trip and dropping the occasional tip my way. Andrew Todd BSc was a mine of information, and was extremely forthcoming with his meticulously taken notes. Dave Neiman, Mr Toot (Richard Palmer), Paul from New Zealand, Erik Jorgensen, Barry, Steve, Fiona, Kaaren and Jackie all provided me with useful information and good times.

From the Publisher

Paul Clifton was responsible for the design, cover design, and maps of this book. Vicki Beale supervised the layout. Alan Tiller edited the text and Simone Calderwood saw the book through production.

Thanks to Tom Smallman for editorial guidance and support and to Dan Levin for his computer help.

Warning & Request

Things change – prices go up, schedules change, good places go bad and bad places go bankrupt – nothing stays the same. So if you find things better or worse, recently opened or long since closed, please write and tell us and help make the next edition better.

Your letters will be used to help update future editions and, where possible, important changes will also be included in a Stop Press section in reprints.

We greatly appreciate all information that is sent to us by travellers. Back at Lonely Planet we employ a hard-working readers' letters team to sort through the many letters we receive. The best ones will be rewarded with a free copy of the next edition or another Lonely Planet guide if you prefer. We give away lots of books, but, unfortunately, not every letter/postcard receives one.

Contents

Introduction

Tokyo is such a huge, sprawling city that you could spend a lifetime exploring it. Perhaps, at first glance, it may strike you as a forgettable labyrinth of concrete housing estates and office blocks traversed by overhead expressways and railway lines; a rather soulless city. Nevertheless, it doesn't take long to realise that, like all great cities, Tokyo is a bizarre conundrum, a riddle of contradictions that springs from the tension between the large-scale ugliness and the meticulous attention to detail that meets the attentive eye at every street corner, and the tensions between the frantic rhythms of 20th-century consumer culture and the quiet moments of stillness that are the legacy of other, older traditions.

Tokyo is Japan Inc and the historical lineages that helped to give rise to the Japanese economic success story rolled into one. Nestled beside fashionable Ginza and administrative Nihombashi is the Imperial Palace, with its gardens and photogenic views. In the heart of Akasaka, surrounded by the international-standard hotels, trendy boutiques and high-class eateries, is Hie-jinja Shrine. The downtown regions of Ueno and Asakusa are home to some splendid museums and to bustling Sensō-ji Temple, possibly Japan's liveliest Buddhist temple. And just two hours from Tokyo by train are the historical areas of Kamakura and Nikkō, and the scenic regions of Hakone and Mt Fuji.

While Tokyo sports some of the world's biggest and most lavish department stores, the average Tokyo suburb hasn't fallen prey to supermarket culture – the streets are lined with tiny specialist shops and restaurants, most of which stay open late into the night. Close to the soaring office blocks in the business districts and commercial centres are entertainment quarters – mazes of narrow alleys that blaze with neon by night and offer an intoxicating escape from the '12 hours a day' working regimen that is the lot of Tokyo's surging crowds of office workers. And in the shadow of the overhead expressways and the office blocks exist pockets of another Tokyo – an old wooden house, a kimono shop, a Japanese inn, an old lady in kimono and geta sweeping the pavement outside her home with a straw broom.

As might be expected of a city that has established itself as one of the economic powerhouses of the modern world, what confronts the visitor more than anything else is the sheer level of energy in Tokyo. Rush hour seems to begin with the first train of the day, sometime after 5 am, when drunken hordes of revellers from the night before start the two or three hour journey back to the so-called 'bedroom suburbs' in which they live.

On the busy train lines, even at 11 pm on a Monday evening there is standing room only. Crowds sweep you up, carry you in their wake, and a barrage of noise assaults you at every turn you make. Train drivers assume mysterious, masked voices to advise you of the next stop. On escalators, female announcers, chirping like an exotic species of rare tropical bird, request (oh so very politely) that you stand within the yellow lines. Shops blast their jingles into the crowded streets, traffic lights and vending machines play digitised melodies, and politicians drive the streets in cars specially fitted with loudspeakers, thanking constituents for having voted for them in the recent elections.

In fact, some of the best sights Tokyo has to offer are often not the kind of things you can put in a guidebook. They jump out at you unexpectedly on a crowded street – the woman dressed in traditional kimono buying a hamburger at McDonald's, and the Buddhist monk with an alms bowl, standing serenely in the midst of jostling crowds of shoppers in Ginza. Tokyo is a living city. It may offer the visitor some splendid sights, but it is less a collection of sights than an experience.

Facts about Tokyo

HISTORY

When the first European visitors, Portuguese traders, came to Japan in the 16th century, Tokyo would have seemed an unlikely destination. True, the area then known as Edo was a sizeable fishing town and even had an abandoned castle, but there was little else to indicate that Edo would one day grow to become the capital of Japan and one of the major cities of the world. Strangely enough, however, the Portuguese visitors were to a certain extent instrumental in the concatenation of events that led to Edo usurping Kyoto's position as Japan's traditional seat of imperial power and becoming Tokyo, or 'Eastern Capital'. Some three centuries later, when Commodore Matthew Perry of the US Navy came to Japan with demands that the country open its doors to commerce with the outside world, it was to the erstwhile fishing town of Edo that he came.

Archeologists have named the earliest period of Japanese culture the Jōmon (cord culture) period after the twined rope-like exteriors of pottery that have been discovered dating back as far as 11,000 BC. Although there is evidence that the island was inhabited much longer than this, its people probably originating in waves of migration from Europe, Central Asia, Siberia, China, South-East Asia and even the islands of Polynesia.

Shintō, a religion based on an awe of natural phenomena and the environment, had its origin in the Yayoi period (300 BC to 300 AD). Its preoccupation with elemental forces and the natural gave rise to a simplicity of artistic expression that is still present in the aesthetic values of contemporary Japan. But the most important event in the early history of Japan was the arrival of Buddhism in the 6th century via China and Korea.

Buddhism brought with it a highly evolved system of metaphysics, codes of law and importantly the Chinese writing system, which in turn served as a conduit for the principles of Confucian state craft. By the 8th century, however, the Buddhist clerical bureaucracy had grown to vast proportions, threatening the authority of the imperial administration. In China the response to similar developments had been periodic suppressions and purges of institutionalised Buddhism. In Japan the emperor responded by relocating the capital from Nara

11

and establishing a new seat of imperial power at Heian
(modern-day Kyoto). Heian was, by and large, to serve
as the seat of imperial power through to the Meiji
Restoration and the establishment of Tokyo as Japan's
capital.

Even from Kyoto's early days, a samurai class in the
employ of feudal lords (*daimyō*) was emerging. Much of
Japan's subsequent history has been the record of struggles for power between the daimyō while, for the most
part, the emperor watched impotently from the haven
of Kyoto's Imperial Palace.

By the time the Portuguese arrived in 1543, Japan was
a divided realm of feudal fiefdoms. One of the daimyō,
Nobunaga Oda, was quick to see how the Portuguese
might have a part to play in his ambitions. He saw
Christianity as a potential weapon against the power of
the Buddhist clergy and made ample use of another
import brought by the God-fearing Portuguese – fire-
arms. By the time he was assassinated in 1581, Nobunaga
had united much of central Japan. He was succeeded by
Toyotomi Hideyoshi, who continued the consolidation
process but looked less favourably on the growing Christian movement, subjecting it to systematic persecution.

Hideyoshi's heir, in fine feudal tradition, was defeated
by one of the Toyotomi clan's former allies, Tokugawa
Ieyasu. Tokugawa was a man of vaulting ambition, and
in 1590 he established his *bakufu* (literally 'battle
encampment') or shogunate in Edo, and carried out a
struggle against the Toyotomi clan that culminated in
the Battle of Sekigahara, in which the Toyotomi forces
were routed.

Edo – Tokugawa Rule (1600-1867)

Tokugawa Ieyasu made Edo his permanent base, and in
1603 he was appointed shogun by the Japanese emperor.
One of the most important acts of the Tokugawa administration in their quest to achieve total control of the
country was to implement the so-called *sankin kōtai*
system. This demanded that all daimyō throughout
Japan spend at least one year out of two in Edo. Their
wives and children were to remain in Edo, kept virtual
prisoners of the Tokugawa regime. This combination of
effectively holding families to ransom and the costs of
continually moving backwards and forwards from the
provinces to Edo, made it difficult for ambitious daimyō
to usurp the Tokugawas. Society was made rigidly hierarchical, comprising (in descending order of importance)
the nobility, who had nominal power, the daimyō and

their samurai, the farmers, and finally the artisans and merchants. Class dress, living quarters and even manner of speech were all strictly codified, and interclass movement prohibited. More importantly for the rest of the world, the Tokugawas embarked on a closed-door policy, or *sakoku*, that was to remove Japan from the world stage for nearly three centuries.

These sudden changes led to a rapid growth of the small town of Edo; so much so that by the early 17th century the population had grown to more than one million, making it the largest city in the world. Meanwhile, the hierarchical nature of the society imposed by Tokugawa rule effectively divided Edo into a high city *(Yamanote)* region and a low city *(Shitamachi)* region. The higher Yamanote (literally 'hand of the mountains') area was home to the samurai and daimyō, while the lower orders of Edo society were forced into the low-lying Shitamachi area.

Shitamachi residents lived in squalid conditions; generally in flimsy wooden constructions with earthen floors. Great conflagrations often swept swathes across these shanty-town regions of the city. For the locals, these fires were known as *Edo no hana*, or the 'flowers of Edo'. The cocky bravura of the saying sums up the spirit of Shitamachi – living under circumstances of great privation and in accordance with a social order set by the Tokugawa regime, the residents of Shitamachi produced a flourishing culture that thumbed its nose at social hardships and the strictures of the shogunate. Today, ukiyo-e woodblock prints give us glimpses into this world in which money counted for more than rank, in which actors and artists were the arbiters of style, and in which prostitutes elevated their accomplishments to a level matching those of the ladies of nobility.

To a certain extent, the Yamanote/Shitamachi distinction has lasted through to the present day, with all of the most important administrative and commercial areas of Tokyo lying on or within the ring of the JR Yamanote line.

Another feature of Edo that has left its mark on contemporary Tokyo was the division of the city into towns *(machi)* according to profession. Even today it is possible to stumble across small enclaves that specialise in some particular ware. Most famous are areas such as Jimbō-cho, the bookshop district; Kappabashi, with its plastic food and kitchen supplies; Asakusabashi, with its toy shops; and Akihabara, which now specialises in electronics but which has variously been a bicycle retailing area, an area specialising in domestic household goods and a freight yard.

Meiji Restoration

The turning point for the city of Edo, and indeed for all of Japan, was the arrival of Commodore Matthew Perry's armada of 'black ships' in 1853. Perry's US Navy expedition demanded that Japan open to foreign trade, and other Western powers were quick to follow the US lead in demanding the Japanese open treaty ports and end the long-held Tokugawa policy of seclusion. In 1867, faced with wide-scale antigovernment feeling and accusations that the Tokugawa regime had failed to prepare Japan for the threat of the West, the last Tokugawa shogun resigned and power reverted to Emperor Meiji.

The Meiji Restoration was not an entirely peaceful handover of power. In Edo some 2000 Tokugawa loyalists put up a futile last-ditch resistance to the imperial forces in the brief Battle of Ueno. The struggle took place around Kanei-ji Temple, which, along with Zōjō-ji Temple, was one of the Edo's two mortuary temples for Tokugawa shoguns.

Opposition was short-lived, and in 1868, the emperor moved the seat of imperial power from Kyoto to Edo, renaming the latter Tokyo in the process. Rapid changes followed on the heels of the restoration of imperial

Emperor Meiji

power. In some ways it was less a restoration than a revolution. A crash course of industrialisation and militarisation was embarked upon, and by 1889 Japan had instituted a Western-style constitution. The zeal with which the Japanese embraced this change can be seen in the short space of time required for the country to claim military victories over China (1894-5) and Russia (1904-5).

The changes that were taking place all over Japan could be seen most prominently in the nation's new capital. Tokyo's rapid industrialisation, uniting around the nascent *zaibatsu* (huge industrial and trading combines), drew job seekers from around the country, causing the population to grow rapidly. Western-style buildings began to spring up in fashionable areas such as Ginza, and in the 1880s electric lighting was introduced. However, if the Meiji Restoration and its concomitant changes sounded the death knell for old Edo, there were two more events that were to erase most traces of the old city.

Tokyo Disasters

The Great Kantō Earthquake struck at noon on 1 September, 1923. Unfortunately, it occurred at a time of the day when many of Tokyo's inhabitants were cooking on charcoal or gas stoves. It was less the earthquake itself than the subsequent fires, lasting some 40 hours, that laid waste to the city. In a tragic turn of events, a third of the earthquake's approximately 120,000 fatalities occurred in one savage firestorm that swept through a clothing depot sheltering some 40,000 people.

In true Edo style, reconstruction was embarked upon almost immediately. The spirit in which this was undertaken is perhaps best summed up in Edward Seidensticker's (author of *Tokyo Rising: The City since the Great Earthquake* – Knopf, New York, 1990) observation that during the great fires of the Edo period it was popular wisdom that any business that did not resume trading within three days of being burnt out did not have a future. It has been argued that opportunities were lost in reconstructing the city – that streets might have been widened and that the capital might have been transformed in to something more of a showcase. As it was, Tokyoites were given a second opportunity.

From the accession of Emperor Hirohito and the initiation of Shōwa period in 1926, Japanese society was marked by a quickening tide of nationalist fervour. In 1931 the Japanese invaded Manchuria, and in 1937, having withdrawn from the League of Nations some four years earlier, they embarked on full-scale hostilities with China. By 1940 a tripartite pact with Germany and Italy had been signed and a new order for all of Asia formulated: the 'Greater Asia Co-Prosperity Sphere'. On the 7 September 1941 the Japanese began their expansionist programme in earnest with a surprise attack on Pearl Harbor, attacking the USA, whose forces and regional interests were seen to be the principal hurdle to Japanese domination in the Asia-Pacific region.

Despite initial successes, the war was disastrous for Japan. The earliest bombing raids on Tokyo took place on 18 April 1942, when B-25 bombers carried out a bombing and strafing raid on the city, bringing about 364 casualties. Much worse was to come. Incendiary bombing commenced in March 1944, notably on the nights of the 9th and 10th, when some two-fifths of the city, mainly in the Shitamachi area, went up in smoke and some 70-80,000 lives were lost. The same raids destroyed Asakusa's Sensō-ji Temple, and later raids destroyed Meiji-jingū Shrine. By the time Emperor Hirohito made his famous address to the Japanese people on 15 August 1945 (much of the population had difficulty comprehending the torturously stilted imperial language), much of Tokyo had been decimated and sections of it almost completely depopulated as surely as if it had shared the same fates (atomic-bomb explosions) as Hiroshima and Nagasaki.

Postwar Years

Tokyo's phoenix-like emergence from the ashes of the WW II bombing and its emergence as one of the world's major cities is something of a miracle. Again, Tokyoites did not take the devastation as an opportunity to redesign their city. Rather they rebuilt where the old had once stood.

In the early postwar years, during the US occupation, Tokyo was something of a honky-tonk town. Now respectable areas such as Yūraku-cho were the haunt of the so-called *pan-pan* girls, and areas such as Ikebukuro and Ueno had thriving black-market areas. The vestigial remains of Ueno's black market can be seen in Ameyoko-cho, which is still a lively market, though there is no longer anything particularly black about it.

By 1951, with a boom in Japanese profits arising from the Korean War, Tokyo, especially the central business district, was being rapidly rebuilt. Arguably, Tokyo has never looked back. From the postwar years through to the present, Tokyo has been a city that is continually in the process of reconstructing itself. An absence of two years is enough to observe a difference in the skyline on every stop of the Japanese Railway (JR) Yamanote line. The years of the Korean War also saw serious work commencing on the construction of Tokyo's excellent subway system – the first stretch, from Ueno to Asakusa, had already opened as early as 1927.

Contemporary Tokyo, as befitting the capital of one of the world's economic success stories, is transforming itself into a high-tech wonder. Reclamation plans are afoot for Tokyo Bay and vast construction projects like the Tokyo Metropolitan Government Offices in Shinjuku are rapidly altering the face of the city. Nevertheless, and against all odds considering its cataclysmic history, Tokyo remains a vibrant city with strong roots in the past. Most of all, it is a singular expression of the contemporary Japanese phenomenon, containing a concentration of industry, business, higher education, the arts and a sheer diversity that are rarely found in other capital cities around the globe.

ORIENTATION

Tokyo is a conurbation spreading out across the Kantō Plain from Tokyo-wan Bay. Nevertheless, for visitors, nearly everything of interest lies either on or within the JR Yamanote line, the rail loop that circles central Tokyo.

Tokyo street scene (TW)

In Edo times, Yamanote referred to 'Uptown', the estates and residences of feudal barons, the military aristocracy and other members of the elite of Edo society in the hilly regions of Edo. Shitamachi, or 'Downtown', was home to the working classes, merchants and artisans. Even today the distinction persists, with the areas west of Ginza being the more modernised, housing the commercial and business centres of modern Tokyo, and the areas east of Ginza, centred in Asakusa, retaining more of the character of old Edo.

Essential for finding your way around Tokyo is a map of Tokyo's subway (found in the fold-out section at the back of this book) and the Japan Railways (JR) network. The JR Yamanote line does a loop through Tokyo above ground that takes you through most of the important centres of the city, both Yamanote and, to a lesser extent, Shitamachi. It is actually possible to do the trip very cheaply, because buying a ticket to the next station for Y120 doesn't stop you going in the less direct of the two possible directions and taking in the whole city on the way.

Starting in Ueno, which is where the Keisei Skyliner from Narita Airport is most likely to deposit you, two stops to the south is Akihabara, the discount electronics capital of Tokyo. Continuing in the same direction, you come to Kanda, which is near Tokyo's second-hand bookshop district, Jimbō-cho. The next stops are Tokyo, close to the Imperial Palace and the Imperial Palace East Garden, and Yūraku-cho, a short walk from Ginza. From there, trains continue through to Ebisu, an expensive area that is home to many of Tokyo's foreign embassies and two stops by subway from Roppongi. A little further down the tracks are the teen-oriented, fashionable shopping areas of Shibuya and Harajuku. Another two stops on is Shinjuku, a massive shopping, entertainment and business district. Between Shinjuku and Ueno the train passes through Ikebukuro (really a down-market version of Shinjuku) and Nippori, one of the few areas left in Tokyo where you can find buildings that have survived Tokyo's 20th-century calamities.

Addresses

In Tokyo, as in the rest of Japan, finding a place from its address can be a near impossibility, even for the Japanese. The problem is twofold – firstly, the address is given by an area rather than a street and secondly, the numbers are not necessarily consecutive. To find an address, the usual process is to ask directions and even taxi drivers often have to do this. The numerous local police boxes are there, in part, to give directions. Businesses often include a small map in their advertisements or on their business cards to show their location.

ECONOMY

The Japanese economic phenomenon is one of those rags to riches stories that has left commentators around the world searching for its whys and wherefores. Indeed, Japanese economic success has taken so many people by surprise that there has been a tendency to overemphasise the scale of Japan's achievements. It's worth bearing in mind that while Japanese exports are extremely visible, they still account for less than 10% of the nation's GNP. Japanese industrial and real-estate investment in the USA, a controversial issue, is still on a far smaller scale than similar investment by countries such as Britain and Canada.

Nevertheless, in the short space of 40 or so years, Japan has gone from defeated nation to the world's largest creditor nation. The reason for this success is complex, but to a large part it can be credited to the industriousness of the Japanese, the export orientation of the economy, controls on imports and the shifting fortunes of the yen.

At the end of WW II, the Japanese economy devastated, the MacArthur occupation government took an important step in restoring the competitiveness of Japanese products by drastically devaluing the yen. The extent of this devaluation can be seen in the difference between the prewar value of the yen at Y4 to US$1 and in its 1949 value at Y360 to US$1. The devaluation had the desired results, and for some time Japanese export items filled the cheap and nasty bins of supermarkets around the world.

An important feature of Japanese industry, however, is its far sightedness. Profits were reinvested into research and development, so that by the mid-70s Japan was filing more patents than the USA. The Japanese began to produce goods that were not just cheap but qualitatively competitive as well. Even events such as the unstable oil prices of the 1970s, which vastly increased the costs of Japan's imported energy needs, conspired to cooperate with Japanese export ambitions. It pushed the yen down even further, increasing the competitiveness of Japanese goods, and made the Japanese-developed, fuel-economic automobiles seem suddenly a lot more attractive than they had before.

It was against this background of the increasingly successful export orientation of the Japanese economy that the US Reagan government in 1984 brought about the Yen-Dollar Agreement, internationalising the yen. The theory behind this move was that international trading of the yen would push its value upwards and make Japanese products less competitive. What it did not take into account was Japan's immense reserves of savings and the willingness of Japan's industry to undergo periods of belt tightening and hardship in order to achieve its ends. Rise the yen did, but as the yen doubled in value so did Japanese reserves of savings. And the creative response of Japanese industry was to use the boost in the value of their assets to make investments in which the profits would offset the losses incurred by raising the prices of their exports. Thus, the prices of exports, which theoretically should have doubled as the dollar value of the yen dropped from Y260 to Y130, actually only rose some 20%, and the Japanese economy became even stronger than it had before.

Of course, one of the major reasons for Japan's much vaunted trade surpluses with its trading partners is not merely the volume of its exports but also the low level of its imports. Japanese imports can be largely accounted for by its energy requirements, of which it imports more than 80%. Even with its high population density, Japan still manages by virtue of highly efficient cultivation and protectionist agricultural policies to provide around 70% of its own food requirements. And here lies the rub. The Japanese could save themselves a great deal of money by buying their food elsewhere, but the combination of the LDP (Liberal Democratic Party) agricultural power base and public sentiment that favours Japanese independence when it comes to feeding themselves, serves to keep US rice off the market and to make Australian beef prohibitively expensive.

Altogether there are a great many elements that have gone into making Japan as successful as it is, but the one that can least afford to be overlooked is not so much the Japanese work ethic but the loyalty ethic that manifests itself in an extraordinary commitment to the companies the people work for. Despite the myths that prevail about the Japanese workplace, anyone who has worked in one will attest that they are generally no more efficiently run than their counterparts in the USA or Europe. The important difference is the hours that Japanese workers put in. Japanese work such long hours for their companies, generally choosing to forego their annual leave, that the condition of *karōshi*, or death by overwork, is starting to receive more and more attention in the local newspapers.

The fortunes of the yen, the long-sighted investment of Japanese industry and the hard work of the Japanese have conspired to bring about an odd situation. While the USA blusters about its role as a model to the free world, it is increasingly the Japanese who have the cash to serve as financiers for countries who aspire to the US model. While for visitors to Japan, the combination of the high value of the yen and protective import policies make the country a very expensive place to take a holiday.

POPULATION

Around 11 million of Japan's more than 123 million people live in metropolitan Tokyo. However, these figures are misleading insofar as there are a lot more people than that commuting into Tokyo on a daily basis – more than 22 million people use Tokyo's transportation system every day. The high cost of land and the unavailability of residential space has pushed many Tokyo commuters far out beyond the suburbs into other cities such as Yokohama and Kawasaki.

Like the rest of Japan, the population of Tokyo is extremely homogeneous. True, recent years have seen a vast influx of foreign workers, but still nothing to match the scale of immigration found in European, Canadian,

Japanese children (TW)

USA and Australian cities. More importantly, foreigners in Tokyo are for the most part temporary, and the laws conspire to keep it that way.

The largest group of non-Japanese permanent residents are the Koreans, for outsiders an invisible minority. Indeed, even the Japanese themselves have no way of knowing that someone is of Korean descent if he or she adopts a Japanese name. Nevertheless, Japanese-born Koreans, in some cases speaking no language other than Japanese, are required to carry ID cards at all times and face discrimination in the work place and other aspects of their daily lives.

Other ethnic groups include the Chinese and a wide cross section of foreigners hitching a ride on the Japanese economic juggernaut. Groups such as the Ainu, the original inhabitants of Japan, have been reduced to very small numbers and are today found almost only in reservations on Hokkaidō. You're certainly not likely to run into any in Tokyo, and if you do, chances are they will have well and truly integrated into the Japanese mainstream.

PEOPLE

According to mythology, the origins of the Japanese people stretch back to a time when a pristine world was the playground of the gods. The Japanese themselves are, according to this scheme of things, divine in origin, being the issue of the sun goddess, Amaterasu Omikami.

In more scientific terms, the Japanese are not a distinct race but belong to the Mongoloid group, like the Koreans and Han Chinese. Scholars have also pointed to other evidence that seems to suggest Japan as the terminus for waves of migration from Europe, Siberia and even the Polynesian islands of the Pacific.

Whatever the truth about their ancestry, the Japanese have developed a complex mythology concerning their origins and their uniqueness. To the rest of us, the Japanese curiosity about themselves and their differences is, at times, nothing short of obsessive. One of the more absurd theories gobbled up by a gullible Japanese public is the idea that the Japanese brain is unique. According to this theory, the 'Japanese brain' processes stimuli in the left hemisphere and is thus emotional and harmonious with nature, while the 'Western brain', with its right-hemisphere bias, is more rational and less harmonious. Where this leaves the rest of the world from Inuit to Zulus is not quite clear!

Are the Japanese really different from the rest of us? As usual, the answer is 'yes ... and no'. If the question is whether the Japanese possess characteristics that are theirs alone (a unique brain, singular features, etc) the answer is obviously no. On the other hand, the sum total of the culturally conditioned aspects of the 'typical' Japanese character can only be found in Japan. In short, it is Japanese culture not Japanese nature that is unique.

Of course, all cultures are unique. It is possible to feel the shock of entering another world simply by flying from Hamburg to Paris, or by driving from California to Texas. The difference is one of degree. Adapting from one European culture to another is a lot simpler than adapting from any of the cultures of the West to one of those of the East. In the case of Japan, the differences are such that some fairly major shifts have to take place in Westerners' thinking if they are to make sense of the Japanese world.

The Group

One of the most widely disseminated ideas regarding the Japanese is the importance of the group over the individual. The image of loyal company workers bellowing out the company anthem and attending collective exercise sessions has become a motif that is almost as powerful as Mt Fuji in calling to mind the Land of the Rising Sun.

It's easy to fall into the spirit of these kinds of images and start seeing the business-suited crowds jostling on the JR Yamanote line as so many ant-like members of a collectivised society that has rigorously suppressed individual tendencies. If this starts to happen, it's useful to remember that in some senses the Japanese are no less individual than their Western counterparts. The difference is that, while individual concerns have a place in the lives of the Japanese, their principal orientation remains that of the group. The Japanese do not see their individual differences as defining.

For the Japanese, the individual has its rights and interests, but in the final analysis, these are subsumed under the interests of the group. Indeed the tension between group and individual interests and the inevitable sacrifices demanded of the latter has been a rich source for Japanese art. The Japanese see the tension as one between *honne*, the individual's personal views, and *tatemae*, the views that are demanded by the individual's position in the group. Among other things the group emphasis gives rise to is the important *uchi* (inside) and *soto* (outside) distinction. For the Japanese all things are either inside or outside. Relationships, for example, are generally restricted to those inside the groups to which they belong. Mr Satō, who works with Nissan, will have a social life comprised entirely of fellow Nissan workers and family. Mrs Satō, if she doesn't work (which is likely), will mix with members of the tea ceremony and jazz ballet clubs to which she belongs.

The whole of Japanese social life is an intricate network of these inside-outside distinctions. Of course, this is hardly unique to Japan; it's just that in Japan being inside a group makes such special demands on the individual. Perhaps foreigners who have spent many years in Japan learning the language and who finally throw up their hands in despair, complaining 'you just can't get inside this culture', should remember that to be 'inside' in Japan is to surrender the self to the priorities of the group – and not many foreigners are willing or able to do that.

Men & Women

Japan may be a modern society in many respects, but don't expect the same level of equality between the genders that you have come to expect in your own country. As everything else in Japan, male-female roles and relationships are strictly codified. Although there's some evidence that this is changing, it's definitely doing so at a much slower pace than it has done in the West. Part of the reason is that 'feminism' is a Western import

Crowds at Sensō-ji Temple (CT)

and in a Japanese context tends to have a different resonance than it does in its culture of origin. Even the word feminist has been co-opted so that a Japanese male can proudly declaim himself a *femunisuto* when he means that he is the kind of man that treats a woman as a 'lady', in the Walter Raleigh sense.

Anyone who visits Japan will be struck by the fact that Japanese women, like women in other parts of the world, are subordinate to men in public life. However, both sexes have their spheres of influence, domains in which they wield power. Basically women are *uchi-no* (of the inside) and men are *soto-no* (of the outside). That is, the woman's domain is the home, and here she will take care of all decisions related to the daily running of domestic affairs. The husband, on the other hand, while he may be the breadwinner, will still hand over his pay packet to his wife, who will then allocate the money according to domestic expenses and provide the husband with an allowance for his daily needs.

In public life, however, it is the men who rule supreme. In this world it is the role of women to listen, to cater to male needs and often to serve as vents for male frustrations. As any Western woman who tries hostessing will discover, women are expected to help men bear the burden of their public-life responsibilities not by offering advice – that would be presumptuous in the extreme – but by listening and making the appropriate sympathetic noises at the right moments.

The codification of women's roles translates over to the marriage market, a perception which has an impact on women's career options – it is widely perceived that they should be married by the age of 25, and in Japan married women are expected to resign from their work. This cut-off point of 25 years is a very serious one. Women who remain unmarried after this age are frequently alluded to as 'Christmas cake', this being a useless commodity after the 25th. By the time a woman is 26 and up, she will be regarded with suspicion by many men, who will wonder what imperfection stood in the way of her being snatched up earlier.

Perhaps most disturbing for Western women visiting Japan is the way in which women feature in so much of the male-oriented mass culture. It's not so much women being depicted as sex objects, which most Western women would at least be accustomed to in their own countries, but the fact that in comic strips, magazines and movies, women are so often shown being brutalised, passive victims in bizarre, sado-masochistic rites.

While these fantasies are disturbing, it is possible to take refuge in the thought that they *are* fantasies, and women are a great deal safer in Japan than they are in other parts of the world. Harassment, when it does occur, is usually furtive, occurring in crowded areas such as trains. However, with direct confrontation, almost all Japanese men will be shamed into withdrawing the groping hand.

Meeting the Japanese

The Japanese have a reputation as being hard to get to know, but even on a short visit to Tokyo there are opportunities to meet them. Perhaps the easiest are those in a more formal setting, such as the conversation lounge or via the home-visit system (described later in this section). Alternatively, just going out for a drink somewhere, usually gives you an opportunity to meet locals in a more relaxed setting (see the Entertainment chapter later in this guide).

Bear in mind when you meet Japanese that they are generally a shy people (unless they've been drinking), and fearful of making embarrassing mistakes. If you need to ask directions, try to appear calm and relaxed, and smile as you do so.

Another thing that should be considered if you are socialising or working with Japanese is Japanese codes of etiquette. With a little sensitivity, however, there is little danger of making a grave faux pas. If you are visiting a Japanese home, it is usual to sit on the floor. Japanese sit with their feet tucked under them in a slouched back kneeling position, and unless you have had a lifetime of training it very quickly becomes excruciatingly painful. If you have to, stretch your legs out discreetly, but be careful not to point your feet at anyone.

When Japanese meet it is customary to bow. Actually, the depth of your bow depends on the status of the person you are meeting. For Westerners, a slight inclination and a bob of the head will do. Usually an exchange of business cards follows this (so it's a good idea to bring some along or have some printed up when you arrive). It's good form to accept cards with both hands and examine them before tucking them away into your wallet.

Finally, a major difference between Japanese and Westerners is that the Japanese do not make a virtue out of being direct. The Japanese tend to feel their way around problems and sound things out in ways that to many foreigners seem impossibly vague. It's a good idea to avoid the use of straight talk when socialising with the Japanese. For them it will be embarrassingly vulgar and is more likely to elicit a nervous giggle than a candid exchange of views.

Home Visit System The home-visit system is publicised in JNTO pamphlets and gives visitors to Tokyo the opportunity to visit a Japanese family in their home. Visits take place in the evening and, while dinner is usually not served, the hosts will often provide tea and sweets. It is polite to bring a small gift with you when you visit to show your appreciation of your hosts' thoughtfulness and hospitality.

Home visits can be organised by the Tokyo branch of the home visit service (☎ 3502-1461). There is also a service in Yokohama (☎ 045-641-5824).

Clubs & Conversation Lounges No matter what your interests are, there will be a club for it in Tokyo. Not surprisingly, clubs have sprung up to give Japanese the opportunity to meet and talk to foreigners. Generally, activities centre around a lounge or a coffee shop, entry to which costs foreigners little or nothing – it is the Japanese who pay.

Mickey House (☎ 3209-9686) is an 'English bar' that offers free coffee and tea as well as reasonably priced beer and food. Entry is free for foreigners and it's a good place to meet young Japanese as well as long-term gaijin residents. It's a lively place with a fairly regular crowd, but it is definitely not a closed scene. This can be a good place to make contacts and pick up tips on living in Tokyo. It's close to the JR Takadanobaba station. Give them a ring any evening of the week for instructions as to how to get there from the station.

Other clubs with similar programmes include the Japan International Friendship Club (☎ 3341-9061) and Cornpopper (☎ 3715-4473), which has different activities on different nights of the week. Give them a ring for the schedule.

ARTS & CULTURE

The arts in Japan have a long and rich history, and like so many aspects of Japanese culture, have been enriched through the integration of outside influences. In the visual arts, for example, early forms of Buddhist narrative painting found their origins in China and Korea; indeed the artists themselves were often intinerant painters from these countries.

The influence of Chinese art on the Japanese visual arts is particularly obvious. Much of the fascination for students of Japanese art derives from the tension of transforming Chinese forms in keeping with Japanese sensibilities and native traditions. From the beginning of the Meiji Restoration in 1867, the West also began to exert a powerful influence on the Japanese arts. Modern Japanese art galleries often display influences of major Western artistic movements, from expressionism to postmodernism.

The traffic has not been all one-way, however. *Ukiyo-e*, or 'pictures from the floating world', while owing something to Chinese innovations such as multi-colour wood-block printing, are distinctively Japanese in their execution and subject matter. By the 1750s ukiyo-e, with its colourful and often bawdy depictions of the Edo entertainment world, had become very popular, and

Temple entrance (CT)

before too long caught the attention of Western artists such as Toulouse-Lautrec and Van Gogh.

Despite the influence of powerful cultural and artistic traditions overseas, in the Japanese arts, there are distinctive Japanese characteristics. It has been argued, for example, that the walkman is as essentially Japanese in its conception and design as the tea ceremony: the purpose of both is to create a personal, contemplative space. The emphasis on the inner private world as a retreat from the rough and tumble of the outer world has led to the utilisation of private space.

This focus on space can also be found in the creation of minature landscapes, as in *bonsai*, *bonkei* and *ikebana*. Bonsai minaturises trees through careful pruning, while bonkei achieves the same with an entire landscape. Ikebana is promoted as a requisite skill for the cultivated young lady, but again it has a stress on personal contemplation. Ikebana is frequently featured in the tea ceremony and the apparently random arrangement of flowers invites the viewer to find a symbolic meaning of the relationships between humans, the earth and the heavens.

In the *chanoyu*, or the tea ceremony, it is possible to find an expression of all these peculiarly Japanese qualities. The most informative influence on chanoyu came from Sen no Rikyū (1521-91). He was responsible for transforming the tea ceremony into an art form. He believed the rough and irregular setting and utensils used in the ceremony reflected the asymmetry of the natural world. This was in contrast to the delicate designs and stylised perfection of Chinese ceramics which would disturb the mind from the quiet contemplation that chanoyu sought to achieve.

Of course there is much more to the arts in Japan than this. It is also possible to find examples of grand public displays that contradict the logic of many Japanese qualities. The temples of Nikkō, for example, are far from understated. The buildings are decorated in a riot of colour, and the only deliberate 'mistakes' were not the result of an aesthetic of imperfection but of a fear that the perfection of the work would arouse the envy of the gods. But these *are* public displays, often owing much to Chinese influences, and are in a different category to most Japanese art forms.

Tokyo is an excellent place to take a look at some of Japan's traditional performing arts such as kabuki and nō, and, at the right time of year, to catch up with a sumō match. For information on where to catch up with any of these while you're in Tokyo, see the Entertainment chapter later in this guide.

Kabuki

The origins of kabuki lie in the early 17th century when it was known as *kabuku odori*, which may loosely be translated as avant-garde dance. Its first exponent was a maiden of a Shintō shrine, who developed the dance as a means to raise funds for the shrine. It quickly caught on and was soon being performed with prostitutes in the leading roles. With performances plumbing ever greater depths of lewdness, the Tokugawa government moved to ban females from the kabuki stage. The young ladies of easy virtue were promptly replaced by attractive young men of no less availability, and the exasperated authorities once again issued a decree; this time ordering that kabuki roles be undertaken by older males.

It was a move that had a profound effect on kabuki, in the sense that roles played by these older male actors demanded great artistry in order be brought off credibly. The result was that, while remaining a popular art form that at least in part gave itself to popular themes, the kabuki also metamorphosed into a serious art form, with the more famous of its practitioners being the stuff of which legends are made.

Kabuki

Kabuki is a theatre of the larger than life gesture and spectacle, and as such employs opulent sets, a boom-crash Japanese-style orchestra, and a ramp through the audience to the stage that allows important actors to get the most mileage out of their melodramatically stylised entrances and exits. Initially it featured plebeian versions of nō classics, but as this displeased the Tokugawa government kabuki was compelled to develop a canon of its own. It did so drawing on disparate themes, both modern and historical; the latter being represented by feudal tragedies of tormented loyalties and the struggles between duty and inner feelings that produced a body of work on the theme of love suicides.

One thing worth bearing in mind if you get to see a performance of kabuki while you are in Tokyo is that unlike the theatre of the West, kabuki is not a theatre in which the playwright is the applauded champion. The entire kabuki spectacle is a vehicle for the genius of the actor and his poses, gestures and animated actions. It is the actor who rules supreme and who is remembered long after the writer who put the words in his mouth has been forgotten.

Nō

Nō is an older form of theatre than kabuki, dating back some 600 years. It seems to have evolved as a cross-pollination between both indigenous Shintō related dance and mime traditions, and dance forms that had their origin elsewhere in Asia. It was adopted as a courtly performing art, and in this capacity underwent numerous refinements. The result was an essentially religious theatre; its aesthetic codes defined by the austerities, the minimalism of Zen. Unlike the spectacle of kabuki, the power of nō lies in the understatement. And in this respect – its use of masks as a mode of expression and the bleak emptiness of the sets, directing all attention to the performers – nō has been a form of Japanese theatre that has fascinated Western artists searching for a more elementally powerful theatre with which to express themselves. Of these, perhaps the most famous is W B Yeats.

One of the more interesting aspects of nō is the formalised structure of its plays. Two performers alone are vital to its business – the one who watches (*waki*) and the one who acts (*shite*). Remembering that nō is a theatre of masks, it is the role of the one who watches to, as it were, demask the one who acts. The reason is that the one who acts is not who he or she seems. Usually the one who acts is a ghost whose spirit has lingered on in a particular place because of some tragedy that took place in the past. The recognition, the demasking by the one who watches, gives way to the second act in which the one who acts dances a re-enactment of the tragedy.

Whether this is a kind of cathartic liberation or whether it is a sorrowful celebration of the lingering pain of the tragedy is partly dependent on whether it is a happy story or not. It also depends partly on how one interprets the sometimes quite bizarre but often spellbinding proceedings of the nō performance.

Sumō

Sumō is a sport that is rooted in tradition. It was originally performed in Shintō shrines as a form of divination, but was already popular as a sport in the 6th century. The rules are simple: the victor causes any part of his opponent's body other than his feet to touch the ground outside the ring. There are no rounds – it is all over often in a matter of seconds – and there are no weight classes – they are all *big*.

Sumō's Shintō origins can still be seen in the shrine-like roof that hangs over the ring and in the brightly attired wizard-like figure of the referee, or *gyōji*. The latter comes complete with a dagger which in times past he might have used to commit *seppuku* (ritual suicide) if he made a bad refereeing decision. Other Shintō related features are the purifying scattering of salt into the ring that precedes the clashing of titans.

Although sumō wrestlers look like enormous flabby infants, their physiques are actually the products of long and intensive training. Part of the training, of course, is eating big. *Chanko-nabe*, a special stew with weight-accruing properties, is a staple of the sumō diet. But the rest of the training is very physical, and all that flab, rippling like jello as two sumō wrestlers locked in mutual obesity paw frantically at each other, conceals a lot of muscle. Just ask a martial arts exponent whether he or she would like to tackle a sumō, and most would agree that it would be a very dangerous proposition.

People seeing sumō for the first time might wonder why they do it. The reasons are simple. A successful sumō, particularly one who joins the top 50 in the *sekitori* status, will have fame and a very comfortable living. Those who reach grand champion, or *yokozuna*, status are made for life and often achieve a kind of cult status during their careers. And for those who don't succeed? Well, it's off to weight watchers and perhaps a career as a furniture removalist.

Sumo wrestlers (RI'A)

Cultural Centres

Libraries There are quite a number of libraries with collections of material in European languages scattered around Tokyo. The British Council (☎ 3235-8031) in Iidabashi has a good collection of books and magazines. It's open from 10 am to 8 pm and is closed weekends. Along similar lines, the American Center (☎ 3436-0901) has a library in Shiba-kōen. It's open from 10.30 am to 6.30 pm and is closed on weekends.

The Japan Foundation Library (☎ 3263-4504) is open only to foreigners and has a collection of some 30,000 English books. It's open from 10 am to 5 pm and is closed Mondays and Sundays. For a wide selection of magazines from around the world, check the Ginza section of the Things to See chapter for information on the World Magazine Gallery.

Church Services There are places of worship around Tokyo where you can attend services in English. Catholic services are held at St Anselm's Benedictine Church (☎ 3491-6966) in Meguro and the Franciscan Chapel Centre (☎ 3401- 2141) in Roppongi. St Alban's (☎ 3431-8534) in Kamiyacho has Anglican services on Sunday at 8 and 10 am. The Tokyo Baptist Church (☎ 3461-8439) also has services on Sunday.

RELIGION

In many respects, the term religion can be misleading for Westerners when it is applied to either China or Japan. In the West and in the Islamic East, religion is connected to the idea of an exclusive faith. Religions in Japan, for the most part, are not exclusive of each other. They tend to mingle and find expression in different facets of daily life, their utility in different daily needs.

Shintō (the native religion of Japan), Buddhism (a much-travelled foreign import originating in India), Confucianism (a Chinese import that some will argue is not a religion), and even Christianity all play a role to some extent in Japanese social life, and are defining in some way of the Japanese world view. And if you're skeptical of the inclusion of Christianity, you need only to attend a Japanese wedding ceremony to see that certain Christian rituals have been slotted in quite comfortably with other more traditional elements.

Ideally the Japanese religions should not be considered one by one as separate entities but as disparate elements that are part of a complex whole. Nevertheless, for visitors to Tokyo it is useful to have some background understanding of the differences between Shintō and Buddhism, as most of the traditional sights will either be Shintō shrines or Buddhist temples.

Shintō

Shintō is an indigenous religion that gained its name 'the way of the gods' to distinguish it from Buddhism, a later import. It seems to have grown out of an awe for manifestations of nature that included the sun, water, rock formations, trees and even sound. All such manifestations were believed to have their god *(kami)*, an outlook that gave rise to a complex pantheon of gods and a rich mythology. Certain sites, however, were designated as particularly sacred, and on these shrines were erected. Important to Shintō is the concept of purification before entering such sacred domains. Even today, as you are about to enter a Shintō shrine, you will see a long trough filled with running water in which you are expected to wash your hands and swill out your mouth with the bamboo scoops provided.

Shintō shrines are generally far more serene places than Buddhist temples, though you will often find examples of both almost next door to each other. Compare the solemnity of Meiji-jingū and Yasukuni-jinja shrines with the bawdy carnival atmosphere that prevails at the Buddhist Sensō-ji Temple in Asakusa.

Buddhism

The founder of Buddhism was Siddhartha Gautama. He was born around 563 BC at Lumbini on the border of present-day Nepal and India. Born of a noble family, he questioned the comforts of his existence and for many years led the life of an ascetic. He was to turn his back on this life too. After a period of intense meditation, he achieved 'enlightenment', which is the essence of Buddhahood.

Buddhism has been greatly complicated by the fact that it has fractured into a vast number of schools of thought. Basically these can be divided into the Hinayana (Lesser Vehicle) and the Mahayana (Greater Vehicle) schools, the former emphasising personal enlightenment and the latter seeking the salvation of all beings. Nevertheless, at the heart of all Buddhism are the teachings of Gautama, the original Buddha.

Buddha's thought was necessarily rooted in Aryan metaphysics and logic, and the premise on which Buddhism rests is to a large extent one of cause and effect. Buddha observed that all of life is suffering, and determined that the cause of this suffering is desire. This desire expresses itself in more than simply the sensual; indeed, the totality of life is desire. Even basic needs, after all, might be seen as a manifestation of the desire or will to live. The concept of nirvana, or enlightenment, then, is not a blissful paradise but an extinction of desire, an exit from the wheel of suffering.

Buddhism in Japan, like China, belongs to the Mahayana school, and has again since its arrival fissured into a great number of smaller schools of thought, the most famous of which in the outside world is Zen. Buddhism in its purest Hinayana form is difficult to reconcile with its popular forms in Japan. Despite Buddhism's place in Japanese culture, there seems little sign that the Japanese are about to cast off their worldly desires and become a nation of fasting monks and nuns. A major part of the reason for this lies in Buddhism's offers of salvation and relief from suffering. In the popular imagination, Buddhist saints (usually Bodhisattvas – those who have postponed their own enlightenment in order to help others along the same path) have become figures to be appealed to for help in even the most worldly of desires – establishing a new soapland (massage parlour) for example.

The end result is that Buddhism, with some crucial differences, provides spiritual help for the average person on the street in much the same way that popular Christianity does in the West. Shintō, with its mythological

Jizō (CT)

associations with the Japanese imperial family, Japanese tradition and the essence of Japaneseness, is embodied in shrines that demand a reverent homage. Buddhism, on the other hand, watches out for the common person, and its temples are the place to go to pray for that long-awaited promotion or for luck in the upcoming examinations.

LANGUAGE

Visitors to Tokyo should not have too many language problems. There are plenty of people around who speak English and who are willing to help. Also, there are a lot more English signs around than there were in the past.

The biggest problem for visitors to Japan who have never studied Japanese is the writing system. Japanese has one of the most complex writing systems in the world, using three different scripts (four if you include the increasingly used Roman script *romaji*). The most difficult of the three, for foreigners and Japanese alike, is *kanji*, the ideographic script developed by the Chinese. There are some 2000 of these Chinese characters in daily usage.

For visitors who would like to make an incursion into the written language before arriving, it would make more sense to learn *hiragana* and *katakana*. There are 48 characters in each, the former being used for native

Japanese words and for verb endings, and the latter for
foreign loan words such as *kōhi* (coffee) and *keiki* (cake)
– very useful for menus.

The romaji used in this book follows the Hepburn
system of romanisation, with macrons being used to
indicate long vowels. Most place names will use a combination of romaji and English – the romaji suffix will in
most cases be separated from the proper name by a
hyphen and followed by its English translation. For
example: Sensō-ji Temple (*ji* is the romaji word for
temple); Izu-hantō Peninsula (*hantō* means peninsula)
and Meiji-jingū Shrine (*jingū* means shrine).

The following selection of Japanese phrases will see
you through some of the more common situations faced
by travellers to Tokyo. For a more comprehensive guide
to making yourself understood in Japan, get a copy of
Lonely Planet's *Japanese Phrasebook*. This book has all the
phrases you need for travelling in Japan, charts for
learning hiragana and katakana, and Japanese script for
all the phrases used in the book.

Pronunciation

a	as the 'a' in 'apple'
e	as the 'e' in 'get'
i	as the 'i' in 'macaroni'
o	as the 'o' in 'lot'
u	as the 'u' in 'flu'

Vowels that have a bar (or macron) over them (ā, ē, ō, ū)
are pronounced the same as standard vowels except that
the sound is held twice as long.

Consonants are generally pronounced as in English,
with the following exceptions:

f	this sound is produced by pursing the lips and blowing lightly
g	as the 'g' in 'goal' at the start of a word; as the 'ng' in 'sing' in the middle of a word
r	more like an 'l' than an 'r'

Greetings & Civilities

The all-purpose title *san* is used after a name as an
honorific, the equivalent of Mr, Miss, Mrs and Ms.

Good morning.
   ohayō gozaimasu
   おはようございます

Good afternoon.
konnichiwa
こんにちは

Good evening.
konbanwa
こんばんは

How are you?
o-genki desuka?
お元気ですか？

Fine. (appropriate response)
okagesamade
おかげさまで

Goodbye.
sayōnara
さようなら

See you later.
ja mata
じゃまた

Excuse me.
sumimasen.
すみません

I'm sorry.
gomen nasai
ごめんなさい

Thank you.
arigatō gozaimasu
ありがとうございます

Please. (when offering something)
dōzo
どうぞ

Please. (when asking for something)
onegai shimasu
お願いします

OK.
kekko desu
けっこです

Yes.
hai
はい

No.
iie
いいえ

No. (literally 'different' – used for disagreeing).
chigaimasu
違います

No. (more conciliatory).
chotto chigaimasu
ちょっと違います

Small Talk

I don't understand.
wakarimasen
わかりません

Please say it again more slowly.
motto yukuri mō ichidō itte kudasai
もっとゆっくりもう一度言って下さい

What is this called?
kore wa nan-to yomimasuka?
これは、何とよみますか？

My name is...
watashi no namae wa...desu
私の名前は…です

What's your name?
o-namae wa nan desuka?
お名前は何ですか？

Where are you from?
dochira kara irasshaimasuka?
どちらからいらっしゃいますか？

Is it OK to take a photo?
sasshin o toru ga, ii desuka?
写真を取るがいいですか？

Getting Around

How much is the fare to...?
...made ikura desuka?
…までいくらですか？

Does this train go to...?
kono densha wa...e ikimasuka?
この電車は…へ行きますか？

Is the next station...?
tsugi no eki wa...desuka?
次の駅は…ですか？

Will you tell me when we get to...?
... ga ketara oshiete kudasaimasuka?
…がけたら教えて下さいますか？

Where is the...exit?
...guchi wa doko desuka?
…口はどこですか？

east/west/north/south
higashi/nishi/kita/minami
東/西/北/南

Do you have an English subway map?
eigo no chikatetsu no chizu ga arimasuka?
英語の地下鉄の地図がありますか？

Where is this address please?
kono jūsho wa doko desuka?
この住所はどこですか？

Excuse me, but can you help me please?
sumimasen ga, watashi o tasukeru ga yoroshi desuka?
すみませんが、私を助けるがよろしですか？

Food

Do you have an English menu?
eigo no menyū ga arimasuka?
英語のメニューがありますか？

I'm a vegetarian.
watashi wa saishoku-shugisha desu
私は菜食主義者です

Do you have any vegetarian meals?
saishoku-shugisha no yō no ryōri wa arimasuka?
菜食主義者の用の料理はありますか？

What do you recommend?
o-susume wa nan desuka?
お勧めは何ですか？

Please bring the bill.
o-kanjō onegaishimasu
お勘定お願いします

Shopping

How much is this?
kore wa ikura desuka?
これはいくらですか？

It's too expensive.
taka-sugimasu
高過ぎます

I'll take this one.
kore o itadakemasu
これをいただけます

I'm just looking.
miru dake desu
見るだけです

Emergencies

Help me!
tasukete!
助けて！

Watch out!
ki o tsukete!
気をつけて！

Thief!
dorobō!
どろぼう！

Call the police!
keisatsu o yonde kudasai!
警察を叫んで下さい！

Call a doctor!
isha o yonde kudasai!
医者を叫んで下さい！

Numbers

0	*zero*	○
1	*ich*	一
2	*ni*	二
3	*san*	三
4	*yon/shi*	四
5	*go*	五
6	*roku*	六
7	*nana/shichi*	七
8	*hachi*	八
9	*kyū/ku*	九
10	*jū*	十
11	*jūichi*	十一
12	*jūni*	十二
13	*jūsan*	十三
14	*jūyon*	十四
20	*nijū*	二十
21	*nijūichi*	二十一
30	*sanjū*	三十
100	*hyaku*	百
200	*nihyaku*	二百
223	*nihyaku nijūsan*	二百二十三
1000	*sen*	千
5000	*gosen*	五千
10,000	*ichiman*	一万
20,000	*niman*	二万
100,000	*jūman*	十万
1,000,000	*hyakuman*	百万

Facts for the Visitor

VISAS & EMBASSIES

Tourist and business visitors of many nationalities staying less than 90 days are not required to obtain a visa. Visits involving employment or other remunerated activity require an appropriate visa.

Japanese Embassies & Consulates

Australia
    112 Empire Circuit, Yarralumla, Canberra, ACT 2600 (☎ (06) 733-244).
    There are also consulates in:
    Brisbane (☎ (07) 221-5188),
    Melbourne (☎ (03) 867-3244),
    Perth (☎ (09) 321-3455),
    Sydney (☎ (02) 231-3455).
Canada
    255 Sussex Drive, Ottawa, Ontario K1N 9E6 (☎ 236-8541).
    There are also consulates in:
    Edmonton (☎ 422-3752),
    Montreal (☎ 866-3429),
    Toronto (☎ 363-7038),
    Vancouver (☎ 684-5868),
    Winnipeg (☎ 943-5554).
France
    7 Ave Hoche, 75008-Paris (☎ 47-66-02-22)
Germany
    Bundeskanzlerplatz, Bonn-Center HI-701, D-5300 Bonn 1 (☎ (0228) 5001)
Hong Kong
    25th Floor, Bank of America Tower, 12 Harcourt Rd, Central (☎ 5-221184)
Ireland
    22 Ailesbury Rd, Dublin 4 (☎ 69-40-33)
Israel
    Asia House, 4 Weizman St, 64 239 Tel-Aviv (☎ 03-257-292)
New Zealand
    7th Floor, Norwich Insurance House, 3-11 Hunter St, Wellington 1 (☎ 731-540).
    There is also a consulate in Auckland (☎ 34-106).
Singapore
    16 Nassim Rd, Singapore 1025 (☎ 235-8855)
Thailand
    1674 New Petchburi Rd, Bangkok 10310 (☎ 252-6151)

UK
   43-46 Grosvenor St, London W1X OBA (☎ (071) 493-6030)
USA
   2520 Massachusetts Ave, NW Washington DC 20008-2869
   (☎ (202) 939-6800).
   There are also consulates in:
   Anchorage (☎ (907) 279-8428),
   Atlanta (☎ (404) 892-2700),
   Boston (☎ (617) 973-9772),
   Chicago (☎ (312) 280-0400),
   Honolulu (☎ (808) 536-2226),
   Houston (☎ (713) 652-2977),
   Kansas City (☎ (816) 471-0111),
   Los Angeles (☎ (213) 624-8305),
   New Orleans (☎ (504) 529-2101),
   New York (☎ (212) 371-8222),
   Portland (☎ (503) 221-1811),
   San Francisco (☎ (415) 777-3533).

Reciprocal Visa Exemptions

Many visitors who are not planning to engage in any
remunerative activities while in Japan are exempt from
obtaining visas. Stays of up to six months are permitted
for citizens of Austria, Germany, Ireland, Mexico, Switzerland and the UK. Stays of up to three months are
permitted for citizens of Argentina, Belgium, Canada,
Denmark, Finland, France, Iceland, Israel, Italy, Malaysia, Netherlands, New Zealand, Norway, Singapore,
Spain, Sweden, the USA and a number of other countries.

Visitors from Australia and South Africa are among
those nationals requiring a visa. This is usually issued
free, but passport photographs are required and a return
or onward ticket must be shown.

Working Holiday Visas

Australians, Canadians and New Zealanders between
the ages of 18 and 25 (the age limit can be pushed up to
29) can apply for a working holiday visa. This visa
allows a six-month stay and two six-month extensions.
The visa's aim is to enable young people to travel exten-
sively during their stay, and for this reason employment
is supposed to be part time or temporary, although in
practice many people work full time. Those arriving on
a working holiday visa may like to contact the Japan
Association for Working Holiday Makers (☎ 3389-0181)
for information about working in Japan.

A working holiday visa is much easier to obtain than
a working visa and is popular with Japanese employers
as it can save them a lot of inconvenience. Applicants

must have the equivalent of A$2000 of funds and an onward ticket from Japan, or A$3000 in funds without the ticket.

Working Visas

The ever-increasing number of foreigners clamouring for a role in the Asian economic miracle has prompted much stricter visa requirements for Japan. New immigration laws introduced in June 1990 designate legal employment categories for foreigners and specify standards of experience and qualifications.

A change of visa status from temporary visitor to working visa will usually be denied. In cases where an employer is willing to sponsor you, it is necessary for the employer to obtain a Certificate of Eligibility. Following this, it is necessary for you to leave the country with the certificate and apply for a working visa at a foreign visa office.

Visa Extensions

It has become quite difficult to extend visas. With the exception of nationals of the few countries whose reciprocal visa exemptions allow for stays of six months (see the previous Reciprocal Visa Exemptions section), 90 days is the limit for most people. Those who do apply should provide two copies of an Application for Extension of Stay (available at the Tokyo Immigration Bureau), a letter stating the reasons for the extension and supporting documentation, as well as your passport. There is a processing fee of Y4000. Many long-term visitors to Japan get around the extension problem by briefly leaving the country, usually going to Hong Kong, South Korea or Taiwan; however, the immigration officials can be very difficult when returning.

The Tokyo Immigration Bureau has a visa information line (☎ 3213-8523), where questions about visas can be answered in English. The service operates Monday to Friday from 9.30 am to 12 noon and 1 pm to 4 pm. The bureau is best reached from Ōtemachi subway station on the Chiyoda line. Take the C2 exit, cross the street at the corner and turn left. Walk past the Japan Development building; the immigration bureau is the next building on your right.

Aliens

Anyone, and this includes tourists, who stays more than 90 days is required to obtain an Alien Registration Card.

The card can be obtained at the municipal office of the city, town or ward in which you're living but moving to another area requires that you re-register within 14 days.

You must carry your Alien Registration Card at all times as the police can stop you and ask to see the card. If you don't have it, you will be taken to the station and will have to wait there until someone fetches it for you.

Face in the crowd (CT)

Consulates & Embassies in Tokyo

Foreign Embassies in Tokyo Most countries have embassies in Tokyo, though visas are generally expensive in Japan.

Australia
    2-1-14 Mita, Minato-ku (☎ 5232-4111)
Austria
    1-1-20 Moto Azabu, Minato-ku (☎ 3451-8281)
Belgium
    5-4 Niban-cho, Chiyoda-ku (☎ 3262-0191)
Canada
    7-3-38 Akasaka, Minato-ku (☎ 3408-2101)
China
    3-4-33 Moto Azabu, Minato-ku (☎ 3403-3380)
Denmark
    29-6 Sarugaku-cho, Shibuya-ku (☎ 3496-3001)
France
    4-11-44 Minami Azabu, Minato-ku (☎ 3473-0171)
Germany
    4-5-10 Minami Azabu, Minato-ku (☎ 3473-0151)
India
    2-2-11 Kudan Minami, Chiyoda-ku (☎ 3262-2391)
Indonesia
    5-2-9 Higashi Gotanda, Shinagawa-ku (☎ 3441-4201)
Ireland
    No 25 Kowa Building, 8-7 Sanban-cho, Chiyoda-ku (☎ 3263-0695)
Israel
    3 Niban-cho, Chiyoda-ku (☎ 3264-0911)
Italy
    2-5-4 Mita, Minato-ku (☎ 3453-5291)
Laos
    3-6-2 Minami-Magome, Ota-ku (☎ 3778-1660)
Malaysia
    2-1-11 Minami-Azabu, Minato-ku (☎ 3280-7601)
Myanmar (Burma)
    4-8-26 Kita Shinagawa, Shinagawa-ku (☎ 3441-9291)
Nepal
    7-14-9 Todoroki, Setagaya-ku (☎ 3705-5558)
New Zealand
    20-40 Kamiyama-cho, Shibuya-ku (☎ 3467-2271)
Norway
    5-12-2 Minami Azabu, Minato-ku (☎ 3440-2611)
Philippines
    11-24 Nanpeidai-cho, Shibuya-ku (☎ 3496-2731)
Russia
    2-1-1 Azabudai, Minato-ku (☎ 3583-4224)
Singapore
    5-12-3 Roppongi, Minato-ku (☎ 3586-9111)
South Korea
    1-2-5 Minami Azabu, Minato-ku (☎ 3452-7611)

Spain
    1-3-29 Roppongi, Minato-ku (☎ 3583-8531)
Sri Lanka
    1-14-1 Akasaka, Minato-ku (☎ 3585-7431)
Sweden
    1-10-3 Roppongi, Minato-ku (☎ 5562-5050)
Switzerland
    5-9-12 Minami Azabu, Minato-ku (☎ 3473-0121)
Taiwan (Association of East Asian Relations)
    5-20-2 Shirogane-dai, Minato-ku, Tokyo (☎ 3280-7811)
Thailand
    3-14-6 Kami Osaki, Shinagawa-ku (☎ 3441-7352)
UK
    1 Ichiban-cho, Chiyoda-ku (☎ 3265-5511)
USA
    1-10-5 Akasaka, Minato-ku (☎ 3224-5000)
Vietnam
    50-11 Moto Yoyogi-cho, Shibuya-ku (☎ 3466- 3311)

CUSTOMS

Customs allowances include the usual tobacco products, three 760 ml bottles of alcoholic beverages, 57 grams of perfume and gifts and souvenirs up to a value of Y200,000 or its equivalent. Liquor is not cheap in Japan, so it's worth bringing some for personal consumption or as a gift; there is no possibility of reselling it for profit. The penalties for importing drugs are very severe.

Customs officers also confiscate literature, such as men's magazines, which shows pubic hair. Depictions of just about every kind of sexual liaison and contortion are readily available at newsagents in Japan, but all pubic hair is carefully erased.

There are no limits on the import of foreign or Japanese currency. The export of foreign currency is also unlimited but a five-million yen limit exists for Japanese currency.

MONEY

Currency

The currency in Japan is the *yen* (Y), and banknotes and coins are easily identifiable. There are Y1, Y5, Y10, Y50, Y100 and Y500 coins, and Y1000, Y5000 and Y10,000 banknotes. The Y1 coin is of lightweight aluminium, and the Y5 and Y50 coins have a hole in the middle.

The Japanese are used to a very low crime rate and often carry wads of cash for the almost sacred ritual of cash payment. Foreign travellers in Japan can safely copy the cash habit, but should still take the usual precautions.

Exchange Rates

A$1	=	Y85
C$1	=	Y100
DM1	=	Y78
HK$1	=	Y16
NZ$1	=	Y66
S$1	=	Y75
UK£1	=	Y190
US$1	=	Y125

Changing Money

You can change cash or travellers' cheques at an 'Authorised Foreign Exchange Bank' (signs will always be displayed in English) or at some of the large hotels and stores. The safest and most practical way to carry your money is in travellers' cheques, preferably in US dollars, although other major currencies are acceptable. Exchanging Korean or Taiwanese currency in Japan is a fruitless task, so avoid bringing any if you're arriving from those countries.

Banking Hours

Banks are open Monday to Friday from 9 am to 3 pm and closed on Saturday, Sunday and national holidays. Procedures can be time consuming at some banks. If you're caught cashless outside regular banking hours, try a large department store or major hotel. The Shinjuku branches of the Isetan and Keio department stores (Map 6) as well as Ikebukuro's Seibu (Map 5), on the 7th floor, will all change travellers' cheques. The Shibuya branch of the the Bank of Tokyo (☎ 3610-7000) also has an after-hours exchange service until 6 pm daily; it's on Meiji-dōri Ave.

Money Transfers

If you are having money sent to a bank in Japan, make sure you know *exactly* where the funds are going: the bank, branch and location. Telex or telegraphic transfers are much faster, though more expensive, than mail transfers. A credit-card cash advance is a worthwhile alternative; American Express transfers require a trusty friend back home.

Bank & Post Office Accounts

If you open a savings account at one of the major banks, you'll receive a savings book and a cash card which will allow you to draw cash at any branch of the bank or from a cash-dispensing machine. Even if you don't speak Japanese, just say *futsū chokin*, or general deposit, and this should get the ball rolling.

An easy option is to open a post office savings account (*yūbin chokin*) at the Tokyo Central Post Office (Map 2); this will allow you to withdraw funds from any post office. A general account with the post office yields slightly higher rates of interest than the banks. A general postal savings account is known as *tsūjō chokin*.

Credit Cards

The use of credit cards is becoming more widespread in Tokyo, but cash is still much more widely used. American Express, Visa, MasterCard and Diners Club are the most widely accepted international cards. The main offices are:

American Express
    Ogikubo Head Office, 4-30-16 Ogikubo, Suginami-ku, Tokyo (☎ 3220-6000; 0120-376-100 toll free, 24 hours)
Diners Club
    Senshu Building, 1-13-7 Shibuya, Shibuya-ku, Tokyo (☎ 3499-1311; 3797-7311 in an emergency; 3499-1181 after hours)
JCB Card
    (☎ 3294-4649 – 24 hours)
MasterCard
    Union Credit Co, 1-10-7 Kaji-cho, Chiyoda-ku, Tokyo (☎ 3254-6751; in an emergency, dial 0051 and ask for a collect call to 1-314-275-6690)
Visa
    Sumitomo Credit Co, Taihei Building, 5-2-10 Shimbashi, Minato-ku, Tokyo (☎ 3459-4800; 3459-4700 in an emergency)

Costs

Tokyo is without a doubt the most expensive city in Asia, if not the world, but this shouldn't be taken as an insuperable barrier to an enjoyable trip. There are always cheaper options in Tokyo – it's just a matter of seeking them out.

A skeleton daily budget – assuming you take the cheapest accommodation (Y4500 per night in one of the cheaper *ryokan*, or Japanese-style inn), eat modestly (Y1800) and spend Y1500 on short-distance travel –

would be Y7800. Add at least Y2000 for extras like snacks, drinks, admission fees and entertainment. More expensive accommodation costs around Y5500 to Y7000 for a business hotel, and anywhere from Y14,000 for something more luxurious.

Food costs can be kept within reasonable limits by taking set meals. A fixed 'morning service' breakfast *(mōningu sābisu* or *setto)* is available in most coffee shops for around Y400. At lunch time there are set meals *(teishoku)* for about Y750. Cheap noodle places, often found at stations or in department stores, charge around Y350 for a filling bowl of noodles. For an evening meal, there's the option of a set course again or a single order – Y800 should cover this. Average prices at youth hostels are Y450 for a Japanese breakfast and Y700 for dinner.

Transport costs for trips to the sights around Tokyo can be expensive. But unless you are going to be travelling to other parts of Japan, it's dubious whether it's worth your while getting a Japan Rail Pass before you arrive. If you want to avoid emptying your wallet at an alarming rate, you should only use taxis as a last resort. Tokyo has a fast, efficient public transport, so it's only on those late-night binges that you need a taxi anyway. Check out some of the transport passes available in the Getting Around chapter later in this guide. For *shinkansen* (bullet train) trips and domestic flights, discounted tickets are available at some theatre ticketing outlets. See the following Getting There & Away chapter for more information.

Tipping & Tax

The total absence of tipping does reduce costs a little; nobody expects a tip so it's best to keep it that way. However, if you feel your maid at a top-flight ryokan has given service surpassing that of a fairy godmother, you can leave her a small present, perhaps a souvenir from your home country. If you give cash, the polite way is to place it in an envelope.

Unfortunately, Japan does have a 3% consumer tax, introduced in 1989 and extremely unpopular with the Japanese public. If you eat at expensive restaurants and stay at 1st-class accommodation you will encounter a service charge – a disguised form of tipping – which varies from 10% to 15%. A local tax of 3% is added for restaurant bills exceeding Y5000 or for hotel bills exceeding Y10,000. This means it is sometimes cheaper to ask for separate bills. At *onsen* (hot-spring) resorts, a separate onsen tax applies. This is usually 3% and applies at cheap accommodation, even youth hostels.

WHEN TO GO

Like the rest of Japan, the best time to visit Tokyo is spring, from March to May. From early April is the cherry blossom season, and even Tokyo can seem quite beautiful at this time of the year. It's a lively time to be in town too, with hordes of revellers heading off to the parks (particularly Ueno-kōen Park) for *hanami* (cherry-blossom viewing) parties. Summer in Tokyo is hot and muggy. It's a time when the overcrowded trains are at their most unbearable; even Japanese tempers get frayed at times. Summer is also monsoon season; four or five days of torrential rain can play havoc with a tight travel itinerary.

Autumn is the next best time to be in Tokyo. Areas like Kamakura and Nikkō are especially beautiful at this time of year. The weather is cool and there's a high proportion of clear days – perfect sightseeing weather. Temperatures occasionally drop below 0°C in winter, but most of the time it's just heavy overcoat weather. Tokyo generally gets a couple of snowfalls every winter, but they're usually over fairly quickly. In many ways, the winter is a better time to be in Tokyo than the height of summer, but this also depends on your own preferences.

It's generally a good idea to avoid visiting Japan during the holiday seasons, in particular Golden Week (29 April to 5 May) and the mid-August Obon festival. However, in some respects it can be a good time to do some sightseeing in Tokyo itself, as most of the locals are on holidays somewhere else and the city metamorphoses into a ghost town (well, almost). If your trip includes other parts of Japan, however, try and reschedule it around these national holidays.

WHAT TO BRING

This is nothing to get unduly flustered about. You can get anything you forgot to bring in Tokyo. Nevertheless, the usual rules apply – bring warm clothing if you're going to be in Tokyo during late autumn, winter or early spring. You'll need light clothes for the summer, and a fold-up umbrella is useful at any time of the year in Tokyo. If you do get stuck in the rain, the convenience stores all sell cheap umbrellas for around Y500. It's a good idea to bring some smart casual clothes. Tokyoites are extremely fashionable, and for wining and dining you'll feel much more comfortable if you dress the part. Finally, a pair of slip-on shoes come in handy anywhere in Japan, simply because it makes taking them off before you enter rooms that much easier.

TOURIST OFFICES

The Japan National Tourist Organisation (JNTO), which
has both Japanese and overseas offices, produces a great
deal of literature.

Tourist Information Centres (TIC)

The JNTO operates two Tourist Information Centres in
the Tokyo area – one at Narita International Airport
(☎ 047- 632-8711), and another in the Ginza in central
Tokyo (☎ 03-3350-21461; Map 2). TIC offices do not make
reservations or bookings, but will direct you to agencies
which can, such as the Japan Travel Bureau (JTB) or the
Nippon Travel Agency (NTA). TIC's Tokyo office (☎ 3503-
2911) operates Teletourist, a round-the-clock taped
information service on current events in town. JNTO also
operate Goodwill Guides, a volunteer programme with
over 30,000 members who wear a blue and white badge
with a dove and globe logo.

The Tokyo TIC is at 1-6-6 Yūraku-cho and can be
reached from the A2 exit of Hibiya subway station or
from the JR Yūraku-cho station. The office has enormous
stocks of material on Tokyo as well as the rest of Japan.
It helps to know what you want, though. You're not
likely to leave with much just by asking for information
on Tokyo. As a starter, pick up copies of the *Tourist Map
of Tokyo* and the *Tokyo City Guide* newspaper. The latter
is free and has good listings of shows, expositions and
sales around town. For more specialised interests, the
TIC has pamphlets on everything from ikebana (flower
arranging) clubs to factory tours. All you have to do is
ask.

Telephone Service

The JNTO operate a telephone service for visitors in need
of assistance in the Tokyo region. English speaking travel
experts can be contacted from 9 am to 5 pm on 3502-1461.
Another excellent service, Japan Hotline, is provided by
Dial Service (☎ 3586-0110). They offer assistance on
travel and all aspects of daily life in Tokyo, and can be
contacted Monday to Friday from 10 am to 4 pm.

Other Information Offices

All the major tourist sights around Tokyo have information offices *(annai-jo)* in prominent locations. Generally
they have brochures and maps, and are able to help with

finding accommodation. If you would like a licensed, professional tourist guide, try TIC, a large travel agency such as JTB, or phone the Japan Guide Association in Tokyo on 3213-2706.

For any information on Japan Railways (JR) including schedules, fares, fastest routings, lost baggage and discounts on railway services, hotels and rent-a-cars, call the JR East-Infoline in Tokyo on 3423-0111. The service is available from 10 am to 6 pm Monday to Friday, but not on holidays.

JNTO Offices Overseas

Some of the JNTO offices overseas include:

Australia
   115 Pitt St, Sydney, NSW 2000 (☎ (02) 232-4522)
Canada
   165 University Ave, Toronto, Ontario M5H 3B8 (☎ (416) 366-7140)
France
   4-8 Rue Sainte-Anne, 75001 Paris (☎ (01) 42-96-20-29)
Germany
   Kaiserstrasse 11, 6000 Frankfurt am Main 1 (☎ (069) 20353
Hong Kong
   Suite 3606, Two Exchange Square, 8 Connaught Place, Central (☎ 5255295)
South Korea
   10 Da-Dong, Chung-Ku, Seoul (☎ (02) 752-7968)
Switzerland
   13 Rue de Berne, 1201 Geneva (☎ (022) 731-81-40)
Thailand
   Wall Street Tower Building, 33/61, Suriwong Rd, Bangkok 10500 (☎ (02) 233-5108)
UK
   167 Regent St, London W1 (☎ (071) 734-9638)
USA
   Chicago – 401 North Michigan Ave, IL 60611 (☎ (312) 222-0874)
   Dallas – 2121 San Jacinto St, Suite 980, LB-53, TX 75201 (☎ (214) 754-1820)
   Los Angeles – 624 South Grand Ave, Suite 2640, CA 90017 (☎ (213) 623-1952)
   New York – Rockefeller Plaza, 630 Fifth Ave, NY 10111 (☎ (212) 757-5640)
   San Francisco – 360 Post St, Suite 401, CA 94108 (☎ (415) 989-7140)

BUSINESS HOURS & HOLIDAYS

Shops are typically open seven days a week from around 10 am to 8 pm. Department stores close slightly earlier, usually 6.30 or 7 pm, and also close one weekday each week. Tokyo's department stores are closed on different days of the week, so that even if, say, Mitsukoshi is closed, Isetan will be open. Large companies usually work a 9 am to 5 pm five-day week, some also operate on Saturday mornings.

National holidays are spread across the year, but beware of the three holidays on 29 April, and 3 and 5 May. Together they make up Golden Week, a time when Japanese are all on international flights or long train and bus journeys, making it very difficult to get around or out of the country. Another difficult time to travel is during *O-Bon* (13-16 of August), the Festival of the Dead, in which most Japanese try to get back to their home town.

Ganjitsu (New Year's Day)
   1 January
Seijin-no-hi (Adult's Day)
   15 January
Kenkoku Kinen-no-bi (National Foundation Day)
   11 February
Shunbun-no-hi (Spring Equinox)
   21 March (approximately)
Midori-no-hi (Green Day)
   29 April
Kenpo Kinen-bi (Constitution Day)
   3 May
Kodomo-no-hi (Children's Day)
   5 May
Keiro-no-hi (Respect-for-the-Aged Day)
   15 September
Shubun-no-hi (Autumn Equinox)
   23 September (approximately)
Taiiku-no-hi (Sports Day)
   10 October
Bunka-no-hi (Culture Day)
   3 November
Kinro Kansha-no-hi (Labour Thanksgiving Day)
   23 November
Tennō Tanjōbi (Emperor's Birthday)
   23 December

CULTURAL EVENTS

The following is a list of the major festivals celebrated in and around Tokyo. There are so many that, no matter when you visit, you're bound to be in time for something.

January-February

Ganjitsu (New Year's Day)

On 1 January, it is customary for Japanese to visit Buddhist and Shintō shrines to pray for luck in the coming year. Go to Meiji-jingū Shrine, Sensō-ji Temple or the Yasukuni-jinja Shrine. The day after New Year's Day is one of the two occasions each year when the Imperial Palace is open to the public. Enter the inner gardens by the Nijū-bashi Bridge between 9 am and 3.30 pm.

Dezome-shiki

On 6 January, firemen dressed in Edo-period costumes put on a parade involving acrobatic stunts on top of bamboo ladders. The parade takes place on Chūō-dōri Ave in Harumi from 10 am onwards.

Seijin-no- hi (Adult's Day)

On 15 January, a traditional display of archery is held at Meiji-jingū Shrine.

Setsubun

On 3 or 4 February, in Tokyo, ceremonies are held at Zōjō-ji Temple, Kanda-jinja Shrine and Sensō-ji Temple. Sensō-ji Temple offers the added attraction of a classical dance.

Hari-kuyō

This festival is usually held in early February. Check with the TIC for the dates of this typically quirky Japanese festival held for pins and needles that have been broken in the preceding year. At Sensō-ji Temple, women lay their pins and needles to rest by 'burying' them in tōfu and radishes.

March-April

Hina Matsuri (Doll Festival)

On 3 March – from about mid-February onwards, a doll fair is held in Asakusabashi; check with the TIC for exact details.

Knickers Giving Day

On 14 March – a recent innovation that could only happen in Japan (although people once said that about karaoke). The idea is that boys reciprocate their Valentine chockies with an article of a lady's most intimate apparel.

Kinryū No Mai

On 18 March, a golden dragon dance is held at Sensō-ji Temple to celebrate the discovery of the golden image of Kannon that now rests there. Two or three dances are performed during the day.

Gōhan Shiki

On 2 April, this is a rice-harvesting festival held at Rinnō-ji Temple, Nikkō, in which men (in days past, samurai lords) are forced to eat great quantities of rice in a tribute to the bounty supplied by the gods. Sacred dances are also performed by the priests as an accompaniment to the ceremonial pig-out.

Hanami (Blossom Viewing)
> In early to mid-April, this is one festival you can't help hearing about if you happen to be in Japan when the blossoms come out. In Tokyo, *the* place to go for Hanami is Ueno-kōen Park. Other famous spots around Tokyo include Yasukuni-jinja Shrine and Koishikawa Kōraku-en Garden.

Kamakura Matsuri
> On the second and third Sunday of April, this is a week of celebrations centred around Hachiman-gū Shrine in Kamakura.

Hana Matsuri (Buddha's Birthday)
> On 8 April, celebrations are held at Buddhist temples all over Japan. In Tokyo, celebrations take place at Sensō-ji Temple and Zōjō-ji Temple, among others.

Jibeta Matsuri
> On 15 April, Kawasaki's famous festival that celebrates the vanquishing of a sharp-toothed demon residing in a young maiden by means of an iron phallus (it's true, really!). The festival commences with a procession, followed by a re-enactment of the forging, and is rounded off with a banquet. The action takes place close to Kawasaki Taishi station.

Yayoi Matsuri
> On 16-17 April, a procession of portable shrines is held at Futāra-san-jinja Shrine in Nikkō.

Ueno Tōshō-gū Taisai
> On 17 April, ceremonies, traditional music and dance are held at Ueno's Tōshō-gū Shrine in memory of Tokugawa Ieyasu.

May-June

Kanda Matsuri
> In mid-May, this festival is held on odd-numbered years on the Saturday and Sunday closest to 15 May and is a traditional Edo festival that celebrates a Tokugawa battle victory. A whole range of activities take place at Kanda-jinja Shrine.

Kuro-fune Matsuri (Black Ship Festival)
> On 16-18 May, this is held in Shimoda on the Izu-hantō Peninsula. It commemorates the first landing of Commodore Perry with parades and fireworks displays.

Tōshō-gū Shrine Grand Festival
> On 17-18 May, this is Nikkō's most important annual festival. It features horseback archery and a 1000-strong costumed re-enactment of the delivery of Ieyasu's remains to Nikkō.

Sanja Matsuri
> In May, on the third Friday, Saturday and Sunday of May, at Sensō-ji Temple in Asakusa, up to 100 mikoshi carried by participants dressed in traditional clothes are paraded through the area in the vicinity of the temple.

Facts for the Visitor

Top: Festival offerings (RI'A)
Bottom: Sanja Festival, Ueno (CT)

Sannō-sai
> On 10-16 June, street stalls, traditional music and dancing, and processions of mikoshi are all part of this Edo Festival, held at Hie-jinja Shrine, near Akasaka-Mitsuke subway station.

July-October

Tarai-nori Kyoso
> On the first Sunday of July, held in Itō on the Izu-hantō Peninsula, this is a race that involves paddling down the Matsukawa River in washtubs using rice scoops as oars; what it's in aid of, no-one seems to know.

O-Bon
> On 13-15 July, this festival takes place at a time when, according to Buddhist belief, the dead briefly revisit the earth. Dances are held and lanterns lighted in their memory. In Tokyo *bon odori* dances are held in different locations around town.

Sumidagawa Hanabi Taikai
> On the last Saturday of July, the biggest fireworks display of its kind in Tokyo is held on the Sumidagawa River in Asakusa.

Tsukudajima Sumiyoshi-jinja Matsuri
> On the Sunday closest to 7 July, this is a tri-annual festival, with activities centred around the Sumiyoshi-jinja Shrine; it includes dragon dances and mikoshi parades among other things. The next festival will take place in 1995.

Ashino-ko Kosui Matsuri
> On 31 July, this festival is held at Hakone-jinja Shrine in Moto-Hakone, and features fireworks displays over Ashino-ko Lake.

Fukagawa Hachiman Matsuri
> On 15 August, in this, another tri-annual, three-day Edo festival, foolhardy mikoshi-bearers charge through eight km of frenzied crowds who dash water on them. The action takes place at Tomioka Hachiman-gū Shrine, next to Monzen-Naka-cho subway station on the Tōzai line. The next festival will be held in 1995.

Hakone Daimonji-yaki Festival
> On 16 August – held in Hakone, torches are lit on Mt Myojoga-take so that they form the shape of the Chinese character for 'big' or 'great'.

Hachiman- gū Matsuri
> On 14-15 September, festivities include a procession of mikoshi and, on the 16th, a display of horseback archery.

Ningyō-kuyō
> On 25 September, childless couples make offerings of dolls to Kannon in the hope that she will bless them with children. More interesting for spectators is the ceremonial burning by priests of all the dolls that remain from previous years. It takes place at Kiyomizu- dō Temple in Ueno Park from 2 pm to 3.30 pm.

Furusato Tokyo Matsuri (Metropolitan Citizen's Day)
On the first Saturday and Sunday in October, a wide range of activities are held at different locations around town. In particular, check out Asakusa's Sensō-ji Temple and Ueno-kōen Park.

Oeshiki
On 12 October, this festival is held in commemoration of Nichiren (1222-82), founder of the Nichiren sect of Buddhism. On the night of the 12th, people bearing large lanterns and paper flower arrangements make their way to Hommon-ji Temple. The nearest station is Ikegami station on the Tōkyū Ikegami line.

Tōshō-gū Shrine Autumn Festival
On 17 October, this requires only the equestrian archery to be an autumnal repeat of Nikkō's grand festival in May.

Meiji Reidaisai
On 30 October to 3 November, a series of events is held at Meiji-jingū Shrine in commemoration of the Meiji emperor's birthday. Particularly interesting to watch are displays of horseback archery in traditional clothes. Other events include classical music and dance.

November-December

Hakone Daimyō Gyoretsu
On 3 November, this is a re-enactment of a feudal lord's procession by 400 costumed locals; it is held in Hakone.

Shichi-go-san (Seven-Five-Three Festival)
On 15 November, as its name suggests, this is for children aged seven, five and three. The children (boys aged five and girls aged three and seven) make a colourful sight, as they are dressed in traditional clothes and taken to different shrines around town, notably Meiji-jingū Shrine, Yasukuni-jinja Shrine and Sannō Hie-jinja Shrine.

Gishi-sai
On 14 December, the day's events commemorate the deaths of the 47 *rōnin* (masterless samurai) who committed seppuku after avenging the death of their master. The activities involve a parade of warriors to Sengaku-ji Temple – the rōnin's burial place – and a memorial service from 7.30 pm onwards.

POST & TELECOMMUNICATIONS

Post

The symbol for post offices is a white and red T with a bar across the top. Red mailboxes are for ordinary mail and blue ones for special delivery. The Japanese postal system is reliable and efficient and, for regular postcards and airmail letters, not markedly more expensive than other advanced countries. The airmail rate for postcards is Y70 to any overseas destination; aerograms cost Y80.

Letters weighing less than 10 grams are Y80 to other countries within Asia, Y100 to North America or Oceania (including Australia and New Zealand) and Y120 to Europe, Africa and South America.

Sending parcels overseas from Japan often works out 30% cheaper with Surface Airlift (SAL) and only takes a week longer.

District post offices (the main post office in a ward or *ku)* are normally open from 9 am to 7 pm on weekdays, 9 am to 3 pm on Saturday and 9 am to 12.30 pm on Sunday and public holidays. Local post offices are open 9 am to 5 pm on weekdays and 9 am to 3 pm on Saturday.

Mail can be sent to Japan, from Japan or within Japan when addressed in our script (romaji) but it should, of course, be written as clearly as possible.

Receiving Mail Mail can be sent to Post Restante, Tokyo International Post Office, 2-3-3 Ōtemachi, Chiyoda-ku, Tokyo (☎ 3241-4869; Map 2). Take the A4 exit of Ōtemachi subway station to get there. It will hold mail for 30 days.

American Express will hold mail for their cardholders or users of American Express travellers' cheques. Normally, mail will be held for 30 days only unless marked 'Please hold for arrival'. American Express offices in Tokyo are:

Ginza 4-Star Building, 4-4-1 Ginza, Chūō-ku, Tokyo 104
Shuwa Kamiya-cho Building (5th floor), 4-3-13 Toranomon, Minato-ku, Tokyo 105
Shuwa Shiba Park Building, 2-4-1 Shiba-kōen, Minato-ku, Tokyo 100-91
3-8-1 Kasumigaseki, Chiyoda-ku, Tokyo 106

Some embassies will hold mail for their nationals – check before you depart. Hotels and youth hostels are another possibility.

Telephone

The Japanese public telephone system is very well developed; there are a great many public phones and they work almost 100% of the time. It is very unusual to see a vandalised phone in Japan. Local calls cost Y10 for three minutes; long-distance or overseas calls require a handful of coins; unused coins are returned at the end of the call.

Most pay phones will also accept prepaid phone cards. It's much easier to buy one of these – typically in Y500, Y1000 and Y3000 denominations – rather than worry about having coins to hand. The cards are readily available from vending machines and convenience stores – coming in a myriad of designs they are also a collectable item.

International Calls In Tokyo, overseas-call telephones have become increasingly common. Both paid and collect overseas calls can only be made from a phone with a gold plate. Once you're through, calls are charged by the unit (no three-minute minimum), each of which is six seconds, so if you've not got much to say you could phone home for just Y100.

As in other parts of the world, you save money by dialling late at night. Economy rates with a discount of 20% apply from 7 pm to 11 pm Monday to Friday and all day to 11 pm on weekends and holidays. From 11 pm to 8 am a discount rate brings the price of international phone calls down by 40% seven days a week.

To place an international call through the operator, dial 0051 – international operators all seem to speak English. To make the call yourself, simply dial 001 then the international country code, the local code and the number. Another option is to dial 0039 for home country direct which takes you straight through to a local operator in the country dialled. You can then make a reverse-charge (collect) call or a credit-card call with a telephone credit card valid in that country. In some hotels or other tourist locations, you may find a home country direct phone where you simply press the button labelled USA, UK, Canada, Australia, NZ, or wherever, to be put through to your operator.

Dialling codes include:

Country	Direct Dial	Home Country Direct
Australia	001-61	0039-611
Canada	001-1	0039-161
Hong Kong	001-852	0039-852
Netherlands	001-31	0039-311
New Zealand	001-64	0039-641
Singapore	001-65	0039-651
Taiwan	001-886	0039-886
UK	001-44	0039-441
USA	001-1	0039-111*

* For mainland USA you can also dial 0039-121, and for Hawaii you can also dial 0039-181.

Fax

An economic miracle Japan may be, but getting access
to fax services in Tokyo can be difficult. If you're staying
in a major hotel you should have no problems. For those
in more down-market digs, the branches of Kokusai
Denshin Denwa, or KDD, in Shinjuku (☎ 3347-5000;
Map 6) and Ōtemachi (☎ 3275-4343) can both receive and
send international faxes from 9 am to 6 pm Monday to
Friday, and to 5 pm on weekends. The KDD branch in
Shinjuku is on the west side of the station; the Ōtemachi
branch is next to the C1 exit of the Ōtemachi subway
station. Sending faxes is easier than receiving them at
KDD. The Ōtemachi branch requires an annual membership fee of Y5000.

Other services are offered by the Alpha Corporation
on the 1st floor of the Tokyo Hilton International Hotel
(☎ 3343-2575; Map 6) in Shinjuku and the Akasaka
Tōkyū Hotel (☎ 3580-1991; Map 9). In Ikebukuro is the
Kimi Information Service (☎ 3986-1604; Map 5), which
will both receive and send faxes. It's popular with foreigners staying in budget accommodation in this area.

TIME

Japan is only on one time zone which is nine hours ahead
of Greenwich Mean Time (GMT). Thus, when it is noon
in Tokyo, it is 3 am in London, 11 am in Hong Kong, 1
pm in Sydney, 3 pm in Auckland, 10 pm the previous
day in New York, 7 pm the previous day in San Francisco
and 5 pm the previous day in Honolulu. Daylight-saving
time is not used in Japan. Times are all expressed on a
24-hour clock.

ELECTRICITY

The Japanese electric current is 100 volts AC, an odd
voltage found almost nowhere else in the world. Fur-
thermore, Tokyo and eastern Japan are on 50 cycles,
western Japan including Nagoya, Kyoto and Osaka is on
60 cycles. Most North American electrical items,
designed to run on 117 volts, will function reasonably
well on Japanese current. The plugs are flat two pin,
identical to US and Canadian plugs.

BOOKS & MAPS

There's no need to stock up on books, particularly books
about Tokyo and Japan in general, before you leave

home. Tokyo has a number of bookshops with excellent selections of books on all aspects of Japanese culture.

Most of the following books should be available in Tokyo, usually in paperback.

History, Culture & Society

For an interesting history of Tokyo from 1867 to 1923, look for Edward Seidensticker's *Low City, High City* (1983). *Tokyo Rising: The City Since the Great Earthquake* (Tuttle, 1991), by the same author, continues the story to the present day.

For a general introduction to Japanese history and society, *Inside Japan* (Penguin, 1987) by Peter Tasker is probably the best wide-ranging introduction to modern Japanese culture, society and the economy. Richard Storey's *A History of Modern Japan* (Penguin) is a concise and consistently interesting history of modern Japan. Less analysis than a series of reflections on life in Meiji Japan, Lafcadio Hearn's *Writings from Japan* (Penguin, 1984) includes what is by common consent some of the best writing on Japan. His eloquent prose captures some of the magic of preindustrial Japan.

Ruth Benedict's *The Chrysanthemum & the Sword*, despite the fact it was written during WW II, is in some ways still regarded as the classic study of Japanese culture and attitudes. *The Japanese Today* (Belknap, 1988) by Edwin O Reischauer is a recently revised standard textbook on Japanese society and a must for those planning to spend time in Japan. Ian Buruma's *A Japanese Mirror* (Penguin) provides an interesting examination of Japanese popular culture. For a slightly academic but consistently interesting history of the Japanese visual arts, see Joan Stanley Baker's *Japanese Art* (Thames & Hudson, 1984).

The two volumes of *Discover Japan – Words, Customs & Concepts* (Kodansha, 1987) were originally published as *A Hundred Things Japanese* and *A Hundred More Things Japanese* and consist of a series of short essays on things Japanese by a wide variety of writers.

The Economic Superpower

As Japan elbows its way to the front of the industrial pack, the countries left behind have produced a flood of 'What was that?' and 'How did it happen?' style books. *The Enigma of Japanese Power* by Karel van Wolferen is an attack on the Japanese 'system' and a book for the finger pointers and accusers who reckon Japan got to the top by playing dirty.

Japan's most forceful recent reply was in *The Japan That Can Say No* by Akio Morita (chairman of Sony) and Shintaro Ishihara (former cabinet minister and politician). They argue that Japan is big enough to play a real role in world politics and need no longer be at the USA's beck and call, and that superior technology has made the USA dependent on Japan.

Other views on the growth of Japan as an economic superpower are found in *Trading Places: How America Allowed Japan to Take the Lead* (Charles E Tuttle) by Clyde

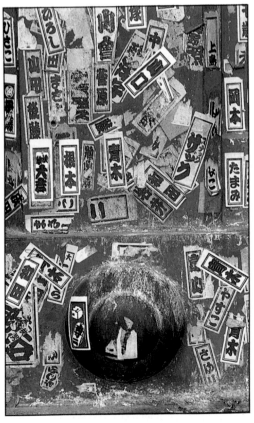

Traditional calling cards (CT)

V Prestowitz Jr and *The New Masters – Can the West Match Japan?* (Hutchinson Business Books, 1990) by Phillip Oppenheim. Ezra Vogel saw it coming more than 10 years ago in *Japan as Number One: Lessons for America* (Harvard University Press, 1979). Of course, Japan has hardly reached the top before someone is foreshadowing its descent – Bill Emmott describes it in *The Sun Also Sets*.

Fiction

Some Japanese classics available in Tokyo bookshops include Murasaki Shikibu's *The Tale of the Genji*, translated by Edward Seidensticker; *The Narrow Road to the Deep North*, a travel classic by the revered Japanese poet Matsuo Bashō; *Kokoro*, by Natsume Sōseki, a modern classic depicting the conflict between old and new Japan in the mind and heart of an aged scholar; *The Makioka Sisters* by Tanizaki Junichirō, a famous family chronicle that has been likened to a modern-day *The Tale of the Genji*; Ibuse Masuji's *Black Rain* (Kodansha, 1969), a response to Japan's defeat in WW II; *Snow Country* by Kawabata Yasunari, a famous story set in Japan's northern regions; and Endō Shūsaku's *Silence*, a historical story of the plight of Japanese Christians following Tokugawa Ieyasu's unification of the country.

Of course no discussion of Japanese fiction would be complete without a mention of the controversial Yukio Mishima. Two of his more well-known works are *The Golden Pavilion*, which reconstructs the life of a novice monk who burned down Kyoto's Golden Temple in 1950, and *The Sailor who Fell from Grace with the Sea*.

Guidebooks

Probably the most enjoyable book to come out on Tokyo is Don Morton and Naoko Tsunoi's *The Best of Tokyo* (Charles E Tuttle, 1989). The book has a comprehensive list of 'best ofs', from the best garlic restaurant and Japanese dolls to the best toilet. It's a good companion with which to explore some of the more idiosyncratic sides of the city.

The *City Source English Telephone Directory* is useful for long-term visitors. It has over 500 pages of telephone numbers and a wealth of useful practical information. The Nippon Telegraph & Telephone (NTT) English Information Service (☎ 3201-1010) will tell you the address of the nearest NTT office, where you can pick up a free copy. Another useful book for those planning on staying in Tokyo for some time is *Living for Less in Tokyo and Liking it!* (Ask Kodansha, 1991). Compiled by the Japan Hotline team, it presents answers to the most commonly asked questions about Tokyo, on everything from visas to ikebana (flower arranging) clubs.

Jean Pearce's *Footloose in Tokyo* (John Weatherhill, 1976) and *More Footloose in Tokyo* (John Weatherhill, 1984) are excellent guides to exploring Tokyo on foot. Even if you don't follow Pearce's routes, her introductions to some of Tokyo's most important areas make for interesting background reading. The first book contains most of the important areas in Tokyo.

Gary Walters' *Day Walks Near Tokyo* (Kodansha International, 1988) covers 25 countryside trails, most of which can be reached from central Tokyo in an hour.

Finally, the APA's *Tokyo Insight Guide* is lavishly illustrated, and provides excellent background reading on Tokyo.

Bookshops

The English-language sections of several of the larger Tokyo bookshops would put entire bookshops in many English-speaking cities to shame.

The main bookshop area in Tokyo is Jimbō-cho (Map 1), and although most of the bookshops there cater only to those who read Japanese, there are a couple of foreign-language bookshops. The best among these is Kitazawa Shoten (☎ 3263- 0011), which has an excellent academic selection on the ground floor and second-hand books on the 2nd floor.

Kinokuniya (☎ 3354-0131; Map 6) in Shinjuku has a good selection of English-language fiction and general titles on the 6th floor, including an extensive selection of books and other aids for learning Japanese. It's closed on the third Wednesday of every month.

Maruzen (☎ 3272-7211; Map 2) in Nihombashi near Ginza has a collection of books almost equal to Kinokuniya's and it is always a lot quieter. This is Japan's oldest Western bookshop, having been established in 1869. It's closed on Sunday.

The 3rd floor of Jena (☎ 3571-2980; Map 2) in Ginza doesn't have quite the range of some other foreign-language bookshops but it does have a good selection of fiction and art books, and it stocks a large number of newspapers and magazines. It's closed on public holidays.

Another bookshop worth taking a look at is Wise Owl (see Map 5), on the east side of Ikebukuro. It's not particularly big, but it has a good selection of material on Japan.

Maps

A *Tourist Map of Tokyo* is available from the TIC (Map 2). Probably the best map available in English for Tokyo is in *Tokyo – A Bilingual Atlas* (Kodansha, 1989). Bus maps of the city are also available (see the Bus section of the Getting Around chapter later in this guide).

MEDIA

Newspapers & Magazines

The *Japan Times*, with its good international news section and unbiased coverage of local Japanese news, is undoubtedly the best of the English-language newspapers. The paper's Monday edition also features an employment section which is the best place for anyone to start looking for work in Japan. The paper costs Y160.

The *Mainichi Daily News* and the *Yomiuri Daily* are a definite second place to the *Japan Times*. If you oversleep and miss the morning papers, the *Asahi Evening News* is not bad. All these newspapers can be picked up from newsstands and hotels around town. On Friday the *Yomiuri Daily* reprints the week's best from the UK *Independent*, a must for anyone starved of high-quality international reporting.

Tokyo also has a number of English-language magazines covering local events, entertainment and cultural listings. The pick of the pack is undoubtedly the *Tokyo Journal*; the Cityscope section alone is worth the Y500 a month for its comprehensive listings of movies, plays, concerts, art exhibitions and unclassifiable 'events'. The *Tokyo Journal's* classified advertisements are particularly useful for those basing themselves in Tokyo for some time. Sections include housing, employment and education. There are also general advertisements for things like moving house on a budget and furniture rental. The *Tokyo Journal* is available in bookshops with English-language sections.

An excellent source of information about more tourist-oriented events is the *Tokyo City Guide*, a free, monthly magazine. However, its listings are nowhere near as comprehensive as those in the *Tokyo Journal*, and it is pitched at well-heeled visitors. Along the same lines is the weekly *Tokyo Weekender*. The monthly *Tokyo Time Out* magazine also costs Y500 but is less of an interesting read than *Tokyo Journal*.

If you're studying Japanese, all the articles in the *Hiragana Times* are in English and Japanese, and all the kanji include *furigana* (Japanese script used to give pronunciation for kanji) readings.

Radio & TV

The common consensus is that Japanese radio is pretty dismal, mainly because it places far more emphasis on DJ jive than it does on music. For English-language broadcasts, the possibilities are pretty much limited to the US armed services' Far East Network (FEN; 810 kHz).

Like radio, most television is inaccessible to the non-Japanese speaker and, even if you do speak the language, most programmes seem to be inane variety shows. It's worth watching a few hours as a window into the culture, but you're unlikely to get addicted.

TVs can be fitted with an adapter so that certain English-language programmes and movies can be received in either Japanese or English. The Japanese Broadcasting Corporation (NHK) even broadcasts a nightly bilingual news report. Unfortunately, Japanese TV news is not the most informative in the world, often running extended reports on the daring rescue of a cat from a tree while the Middle East teeters on the brink of another all-out war.

Finally, many Japanese hotel rooms will have a pay cable TV with video channels. In the more down-market business hotels, it's unlikely that English-language movies will be available but the porn channel which is often available needs no translation!

FILM & PHOTOGRAPHY

The Japanese are a nation of photographers. No social occasion is complete without a few snaps and an exchange of the photos taken at the last get together. This, combined with the fact that the Japanese are major producers of camera equipment and film, means there is no problem obtaining photographic equipment or film in Tokyo. See the Shinjuku section of the Things to See chapter for some information on photographic supplies. The Bic Camera store on Ikebukuro's east side (Map 5) is also renowned for its cheap deals on everything from film to cameras.

A 36-exposure Kodachrome 64 slide film costs about Y950 without processing. The very popular disposable cameras are even sold from vending machines. They typically cost from Y1500 to Y2000; more expensive ones have a built-in flash.

Processing

Processing print film is fast and economical in Tokyo, and generally of fairly high quality. Kodachrome slide film can only be processed by the Imagica Kodak depot in Ginza. The processing is fast (24 hours) and the results are good. There is no problem honouring prepaid Kodachrome film either.

HEALTH

Travel health depends on your predeparture preparations, your day-to-day health care and how you handle any medical problem or emergency that develops. However, looking after your health in Tokyo should pose few problems since hygiene standards are high and medical facilities are widely available, though expensive.

No immunisations are required for Japan. Tap water is safe to drink and the food is almost uniformly prepared with high standards of hygiene.

A small medical kit is a good thing to carry even though most items will usually be readily available in Japan. Your kit could include:

- Aspirin or panadol – for pain or fever.
- Antihistamine (such as Benadryl) – useful as a decongestant for colds, allergies, to ease the itch from insect bites or stings or to help prevent motion sickness.
- Kaolin preparation (Pepto-Bismol), Imodium or Lomotil – for stomach upsets.
- Antiseptic, mercurochrome and antibiotic powder or similar 'dry' spray – for cuts and grazes.
- Calamine lotion – to ease irritation from bites or stings.
- Bandages and band-aids – for minor injuries.
- Scissors, tweezers and a thermometer – mercury thermometers are prohibited by airlines.
- Insect repellent, sunblock cream (can be difficult to find in Japan), suntan lotion and chapstick.

If you're shortsighted bring a spare pair of glasses and your prescription. If you require a particular medication take an adequate supply as it may not be available locally. Take the prescription with the generic rather than the brand name, which may be unavailable, as it will make getting replacements easier. It's a wise idea to have the prescription with you to show you legally use the medication.

Although oral contraceptives are available from clinics specialising in medical care for foreigners, it is

Toilets

Western toilets are on the increase in Japan. On one trip aboard the bullet train, I was intrigued to see queues outside the Western toilet whilst the Japanese one remained vacant. A Dutch couple told me that back in the '70s, there were instructive diagrams on the correct use of Western toilets as part of a drive to dissuade toilet-goers from standing on the seat and aiming from on high.

It's quite common to see men urinating in public, typically in the evening in a bar district. In Shinjuku (Tokyo) I watched a tipsy, soberly suited salaryman slip behind a policeman and pee against the wall a couple of feet behind him. When the salaryman was finished, he turned round, thanked the policeman, exchanged bows and tottered into the station.

Japanese toilets are Asian style – level with, or in the floor. The correct position is to squat facing the hood, away from the door. This is the opposite to squat toilets in most other places in Asia. Make sure the contents of your pockets don't spill out. Toilet paper isn't always provided so carry tissues with you. Separate toilet slippers are often provided just inside the toilet door. These are for use in the toilet only, so remember to change out of them when you leave.

Mixed toilets also exist. Men and women often go through separately marked entrances, but land up in the same place. No-one feels worried and privacy is provided by cubicles and women are supposed to simply ignore the backs turned to them at the urinals. The kanji script for 'toilet' is 洗手間, for 'men' 男 and for 'women' 女 .

A recent newspaper article claimed that in about four years, research on the 'intelligent lavatory' would be complete. According to the article, these lavatories will use the latest microchip technology to check the user's waste products, weight, temperature and even blood pressure. Further research will also investigate the possibility of direct links between these smart conveniences and the closest hospitals so that suspicious symptoms are reported instantly and nipped in the bud. Of course, there are wide implications in this merging of private moments and public data. Perhaps, in the realms of litigation, constipation will be considered as the withholding of information!

My favourite establishment is a musical rest room at the remote tip of Sukoton Peninsula on Rebuntō Island, Hokkaidō. In the middle of nowhere stands this brand-new, windswept rest room. As you enter, an electric eye starts a tape, which plays classical guitar music or the recorded swishing of the sea which is outside the door.

Robert Strauss

preferable to bring adequate supplies with you. Only in 1990 was the marketing of oral contraceptives officially authorised in Japan. Condoms are widely available, but visitors are advised to bring their own or buy a foreign brand from the American Pharmacy (Map 2) in Ginza. Foreigners frequently complain that Japanese brands are too small!

Health Insurance

A travel insurance policy to cover theft, property loss and medical problems is a wise idea. With such a wide variety of policies available, it may be best to consult your travel agent for recommendations. The international student travel policies handled by the STA agencies or other student travel organisations are usually good value. Some policies offer a choice between lower and higher medical expense options; choose the high-cost option for Japan.

Medical Assistance

The Tourist Information Centre (TIC) has lists of English-speaking hospitals and doctors in Tokyo. Dental care is widely available at steep prices. If you need a medicine not readily available in local pharmacies, try the American Pharmacy (☎ 3271-4034; Map 2) close to the TIC in Tokyo. A peculiarity of the Japanese medical system is that most drugs are supplied not by pharmacies but by doctors. Critics say that as a result, doctors are prone to over-prescribe and choose the most expensive drugs.

If you need medical help in English, the Tokyo Medical & Surgical Clinic (☎ 3436-3028) in Kamiya-cho on the Hibiya subway line has foreign doctors. Appointments can be made Monday to Friday from 9 am to 4.45 pm and until 1 pm on Saturdays. The International Clinic (☎ 3583-7831) in Roppongi is another place where you can get medical attention in English. It is open from 9 am to 5 pm Monday to Friday, and from 9 am to noon on Saturday. When making your appointment, ask for exact directions to get to the clinics. Both clinics are closed Sundays and holidays.

Emergencies

Emergency services in Tokyo will usually only react fast if you speak Japanese. You can dial 119 for an ambulance, though the person answering the phone may not speak English. For information on your nearest medical treatment centre, ring the information desk of the Tokyo Fire

Department (☎ 3212-2323); English is spoken. Other alternatives include the Tokyo English Lifeline, or TELL (☎ 3403-7106), and Japan Helpline (☎ 0120-461-997), an emergency number which operates 24 hours a day, seven days a week. Don't clog the line unless you really do have an emergency.

Counselling & Advice

Adjusting to life in Japan can be tough but there are several places to turn for help. The TELL phone service provides confidential and anonymous help. If they don't have the right answers at hand, they can pass you on to someone who might. Tokyo Tapes (☎ 3262-0224) has a wide variety of tapes available to help you deal with problems.

WOMEN TRAVELLERS

By international standards Tokyo is an extremely safe city for women travellers. The major concern of women travellers in many countries – 'Will I be physically safe?' – is not a worry in Tokyo, though jam-packed rush-hour subways or buses can still bring out the worst in the Japanese male. When movement is impossible, roving hands are frequently at work and women often put up with this interference because in Japan, it would simply be impolite or unseemly to make a fuss! One woman visitor has suggested that it is not a Western woman's duty to reinforce Japanese customs and, if possible, the offending hand should be grabbed, held up and the whereabouts of its owner inquired about.

DANGERS & ANNOYANCES

Tokyo is generally an extremely safe city, though it has its share of annoyances. Most of the latter are things that you are simply going to have to live with, and which for the most part are not going to endanger your health. An exception is passive smoking, which is hard not to indulge in while in Tokyo. If this worries you a lot, it's going to make a lot of restaurants and coffee shops less pleasurable than they might have been. Nonsmoking areas are a lot more common than they once were, but Tokyo and the rest of Japan lags a long way behind places like California and Singapore.

Lost & Found

One wonderful thing about Tokyo is that lost property is more often than not returned by the finder. If you've left something on a train, a bus, a taxi or even the restaurant you were eating at last night, don't give it up as lost for good. For things lost at JR trains and stations, ring the JR East Infoline (☎ 3423-0111); for TRTA subway trains and stations, ring their Lost & Found Centre (☎ 3834- 5577); Toei subway trains, stations and buses have a Lost & Found Service Corner (☎ 5600-2020); and for property lost on taxis, ring the Tokyo Taxi Kindaika Centre (☎ 3648-0300).

Theft

The low incidence of theft and crime in general in Japan is frequently commented on, though of course, theft does exist and its unlikelihood is no reason for carelessness. Airports are reputed to be among the worst places in Japan for pickpockets and other sneak thieves, so take extra care in these places. It's probable the stolen goods are on their way overseas before the owner even realises their disappearance.

Earthquakes

Earthquakes are a risk throughout Japan, but the Tokyo region is particularly prone to them. Since major earthquakes occur every 60 years on average, a big one is overdue. There is no point in being paranoid, but it is worthwhile checking the emergency exits in your hotel and being aware of earthquake safety procedures. These include turning off anything that might cause a fire, opening a door or window to secure your exit and sheltering in a doorway or under a sturdy table – not easy when many Japanese tables are about 15 cm high. If an earthquake occurs, NHK (the Japanese Broadcasting Corporation) will broadcast information and instructions in English on all its TV and radio networks. Tune to Channel 1 on your television, or to NHK (639 AM) or FEN (810 AM) on your radio.

WORK

Finding a job in Japan is not as easy as it once was. Japanese employers have become more discriminating, and the job market has become increasingly saturated with young hopefuls looking for a bit-part in the Japanese economic success story. This is particularly true of English teaching: if you don't have teaching qualifications, you should think seriously about trying your luck elsewhere. If you don't have a college or university degree, forget it. Even people with MA degrees in TEFL (Teaching English as a Foreign Language) often spend a month or so answering advertisements before they finally get accepted somewhere.

If you are set on teaching in Japan and are qualified, one option is to inquire at your nearest Japanese embassy about teaching in one of Japan's government schools. At present, there are 2000 positions a year available for foreign teachers.

Other employment options in Tokyo include technical rewriting and modelling. For those with high-level Japanese skills, translation work is frequently advertised in the Employment section of the *Japan Times* on Monday. Illegal possibilities include hostessing (for women), street selling and busking, all three of which have become increasingly common over recent years.

STUDYING IN JAPAN

The Tokyo Tourist Information Centre (TIC) has a wealth of information material on courses relating to many aspects of Japanese culture. Applicants for cultural visas should note that attendance at 20 class hours per week is required.

Japanese Language

Studying Japanese has become so popular that schools cannot keep up with demand and there are long waiting lists of foreign students. The TIC leaflet *Japanese & Japanese Studies* lists government-accredited schools that belong to the Association of International Education (☎ 3485-6827). The association can also be contacted directly. Another organisation worth contacting is the Association for the Promotion of Japanese Language Education (☎ 5386-0080).

Costs at private Japanese-language schools vary enormously depending on the school's status and facilities. There is usually an application fee of Y5000 to Y30,000, an administration charge of Y50,000 to Y100,000, and annual tuition fees of Y400,000 to Y750,000. Add accommodation and food, and it is easy to see that studying is not a viable option for most people unless they also have an opportunity to work.

Martial Arts

Aikidō, jūdō, karate and kendō can be studied in Japan
as well as less popular fields such as *kyūdō* (Japanese
archery) and sumō. Relevant addresses include:

All-Japan Jūdō Federation, c/o Kodokan, 1-16-30 Kasuga,
Bukyō-ku, Tokyo (☎ 3812-9580)

Amateur Archery Federation of Japan, Kishi Memorial Hall,
4th Floor, 1-1-1 Jinan, Shibuya-ku, Tokyo (☎ 3481-2387)

International Aikidō Federation, 17-18 Wakamatsu-cho,
Shinjuku-ku, Tokyo (☎ 3203-9236)

Japan Karate Association (☎ 3462-1415). For information on
how to get there, ring Mr Yamamoto, Mr Hashimoto or
Mr Yagyu at Wise International (☎ 3436-4567) – all three
speak English.

Japan Kendō Federation, c/o Nippon Budokan, 2-3
Kitanomaru-kōen, Chiyoda-ku, Tokyo (☎ 3211-58045)

Nihon Sumō Kyokai, c/o Kokugikan Sumō Hall, 1-3-28
Yokoami, Sumida-ku, Tokyo (☎ 3623-5111)

Cultural

Tokyo is an excellent place to study anything related to
Japanese culture, from Zen meditation to ikebana. The
following are some contact numbers for schools around
Tokyo.

Calligraphy Known in Japanese as *shūji*, calligraphy
lessons are available at the Koyo Calligraphy Art School
(☎ 3941-3809) in Ōtsuka.

Ikebana The study of flower arrangement is popular
among Japanese and consequently there are numerous
ikebana schools around Tokyo. Some of them are even
able to provide a one-off lesson in English. These include
the Ohara School (% 3499-1200) in Harajuku and the
Sogetsu School (% 3408-1126) in Aoyama. The price for
a single lesson, including the flowers, ranges from Y3500
to Y5000.

Shiatsu Lessons in English are available for shiatsu, or
finger-pressure massage. For more information, contact
Dr Kimura at the Iokai Shiatsu Centre (☎ 3832-2983).

Tea Ceremony Both courses and opportunities to
participate in the tea ceremony are available to foreigners in Tokyo. The Kenkyusha Eigo Centre (☎ 5261-8940)
in Iidabashi has both one-off lessons (Y5000) and three-
month courses (Y34,000) in English. To participate in a

tea ceremony, contact the Hotel New Otani (☎ 3265-1111), the Imperial Hotel (☎ 3504-1111) or the Hotel Okura (☎ 3582-0111). These hotels have tea ceremonies you can join for about Y1000 on weekdays. Ring ahead to make an appointment.

Zen There are some organisations and temples around Tokyo that hold talks and zen meditation sessions in English. These include Dogen Sanga (☎ 3235-0701) in Hongo San-chome and Soun-in (☎ 3844-3711) in Ueno. For general Buddhist services in English, Hongan-ji Temple in Tsukiji has a sermon in English on the second and fourth Sunday of every month at 5 pm.

FOOD

It is unlikely that Japanese restaurants outside Japan could possibly prepare the visitor for the sheer diversity of cuisines available in Tokyo. For one, there is an enormous range of Japanese regional cuisines, all of which are represented somewhere in Tokyo. The Japanese are also adept at modifying foreign dishes and making them their own; the pizza you order at the little 'Italian' place on the corner in Tokyo will probably be unlike any pizza you've had before.

Sembei makers (CT)

The following is an introduction to some of the Japanese cuisines that are available in Tokyo. For specific information on where to eat and other cuisines, see the Places to Eat chapter later in this guide.

Okonomiyaki   お好みやき

This is an inexpensive Japanese cuisine, somewhat like a pancake or omelette with anything that's lying around in the kitchen thrown in. The dish is usually prepared by the diner on a hotplate on the table. Typical ingredients include vegetables, pork, beef and prawns.

Rāmen   ラーメン

This is a Chinese cuisine that has been taken over by the Japanese and made their own. These restaurants are generally the cheapest places to fill yourself up in Japan. Rāmen dishes are big bowls of noodles in a chicken stock with vegetables and/or meat and are priced from around Y350.

chāshūmen   叉焼メン
  rāmen with roasted pork
gomokumen   五目メン
  rāmen with a combination of five ingredients (meat, egg and vegetables)
gyōza   餃子
  Chinese fried meat and vegetable dumpling
miso rāmen   みそラーメン
  rāmen with miso

Soba   そば

This is a traditional Tokyo noodle dish, made with buckwheat noodles. The noodles come in a hot or cold fish-stock soup with various other ingredients.

kake   かけそば
  soba with slices of spring onion
kamo-namban   かもなんばんそば
  soba with spring onion and chicken
kitsune   きつねそば
  soba with thinly sliced tōfu
tempura   天ぷらそば
  soba with prawn tempura

tsukimi　月見そば
 soba with a raw egg on top (literally 'moon viewing')

Udon　うどん
This Osaka dish is similar to soba, except that the noodles are white and thicker.

kake-udon　かけうどん
 udon with spring onions
kamo-namban　かもなんばんうどん
 udon with chicken and spring onions
nabeyaki-udon　なべやきうどん
 udon with tempura

Sukiyaki & Shabu-Shabu
すき焼としゃぶしゃぶ
Restaurants usually specialise in both these dishes. Sukiyaki is generally cooked on the table in front of the diner. It is prepared by cooking thinly sliced beef, vegetables and tōfu in a slightly sweetened soya sauce broth. The difference between sukiyaki and shabu-shabu is in the broth that is used. Shabu-shabu is made with a stock-based broth.

Sushi & Sashimi　すしとさしみ
These are probably the most famous of Japanese dishes. The difference between them is that sashimi is thin slivers of raw fish served with soy sauce and *wasabi* (hot horseradish), while for sushi, the raw fish is set atop a small pillow of lightly vinegared rice.

amaebi　甘海老
 sweet prawn (raw)
awabi　あわび
 abalone
ebi　海老
 prawn or shrimp
hamachi　はまち
 yellowtail
ika　いか
 squid
ikura　いくら
 salmon roe

kappa maki　かっぱ巻
　cucumber in *norimaki* (seaweed roll)
maguro　まぐろ
　tuna
tai　たい
　sea bream
tamago　たまご
　sweetened egg
toro　とろ
　fatty tuna
uni　うに
　sea urchin roe

Tempura　天ぷら

This dish has controversial origins, some maintaining that it is a Portuguese import. Tempura is what fish & chips might have been – fluffy, nongreasy batter and delicate, melt-in-your mouth portions of fish, prawns and vegetables.

Yakitori　焼き鳥

This cuisine comprises various parts of the chicken, skewered on a stick and cooked over a charcoal fire. Yakitori is great drinking food, and the restaurants will serve beer and saké with the food. Some common yakitori dishes:

kawa　やきとり
　chicken skin
negima　ねぎま
　chicken and spring onion
piiman　ピーマン
　green capsicum
rebā　レバー
　liver
sei-niku　せい肉
　dark chicken meat
sasami　ささみ
　chicken breast
tsukune　つくね
　chicken meat balls

Robatayaki　ろばた焼

Robatayaki restaurants are celebrated as the noisiest in the world. Enter and you will be hailed by a chorus of welcoming *irasshaimases*, as if you were some long-lost relative. Orders are usually made by shouting. The food, a variety of things including seafood, tōfu, beef, chicken and vegetables, is cooked over a grill. Again, this is a drinking cuisine. Both sashimi and yakitori are popular robatayaki dishes – others include:

agedashi-dōfu　揚げ出し豆腐
   deep fried tōfu in a fish-stock soup
jagabatā　じゃがバター
   potatoes grilled with butter
niku-jaga　肉じゃが
   broiled meat and potato
shio-yaki　塩焼
   a whole fish grilled with salt
tōmorokoshi　とうもろこし
   corn on the cob
yaki-onigiri　焼おにぎり
   broiled rice balls

When Japan was getting me down, a robatayaki was always my favorite choice of a place to eat. The noisy bonhomie may simply be a part of the background décor but it certainly made me feel better. The food was familiar and recognisable, and ordering was never any problem at all as everything was either out on view and you could simply point or the menu was illustrated.

Tony Wheeler

Nabemono　なべもの

This winter cuisine consists of a stew cooked in a heavy earthenware pot. Like sukiyaki, it is a dish cooked on the table in front of the diner.

Fugu　ふぐ

Only the Japanese could make a culinary speciality out of a dish which could kill you. The fugu, pufferfish or globefish, puffs itself up into an almost spherical shape to deter its enemies. Its delicate flesh is highly esteemed and traditionally served in carefully arranged fans of thinly sliced segments. Eat the wrong part of the humble pufferfish, however, and you drop dead. It is said a slight numbness of the lips indicates you were close to the most exciting meal of your life. However, fugu fish chefs are carefully licensed, and losing customers is not encour-

Ameyoko-cho market, Ueno (CT)

aged. Every year there are a few deaths from pufferfish poisoning but they are usually from fish prepared in homes. Fugu can only be eaten for a few months each year and the very best fugu restaurants, places which specialise in nothing else, close down for the rest of the year. It's said that the fugu chef who loses a customer is honour bound to take his own life.

Unagi　うなぎ

This is Japanese for 'eel'. Cooked Japanese style, over hot coals and brushed with soy sauce and sweet saké, this is a popular and delicious dish.

Kaiseki　懐石料理

The origins of kaiseki are in the tea ceremony, where a number of light and aesthetically prepared morsels would accompany the proceedings. True kaiseki is *very* expensive – the diner is paying for the whole experience, the traditional setting and so on.

Etiquette

When it comes to eating in Japan, there are quite a number of implicit rules, but they're fairly easy to remember. If you're worried about putting your foot in it, relax – the Japanese almost expect foreigners to make fools of themselves in formal situations and are unlikely to be offended as long as you follow the standards of politeness of your own country.

Among the more important eating 'rules' are those regarding chopsticks. Sticking them upright in your rice is considered very bad form, that's how rice is offered to the dead! So is passing food from your chopsticks to someone else's – another Buddhist death rite involves passing the bones of the cremated deceased among members of the family using chopsticks.

When eating with other people, the general practice is to preface actually digging into the food with the expression *itadakimasu*, literally 'I will receive'. Similarly, at the end of the meal someone will probably say *gochisōsama deshita*, a respectful way of saying that the meal was good and satisfying.

In Japan, there is a definite etiquette to bill-paying. If someone invites you to eat or drink with them, they will

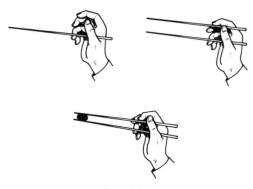

Chopsticks

be paying. Even among groups eating together it is unusual for bills to be split. Generally, at the end of the meal, something of a struggle will ensue to see who gets the privilege of paying the bill. If this happens, it is polite to at least make an effort to pay the bill – it is extremely unlikely that your Japanese 'hosts' will acquiesce. Exceptions to this rule are likely among young Japanese such as students.

DRINK

Alcoholic Drinks

The Japanese are serious about drinking and, unlike most other Asian countries, drinking is a popular pastime for both sexes. It is routinely taken to excess, presumably as a release from the straitjacket of proper conduct at work. Office workers are expected to join their group's boozing sessions to promote bonding. Although recently, with *karōshi* (death from overwork) featuring prominently in the news, opposition to the company drinking rituals is starting to materialise.

If you're out for a few drinks with Japanese friends, remember that you're expected to keep the drinks of your fellow drinkers topped up. Don't fill your own glass: wait for someone to do this for you. It's polite to hold the glass with both hands while it is being filled. The Japanese equivalent of cheers is *Kampai!*

Beer, the most popular alcohol available, is even available from vending machines, where a standard-size can generally costs between Y280 and Y300. The quality is generally excellent and the most popular type is a light lager. The major brewers are Asahi, Suntory, Sapporo and Kirin.

Saké is of course the traditional Japanese brew, but in recent years beer has overtaken it in popularity. Nevertheless, it is still a standard item in homes, restaurants and drinking dens. There are three grades of saké: tokkyū (premium), ikkyū (first grade) and nikyū (second grade). Nikyū is the routine choice. Large casks of saké are often seen piled up as offerings outside a shrine or temple and it plays a part in most celebrations or festivals. Although saké doesn't have quite the cultural significance that wine does in the West, it is still taken very seriously by many Japanese.

For those looking for a quick and cheap escape route from the world of sorrows, *shōchū* is the answer. It's a distilled spirit (averaging 30% alcohol content) which has been resurrected from its previous low-class esteem – it was used as a disinfectant in the Edo period – to the status of a trendy drink. You can drink it as *oyuwari* (with hot water) or as a highball *chūhai* (with soda and lemon). A bottle (720 ml) sells for about Y650 which makes it a relatively cheap option compared to other spirits.

Japanese wines are available and are often blended with imports from South America or Eastern Europe. The major producers are Suntory, Mann's and Mercian. Prices are expensive – expect to pay at least Y1300 for a bottle of something drinkable.

The Japanese produce whisky that measures up to international standards. Prices for imported spirits of any kind are usually astronomical. Make use of your duty-free allotment.

Non-Alcoholic Drinks

Most of the drinks you're used to at home, or at least varieties of them anyway, will be available in Japan. One convenient aspect of pounding city sidewalks, especially in warm weather, is the ubiquitous drink-dispensing machine. These have everything from hot coffee to the popular soft drinks, Pocari Sweat and Jolt – 'with twice the caffeine'.

Coffee drinkers will have no problems getting a fix in Tokyo – there are coffee shops everywhere you look. If you object to the high prices, look out for the discount chains Doutor and Pronto, where a coffee is Y180. And watch out for your lips on the hot cans of coffee from the vending machines.

Finally, as everyone knows, the Japanese are tea drinkers. Unlike the tea Westerners drink, Japanese tea is green and does not contain caffeine. As a visit to the tea section of any Japanese department store will show, Japanese tea comes in a variety of forms; among these green leaf, ground green leaf and green leaf with bits of rice in it. During the summer many Japanese drink *mugicha*, a cold barley-water drink.

Getting There & Away

AIR

To/From USA & Canada

West-coast flights to Tokyo go straight across the Pacific and take about 10 hours. From the east coast, flights usually take the northern route over Alaska – the new nonstop flights take about 13 hours. The large time change on the trans-Pacific flights is a sure-fire recipe for jet lag and there's also a date change as you cross the International Date Line.

Seven-day advance purchase return fares are from US$850 from the west coast (depending on the season) and US$1080 from the east. Regular economy fares are much higher – US$874 to US$935 (one way) from the west coast, and US$1195 to US$1279 from the east coast.

Better deals are available if you shop around. From the east coast, return fares as low as US$845 and one-way fares of US$540 are possible. From the west coast return fares can drop from US$689 to US$559 with carriers like Korean Airlines. There are also good deals available via Vancouver with Canadian Airlines International. From San Francisco or Los Angeles, return fares to Tokyo range from US$629 to US$769. Check the Sunday travel sections of papers like the *Los Angeles Times* or the *New York Times* for travel bargains. Council Travel and STA are two good discount operations specialising in student fares and other cheap deals. They have offices all across USA and Canada.

Fares from Canada are similar to those from the USA. Canadian Airlines International, which operates out of Vancouver, often matches or beats the best fares available from the USA. A return flight from Vancouver starts from C$1130. Travel Cuts, the Canadian student travel organisation, offers cheap one-way and return Vancouver-Tokyo flights depending on the season.

To/From Europe

Flight times between Europe and Tokyo vary widely depending on the route taken. The most direct route is across Scandinavia and Russia. The fastest nonstop

London-Tokyo flights taking this route take just under 12 hours. Flights that stop in Moscow take an extra 2½ hours. Finnair's Helsinki-Tokyo flight over the North Pole and the Bering Strait takes 13½ hours. Before the Russians opened their skies, the popular route was via Anchorage, Alaska. Some flights still operate that way and take about 17 hours, including the Anchorage stop-over. Finally, there are the old trans-Asian routes across the Middle East and south Asia, which take anything from 18 to 30 hours depending on the number of stops en route.

Return economy air fares between London and Tokyo are around UK£1150 and are valid for 14 days to three months. There are also tickets valid for 7 days to six months which are around £1140. Although a wide variety of cheaper deals are available, generally, the lower the price, the less convenient the route. Expect to pay around £1360 for a full return ticket with no time restrictions and with a good airline via a fast route. For a less convenient trans-Asian route, count on £700 or lower and about half that for one-way tickets.

In London, STA Travel (☎ (071) 937-9962) at 74 Old Brompton Rd, London SW7 or 117 Euston Rd, London NW1, Trailfinders (☎ (071) 938-3366) at 46 Earls Court Rd and at 194 Kensington High St, London W8 7RG (☎ (071) 938-3444), and Travel Bug (☎ (061) 721-4000), all offer rock-bottom return flights to Tokyo and can also put together interesting Round-the-World routes incorporating Tokyo on the itinerary. The weekly 'what's on' magazine *Time Out* or the various giveaway papers are good places to look for travel bargains but take care with shonky bucket shops and prices that seem too low to believe. The really cheap fares will probably involve cash-strapped Eastern European or Middle Eastern airlines and may involve complicated transfers and long waits along the way.

The Far East Travel Centre, or FETC (☎ (071) 734-9318), at 3 Lower John St, London W1A 4XE, specialises in Korean Airline ticketing and can fly you from London Gatwick via Seoul to Tokyo. The Japan Centre (☎ (071) 437-6445), 66-68 Brewer St, London W1R 3PJ, handles all sorts of ticket permutations. Its basement has a shop section (☎ (071) 439-8035) with books and assorted Japanese paraphernalia as well as a Japanese restaurant with reasonable prices. It's worth a visit for a taste of Japan.

An alternative route to Japan from Europe is to fly to Hong Kong and buy an onward ticket from one of Hong Kong's very competitive travel agencies. London-Hong Kong flights are much more competitively priced than

London-Tokyo ones. If you have to go to Hong Kong en route to Tokyo, a London-Hong Kong-London ticket plus a Hong Kong-Tokyo-Hong Kong ticket can work out much cheaper than a London-Hong Kong-Tokyo-London ticket.

London remains one of the best places in Europe to purchase keenly priced airline tickets, although Amsterdam is also very good.

To/From Australasia

Japan Airlines (JAL), All Nippon Airways (ANA) and Qantas all have direct flights between Australia and Tokyo, flying from most Australia state capitals. There's only a one-hour time change between Australia and Japan and a direct Sydney-Tokyo flight takes about nine hours.

A return excursion Sydney-Tokyo fare is around A$1600. Discount deals will involve round about routes via other Asian capitals like Kuala Lumpur (Malaysia), Manila (Philippines) or Bali (Indonesia). If you shop around, you can find one-way flights from Sydney or Melbourne for around A$950, and return flights for A$1250. STA travel offices or the numerous Flight Centres International are good places to look for discount ticket deals.

From New Zealand, Auckland-Tokyo return excursion fares are around NZ$1750 in the low season rising to NZ$2200 in the high.

To/From Asia

Most Asian nations have air links with Japan. South Korea is particularly popular because it's used by many travellers as a place to take a short holiday from Japan when their visas are close to expiring. The immigration authorities treat travellers returning to Japan after a short break in South Korea with great suspicion. Hong Kong is popular because it is such a bargain basement for airline ticketing.

South Korea Numerous flights link Seoul and Pusan with Tokyo. A one-way/return Seoul-Tokyo flight costs around US$180/340. There are also ferry links connecting South Korea with Shimonoseki, Osaka and Fukuoka, but if you include the onward travel from these places to Tokyo, you'd be better off flying direct.

Hong Kong There is no shortage of direct flights between Hong Kong and Tokyo, though the cheapest will involve a stopover. Agents like the Hong Kong Student Travel Bureau (☎ 7303269) or Phoenix Travel (☎ 7227378) can offer one-way tickets from around HK$2400, and return tickets from HK$3500 to HK$4500, depending on the route and the period of validity.

Taiwan Agents handling discounted tickets advertise in the English-language *China Post*. The average price for return flight from Taipei to Tokyo is NT$9700.

Other Asian Centres There are regular flights between Japan and other major centres like Manila, Bangkok, Kuala Lumpur, Singapore and Jakarta. Bangkok and Penang offer the cheapest prices for flights to Tokyo.

To/From Other Regions

There are also flights between Japan and South America, Africa and the Middle East.

Round-the-World & Circle Pacific Tickets

Round-the-World (RTW) fares are put together by two or more airlines and allow you to make a circuit of the world using their combined routes. A typical RTW ticket is valid for one year, allows unlimited stopovers along the way and costs about UK£1400, A$3500 or US$2700. An example, including Tokyo, would be a British Airways/United Airways combination flying London-New York-Tokyo-Singapore-London. A South Pacific version might take you London-New York-Los Angeles-Tahiti-Sydney-Tokyo-London. There are many options involving different combinations of airlines and different routes. Generally, routes which stay north of the equator are usually a little cheaper than routes that include countries like Australia or South America.

Circle Pacific fares are a similar idea and allow you to make a circuit of the Pacific. A typical combination involves Qantas and Japan Airlines flying Los Angeles-Tahiti-Sydney-Tokyo-Los Angeles. Circle Pacific fares are around A$2900 or US$2300.

Enterprising travel agents put together their own RTW and Circle Pacific fares at much lower prices than the joint airline deals but, of course, the cheapest fares will involve unpopular airlines and less popular routes. It's possible to put together a RTW from London for as little as UK£700. RTW or Circle Pacific fares from Aus-

Looking good (CT)

tralia start from around A$2100. Travel agents in London have also come up with another variation on these combination fares – the Circle Asia fare. A possible route is London-Hong Kong-Tokyo-Manila-Singapore-Bangkok- London.

Airline Offices

Following is a list of the major airline offices in Tokyo.

Aeroflot
    No 2 Matsuda Building, 3-4-8 Toranomon, Minato-ku (☎ 3434-9671)
Air China (formerly CAAC)
    AO1 Building, 3-2-7 Akasaka, Minato-ku (☎ 3505-2021)
Air India
    Hibiya Park Building, 1-8-1 Yūraku-cho, Chiyoda-ku (☎ 3214-1981)
Air Lanka
    Dowa Building, 7-2-22 Ginza, Chūō-ku (☎ 3573-4261)
Air New Zealand
    Shin Kokusai Building, 3-4-1 Marunouchi, Chiyoda-ku (☎ 3287-1641)
Alitalia
    Tokyo Club Building, 3-2-6 Kasumigaseki, Chiyoda-ku (☎ 3580-2181)
All Nippon Airways (ANA)
    Kasumigaseki Building, 3-2-5 Kasumigaseki, Chiyoda-ku (☎ 3272-1212, international; 3552-8800, domestic)

American Airlines
  201 Kokusai Building, 3-1-1 Marunouchi, Chiyoda-ku (☎ 3248-2011)
Bangladesh Biman
  Kasumigaseki Building, 3-2-5 Kasumigaseki, Chiyoda-ku (☎ 3593-1252)
British Airways
  Sanshin Building, 1-4-1 Yūraku-cho, Chiyoda-ku (☎ 3593-8811)
Canadian Airlines International
  Hibiya Park Building, 1-8-1 Yūraku-cho, Chiyoda-ku (☎ 3281-7426)
Cathay Pacific
  Toho Twin Tower Building, 1-5-2 Yūraku-cho, Chiyoda-ku (☎ 3504-1531)
China Airlines
  Matsuoka Building, 5-22-10 Shimbashi, Minato-ku (☎ 3436-1661)
Continental Airlines
  Suite 517, Sanno Grand Building, 2-14-2 Nagata-cho, Chiyoda-ku (☎ 3592-1631)
Delta Airlines
  Kokusai Building, 3-1-1 Marunouchi, Chiyoda-ku (☎ 3275-7000)
Finnair
  NK Building, 2-14-2 Kojimachi, Chūō-ku (☎ 3222-6801)
Garuda Indonesian Airways
  Kasumigaseki Building, 3-2-5 Kasumigaseki, Chiyoda-ku (☎ 3593-1181)
Japan Airlines (JAL)
  Tokyo Building, 2-7-3 Marunouchi, Chiyoda-ku (☎ 3489-1111, international; 3456-2111 domestic)
Japan Air System (JAS)
  No 18 Mori Building, 2-3-13 Toranomon, Minato-ku (☎ 3438-1155)
KLM
  Yūraku-cho Denki Building, 1-7-1 Yūraku- cho, Chiyoda-ku (☎ 3216-0771)
Korean Air
  Shin Kokusai Building, 3-4-1 Marunouchi, Chiyoda-ku (☎ 3211-3311)
Lufthansa
  3-2-6 Kasumigaseki, Chiyoda-ku (☎ 3580-2111)
Malaysian Airlines (MAS)
  3rd Floor, No 29 Mori Building, 4-2 Shimbashi, Minato-ku (☎ 3503-5961)
Northwest Orient Airlines
  5-12-12 Toranomon, Minato-ku (☎ 3533-6000)
Philippine Airlines
  Sanno Grand Building, 2-14-2 Nagata-cho, Chiyoda-ku (☎ 3593-2421)
Qantas
  Tokyo Shoko Kaigisho Building, 3-2-2 Marunouchi, Chiyoda-ku (☎ 3593-7000)

Sabena Belgian World Airlines
  Address Building, 2-2-19 Akasaka, Minato-ku (☎ 3585-6151)
Scandinavian Airlines (SAS)
  Toho Twin Tower Building, 1-5-2 Yūraku-cho, Chiyoda-ku (☎ 3503-8101)
Singapore Airlines
  Yūraku-cho Building 709, 1-10-1 Yūraku-cho, Chiyoda-ku (☎ 3213-3431)
Swissair
  Hibiya Park Building, 1-8-1 Yūraku-cho, Chiyoda-ku (☎ 3212-1016)
Thai Airways International
  Asahi Seimei Hibiya Building, 1-5-1 Yūraku-cho, Chiyoda-ku (☎ 3503-3311)
United Airlines
  Kokusai Building, 3-1-1 Marunouchi, Chiyoda-ku (☎ 3817-4411)
Virgin Atlantic Airways
  3-13 Yotsuya, Shinjuku-ku (☎ 5269-2680)

Arriving in Tokyo

With the exception of China Airlines, all international airlines touch down at Narita Airport rather than at the more conveniently located. Narita Airport has had a controversial history, its construction having met with considerable opposition from farmers it displaced and from student radicals. Even today, it is very security conscious, which can slow down progress in and out of the airport.

Immigration and customs procedures are usually straightforward, although they can be very time consuming for non-Japanese. Everything is clearly signposted in English and you can change money in the customs hall after having cleared customs or in the arrival hall. The rates will be the same as those offered in town.

The airport Tourist Information Centre (TIC) (☎ 0476-32-8711) is an important stop. It has a wealth of invaluable information – at the very least, pick up a subway map and the *Tourist Map of Tokyo*. The office is open Monday to Friday from 9 am to 8 pm and on Saturday from 9 am to noon; it is closed on Sunday and public holidays. The centre is to the right as you exit the customs hall, between the main building and the southern wing.

In the middle of the central block there is a JR office where you can make bookings and exchange your Japan Rail Pass voucher for a pass if you're planning to start travelling straight away. For information on getting from

Narita and Haneda airports into Tokyo see the following Getting Around chapter.

Leaving Tokyo

Departure Tax There is a Y2000 departure tax at Narita airport, while all those lucky people flying China Airways from Haneda airport get out of the country for nothing.

Travel Agents & Airline Tickets Tokyo is a particularly expensive place to buy airline tickets, though it is possible to occasionally come across a bargain. Some typical prices for return air tickets from Tokyo in the travel agents specialising in tickets for foreigners (generally cheaper than the agents set up for locals) are: Seoul Y36,000; Hong Kong Y59,000; Bangkok Y60,000; London Y150,000; Los Angeles Y65,000; New York Y110,000; and Sydney Y96,000.

Probably the best place to check out the travel deals in town is the *Tokyo Journal*. The Classified section has advertisements for some of the travel agents offering cut-price air tickets. Three well established travel agents where English is spoken are: STA in Yotsuya (☎ 5269-0751), Shibuya (☎ 5485-8380) and Ikebukuro (☎ 5391-2922); Across Traveller's Bureau in Shinjuku (☎ 3374-8721) and Ikebukuro (☎ 5391- 2871); and Just Travel in Takadanobaba (☎ 3207-8311).

Some theatre ticket outlets are also able to provide discounted tickets for domestic air flights and shinkansen (bullet train) journeys. A good place to try is Ikari (☎ 3407-3554) opposite Shibuya post office on the 3rd floor of the Gloria Shibuya building.

LAND

Bus

There are buses plying the expressways between Tokyo and various other parts of Japan. Generally they are little or no cheaper than the trains but are sometimes a good alternative for long-distance trips to areas serviced by expressways. The buses will often run direct, so that you can relax instead of watching for your stop as you would have to do on an ordinary train service.

There are a number of express buses running between Tokyo, Kyoto and Osaka. Overnight buses leave at 10 pm from Tokyo station and arrive at Kyoto and Osaka between 6 and 7 am the following morning. They cost from Y8000 to Y8500. If you plan on coming back the same way, a return ticket can save you quite a bit of money. An example is Tokyo-Kyoto: a one-way ticket costs Y8030, while a return is Y14,200. The buses are a Japanese Railways (JR) service and can be booked at one of the Green Windows in a JR station. Direct buses also run from Tokyo station to Nara and Kōbe. And from Shinjuku station there are buses running to the Fuji and Hakone regions, including, for Mt Fuji climbers, direct services to the fifth stations, from where you have to walk.

Train

Arriving in Tokyo by train is a simple affair. Most of the major train lines terminate at either Tokyo or Ueno stations, both of which are on the JR Yamanote line. As a general rule of thumb, trains for the north and north-east start at Ueno station and southbound trains start at Tokyo station. For day trips to areas such as Kamakura, Nikkō, Hakone and Yokohama, the most convenient means of transport is usually one of the private lines. With the exception of the Tōbu Nikkō line, which starts in Asakusa, all of them start from somewhere on the Yamanote line.

Shinkansen There are three shinkansen, or bullet train, lines that connect Tokyo with the rest of Japan: the Tōkaidō line passes through Central Honshū, changing name along the way to the San-yō line before terminating at Hakata in Northern Kyūshū; the Tōhoku line runs north-east via Utsunomiya and Sendai as far as Morioka; and the Jōetsu line runs north to Niigata. Of these lines, the one most likely to be used by visitors to Japan is the Tōkaidō line, as it passes through Kyoto and Osaka in the Kansai region. The Tōkaidō line starts at Tokyo station, while the Tōhoku and Jōetsu lines start at Ueno station.

Other JR Lines As well as the Tōkaidō shinkansen line there is a Tōkaidō line servicing the same areas but stopping at all the stations that the shinkansen zips through without so much as a toot of its horn. Trains start at Tokyo station and pass through Shimbashi and Shinagawa stations on their way out of town. There are express services to Yokohama and the Izu-hantō Peninsula, via Atami, and from there trains continue to Nagoya, Kyoto and Osaka.

If you are keeping expenses down and travelling long distance on the Tōkaidō line, there are some late-night services that do the Tokyo to Osaka run, arriving early the next morning. One of them will have sleepers available.

Travelling in the same direction as the initial stages of the Tōkaidō line, the Yokosuka line offers a much cheaper service to Yokohama and Kamakura. Like the Tōkaidō line, the Yokosuka line starts at Tokyo station and passes through Shimbashi and Shinagawa stations on its way out of Tokyo.

Northbound trains start in Ueno. The Takasaki line goes to Kumagaya and Takasaki, with onward connections from Takasaki to Niigata. The Tōhoku line follows the Takasaki line as far north as Ōmiya, from where it heads to the far north of Honshū via Sendai and Aomori. Getting to Sendai without paying any express surcharges will involve changes at Utsunomiya and Fukushima. Overnight services also operate for those intent on saving the expense of a night's accommodation.

Private Lines The private lines generally service Tokyo's sprawling suburbia and very few of them go to any areas that visitors to Japan would care to visit. Still, where private lines do pass through tourist areas, they are usually a cheaper option than the JR lines. Particularly good bargains are the Tōkyū Toyoko line, running between Shibuya station and Yokohama; the Odakyū line, running from Shinjuku to Odawara and the Hakone region; the Tōbu Nikkō line, running from Asakusa to Nikkō; and the Seibu Shinjuku line from Shinjuku to Kawagoe.

SEA

There are no direct international sea links with Tokyo, but there are two services running to Yokohama nearby. The Trans-Siberian rail service allows for a connection between Nakhodka (Russia) and Yokohama from June to September. Tickets for the complete rail/sea journey cost around US$900 for a 2nd-class sleeper on the train and a four-berth cabin on the ship. Intourist recommends a minimum of four weeks notice to take care of visas, hotel bookings and train reservations. For information on travelling the other direction contact Uniorient (☎ 3294-3351) in Tokyo. Ticket prices from Yokohama to Nakhodka start at ¥60,800.

The other international sea link with Yokohama is a ferry service running to and from Shanghai (China). The service runs only once a month and tickets start at

Y27,000. For more information ring Japan-China International Ferry (☎ 3294-3351) in Tokyo.

From Tokyo, there are also long-distance ferry services to other parts of Japan: Kushiro on Hokkaidō (Y14,420); to Kōchi (Y13,910) and Tokushima (Y8200) on Shikoku; to Kokura in Northern Kyūshū (Y12,000); and to Naha on Okinawa (Y19,670). For information on these services, ring the Ferry Service Centre (☎ 3501-0806) in Tokyo.

Getting Around

Tokyo has an excellent public transport system. There are very few worthwhile spots around town that aren't conveniently close to a subway or Japanese Railway (JR) station. When the rail network lets you down, there are generally bus services, though these are harder to use if you can't read kanji.

Most residents of and visitors to Tokyo find themselves using the railway system far more than any other means of transport. In fact, the only real drawback with the Tokyo railway network is that it shuts down somewhere between midnight and 1 am and doesn't start up again until 5 or 6 am. Subway trains have a habit of stopping halfway along their route when closing time arrives. People who get stranded face the prospect of an expensive taxi ride home or of waiting the rest of the night for the first morning train.

Avoiding Tokyo's rush hour is a good idea, but unfortunately almost impossible. Things tend to quieten down between 10 am and 4 pm, when travelling around Tokyo can actually be quite pleasant, but before 9.30 am and from about 4.30 pm onwards there are likely to be cheek-to-jowl crowds on all the major train and bus lines. The best advice for coping with the late-evening crowds is probably to be as drunk as everyone else.

TO/FROM NARITA AIRPORT

Narita International Airport is used by almost all the international airlines but only by a small number of domestic operators. The airport is 66 km from central Tokyo, which means that getting into town is going to take from 50 minutes to 1½ hours, depending on your mode of transport.

Train

The JR Narita line has express services (JR NEX) to Tokyo central station (Y2890, 53 minutes); to Shinjuku station (Y3050, 74 minutes); to Ikebukuro station (Y3050, 90 minutes); and Yokohama station (Y4100, 84 minutes). The rapid train (kaisoku) takes 80 minutes and costs Y1260 to Tokyo central.

On the private Keisei line, there are two trains running between Narita Airport and Ueno stations: the Skyliner, which runs nonstop and takes one hour (Y1740); and the limited express (tokkyū) service, which takes 70 minutes (Y940). You can buy tickets at the Keisei ticket office in the northern wing of the arrival lounge at Narita Airport or at the station. Ueno is the final destination of the train and is on the JR Yamanote line and on the Hibiya and Ginza subway lines.

Going to the airport from Ueno, the Keisei station is right next to the JR Ueno station. You can buy advance tickets for the Skyliner service at the ticket counter, while limited express and express tickets are available from the ticket dispensing machines. From the JR station on the Yamanote line, take the southern exit (you should come out under the railway bridge, more or less opposite the Ameyoko market area) and turn right. The station is about 50 metres away on your right.

Limousine Bus

Ticket offices, marked with the sign 'limousine', can be found in both wings of the arrival building. The limousine buses are just ordinary buses and take 1½ to two hours (depending on the traffic) to travel between Narita Airport and a number of major hotels around Tokyo. Check departure times before buying your ticket, as services are not all that frequent. The fare to hotels in eastern Tokyo is Y2500, while to Ikebukuro, Akasaka, Ginza, Shiba, Shinagawa, Shinjuku or Haneda Airport it is Y2700. There is also a bus service straight to Yokohama which costs Y3100. The trip to Yokohama City Air Terminal (YCAT) takes at least two hours.

There are also buses every 20 minutes to the Tokyo City Air Terminal (TCAT), costing Y2500. The TCAT is inconveniently located in Nihombashi, about a 15-minute walk from the nearest subway stations at Ningyō-cho and Kayaba-cho. There is a frequent shuttle bus service between the TCAT and Tokyo station, costing Y200 and departing from the Yaesu side at Tokyo station (look for the signs). If you are leaving Tokyo, you can check in your luggage at the TCAT before taking the bus out to the airport. Allow some extra time if you plan to do this.

A taxi to Tokyo will cost about Y20,000.

TO/FROM HANEDA AIRPORT

Most domestic flights and China Airlines (Taiwan) flights use the convenient Haneda Airport.

Getting from Haneda Airport to Tokyo is a simple matter of taking the monorail to Hamamatsu-cho station on the JR Yamanote line. The trip takes just under 20

minutes; trains leave every 10 minutes and cost Y270.
Taxis to places around central Tokyo will cost around
Y6000.

If you're arriving at Haneda by China Airlines, it is a
10-minute walk from the international terminal to the
monorail station. Turn right when you exit the terminal
and walk down to the domestic terminal. Look out for
the monorail sign and the flight of stairs down into the
station area.

There is also a direct bus service between Haneda and
Narita which can take up to two hours, depending on
the traffic. The alternative is to take the monorail in to
Tokyo, then the Yamanote line to Ueno and the Keisei
line from there, but this is much more time-consuming.

BUS

Many Tokyo residents and visitors spend a considerable
amount of time in the city without ever using the bus
network. This is partly because the train services are so
good and partly because the buses are much more difficult to use. In addition, buses are at the mercy of Tokyo's
sluggish traffic flow. Services also tend to finish fairly
early in the evening, making buses a pretty poor alternative all round.

Bus fares are Y160 and are paid into the fare box next
to the driver as you enter the bus. Change of Y1000 notes
will be given. A tape recording announces the name of
each stop as it is reached, so listen carefully and press
the button next to your seat if yours is announced. If you
are planning to make use of the bus system, pick up a
bus route map from the bus terminal in the basement at
the west exit of Shinjuku station. Ask for a *toei kōtsu no
goannai*.

TRAIN

The Tokyo train system can be a bit daunting at first, but
you soon get the hang of it. All the subway lines are
colour coded, so even if you can't read a thing you soon
learn that the Ginza line is orange. For all local journeys,
tickets are sold by vending machines called *jidō kippu
uriba*. Above the vending machines will be a rail map
with fares indicated next to the station names. Unfortunately for visiting illiterates, the names are often in kanji
only. Probably the best way around this problem is to
put your money in the machine and push the lowest fare
button (usually Y120). This will get you on the train and
when you get to your destination you can correct the fare

at the fare adjustment office. You can get your money back before you press the ticket button by pressing the button marked *torikeshi*.

If you get tired of fumbling for change every time you buy a ticket, the JR system offers the option of 'orange cards'. The cards are available in denominations of Y1000, Y3000, Y5000 and Y10,000. With a Y5000 card you get an extra credit of Y300 and a Y10,000 card gives you a credit of Y700. Fares are automatically deducted from the cards when you use them in the orange-card vending machines. Also now available for the automatic ticket gates is an io card, which automatically deducts the fare for your journey as you pass through the turnstile.

For long-term residents, passes called *teiki-ken* are available between two stops over a fixed period of time, but you really have to use the ticket at least once a day for it to pay off. The incentive for buying one is as much for the saving in time spent queuing for tickets as for any pecuniary advantage.

A Tokyo Free Kippu is a day pass that can be used on all JR, subways and bus lines within the Tokyo metropolitan area. It costs Y1460.

Japanese Railways (JR)

Undoubtedly the most useful line in Tokyo is the JR Yamanote line which does a loop around the city, taking in most of the important areas. The trains are either green or silver with a green stripe. You can do the whole circuit in an hour for the Y120 minimum fare – a great introduction to the city.

Another useful JR route is the Chūō line which cuts through the centre of the Yamanote line between Shinjuku and Akihabara and also services western suburban areas.

The Yokosuka line runs to Kamakura from Tokyo, Shimbashi and Shinagawa stations. The Tōkaidō line travels in the same direction from Tokyo station, providing access to the Izu-hantō Peninsula.

Private

Most of the private lines service suburban areas outside Tokyo, but some of them also connect with popular sightseeing areas. The private lines almost always represent better value for money than the JR lines. The ones you are most likely to use are Shinjuku's Odakyū line, which runs out to Hakone, and Asakusa's Tōbu Nikkō line, which runs out to Nikkō.

Tokyo Subway (TW)

Subway

There are 10 subway lines, of which seven are TRTA lines and three are TOEI lines. This is not particularly import- ant to remember, as the subway services are essentially the same, have good connections from one to the other and allow for ticket transfer between the two systems. The colour-coding and English signposting make the system easy to use. Perhaps the most confusing part is figuring out where to surface when you have reached your destination. There are almost always a large number of subway exits at every station. Fortunately there are maps posted, usually close to the ticket turn- stiles.

Generally, the subway system is indispensable for getting to areas that lay within the loop of the JR Yamanote line. The central Tokyo area is served by a large number of lines that intersect at Nihombashi, Ōtemachi and Ginza, making it possible to get to this part of town from almost anywhere. Most fares within the JR Yamanote loop are either Y140 or Y160.

TRAM

Tokyo has one solitary tram service still in operation. It doesn't really go anywhere of interest, but it does pass through a couple of areas that haven't been claimed by the promiscuous development of the Tokyo real estate

boom. The Toden Arakawa line leaves from opposite
Ōtsuka station on the JR Yamanote line. The line passes
the Sunshine City building before passing though
Zoshigaya. The latter is an interesting area dotted with
small temples and shrines. It is perhaps best known for
Zoshigaya Cemetery, the resting place of Lafcadio
Hearn, the remarkable British chronicler of everyday
Meiji Japan, and the famous writer Natsume Sōseki.
From here the tram travels on to its terminus in Waseda,
not far from Waseda University.

TAXI

Taxis are so expensive that you should only use them
when there is no alternative. Rates start at Y600, which
buys you two km (after 11 pm it's 1.5 km) before the
meter starts to rise by Y90 for every 347 metres (every
273 metres after 11 pm). You also click up Y90 approximately every two minutes while you relax in a
motionless taxi in a typical Tokyo traffic jam.

If you have to get a taxi late on a Friday or Saturday
night, be prepared for delays and higher prices. At these
difficult times, gaijin (foreigners) may find themselves
shunned like lepers because their ride is likely to be a
short one, whereas the drunken worker holding up two
fingers (to indicate his willingness to pay twice the meter
fare) is probably bound for a distant suburb. Finally,
don't get annoyed. With only around 50,000 taxis operating in Tokyo, complaints of a taxi shortage are rife –
even the locals have problems flagging one down once
the trains have shut down for the night.

CAR RENTAL

Driving in Tokyo is not a good idea, even if your health
insurance covers the costs of nursing you through the
ensuing nervous breakdown. For a start you will definitely get wherever you want to go a lot quicker on the
trains, and if that's not argument enough just take a look
at a Tokyo road map for an even more persuasive argument for leaving your International Driving Licence at
home. Imagine negotiating that tangle of expressways
and winding side streets with minimal English signposting.

If you like a challenge, however, there are car rental
agencies in Tokyo that will hire you one of their vehicles
upon presentation of an international license. Nippon
Rent-a-Car (☎ 3485-7196) is the largest agency, with
some 150 branches in Tokyo. Two other agencies are

Nissan Rent-a-Car (☎ 3587-4123) and Orix Rent-a-Car (☎ 3779-0543). Daily rental for a 1500 cc vehicle range from Y12,200 to Y15,000, plus an insurance fee of Y1000.

Anyone planning on driving in Tokyo would be well advised to get a copy of *Rules of the Road*, available from the Japan Automobile Federation, or JAF (☎ 3436-2454), for Y1860. The JAF is close to Kamiya-cho subway station on the Hibiya line.

MOTORCYCLE

Many foreigners living in Tokyo end up getting themselves a motorcycle. It can be a good way to get around town, especially after the trains have stopped running. The best place to take a look at what's available and get some information in English is the area of motorbike shops on Corin-cho Rd, near Ueno station. Some of the shops there have foreign staff. If you have a motorcycle licence, you could also try hiring a motorcycle. SCS (☎ 3827-5432) hire out scooters for around Y5000 per day, and 250cc bikes from around Y11,000 and up per day.

Remember, if you buy a motorcycle you will need a motorcyle licence (for up to 400cc, your foreign licence is transferable) and your bike will need to be registered. Bikes up to 125cc are to be registered at your ward office, and bikes over 125cc with the Bureau of Traffic. See the previous Car Rental section for information on getting a copy of *Rules of the Road*.

BICYCLE

Bicycles are much more likely to be used by Tokyo residents than visitors to the city. Some readers have written in suggesting that it is possible to pick up a bike for nothing from the disused bicycle racks near railway stations or the little bicycle grave yards one occasionally comes across. This is not really such a good idea. Police often stop foreigners on bicycles, and as all bicycles are registered with the local police they won't take long to find out whether it's yours or not. OK, it's an unwanted bike! Unfortunately this doesn't cut any ice with the long arm of the law in Tokyo.

The general procedure is for the police to take you down to the office and ring up the owner who disposed of the bike and ask whether he or she would like to transfer it to your name.

When this happened to a friend of mine, the Japanese owner thought about it for a while before deciding no, he would prefer it to go back to the dump! If you buy a bicycle make sure that the shop you buy it from reports the sale and your name and address to the local police office.

FERRIES & CRUISES

See the Asakusa section of the Things to See chapter for information on cruises down the Sumida-gawa River. Vingt-et-un (☎ 3436-2121) offers cruises from Tokyo Bay as either a straight cruise (Y2500) or including a meal (Y7500). Cruises leave twice a day.

Things to See & Do

There is a wealth of things to see and do in Tokyo. All it takes is a little courage to brave the crowds and the commuting experience. The good news is that almost every worthwhile sight in Tokyo is within easy access of a train station. Basically your railway map is your key to the city.

Tokyo offers both a glimpse into the future, as the modern metropolis *par excellence*, as well as a glimpse into Japan's more traditional past. Any trip to Tokyo should try to take in both. For the high-tech experience, visit some of the showrooms located mainly in the Ginza area or perhaps some of the towering multifunction buildings that have sprung up in western Shinjuku. Tokyo also has some quirky museums with a high-tech orientation, such as the Laforet Museum in Akasaka. A taste of traditional Japan can be provided by a visit to Meiji-jingū Shrine in Harajuku, Sensō-ji Temple in

Tokyo's Top Ten

Meiji-jinjū Shrine
Sunday afternoon at Yoyogi-kōen Park
Sensō-ji Temple
Ueno-kōen Park
Tsukiji Fish Market
Hama Rikyū Detached Palace Garden
Tokyo Disneyland
Yasukuni-jinja Shrine
Seibu Department Store (Ikebukuro)
Ginza

Tokyo's Alternative Top Ten

Dr Jeekhan's
Friday night at the Rolling Stone
Small Museum of Musical Boxes
Sleep Culture Gallery Alpha
Vibrating seats at Déjà Vu
Oh God!
Loft
Garlic Restaurants
Tokyo Kaisen Ichiba (Fish Market - late)
Kappabashi Plastic Food

Asakusa or any of the many other temples and gardens that are tucked away throughout the city.

Although Tokyo cannot compare with Kyoto in this respect, it still has some splendid gardens, such as the Hama Rikyū Detached Palace Garden near Ginza and the wonderful Japanese-style garden in the New Otani Hotel. For Japanese consumer culture at full tilt, take a stroll in any or all of the fashionable areas of Ginza, Shibuya, Harajuku, Aoyama and Akasaka, not to mention Akihabara, the garish discount 'Electric Town'. Finally, some of your best experiences will be of Tokyo by night. Try out the east side of Shinjuku, with its innumerable restaurants and salaryman watering holes, along with its infamous red-light area, Kabuki-cho – sleazy but safe. For real late-night action, check out the bright lights of Roppongi, an area that parties through till the first train of the morning.

CENTRAL TOKYO　東京中心

Central Tokyo combines the modern opulence of the Ginza, with its high-class department stores, art galleries, top-notch restaurants and show rooms, with the grandeur of the Imperial Palace and the picturesque views of the Imperial Palace East Garden. Just to the north of the Imperial Palace East Garden and close to

Imperial Palace (TW)

Kudanshita subway station are Kitanomaru-kōen Park, with its museums, and the Yasukuni-jinja Shrine (Map 1), a Shintō shrine that has been the continuing focus of controversy over the connection between politics and Shintō, a legacy of the years leading up to and including WW II.

Imperial Palace (Map 2)

The Imperial Palace is the home of Japan's emperor and the imperial family. Unfortunately the palace itself is closed to the public for all but two days of the year – 2 January (New Year's Day) and 23 December (the emperor's birthday). Nevertheless, it is possible to wander around its outskirts and visit the gardens, from which you can at least get a good view of the palace with the **Nijū-bashi Bridge** in the foreground.

On the grounds of the Imperial Palace once stood Edo-jō Castle, in its time the largest castle in the world. The palace we see today is a reconstruction, completed in 1968, of the Meiji Imperial Palace, destroyed during the aerial bombing of WW II. Originally Edo-jō Castle was home to a feudal lord who was assassinated in 1486. The castle fell into disuse until 1590, when Tokugawa Ieyasu chose it as the site for an impregnable castle from which the Shogunate was to rule all Japan until the Meiji Restoration.

Edo-jō Castle was fortified by a complex system of moats and the grounds included large numbers of watch towers and armouries. By the time the Meiji Emperor moved to Edo in 1868, making it the seat of imperial power and changing its name to Tokyo, large sections of Edo-jō Castle had already been destroyed in the upheavals leading to the transfer of power. Much that remained was torn down to make way for the new Imperial Palace.

It is an easy walk from Tokyo station, or Hibiya or Nijū-bashi-mae subway stations, to the Nijū-bashi Bridge. The walk involves crossing **Babasaki Moat** and the expansive **Imperial Palace Plaza**. This vantage point, which is popular with photographers, gives you a picture-postcard view of the palace peeking over its fortifications, with the Nijū-bashi Bridge in the foreground.

Imperial Palace East Garden (Map 2)

This is a very pleasant retreat after wandering around the outskirts of the Imperial Palace or sightseeing in Ginza. Enter through the **Ote-mon Gate** (one of the three entrances to the garden – all three were formerly entrances to Edo-jō Castle), a 10-minute walk north of the Nijū-bashi Bridge. This was once the principal gate of Edo-jō Castle, while the garden is situated at what was once the centre of the old castle. The garden includes a tea pavilion, a Japanese garden and expansive lawns. If you really want to explore the place properly, it is worth picking up a map for Y150 at the rest house which appears on your right shortly after you enter through the Ōte-mon Gate. Remarkably, there is no entry fee for the park, which is open daily except Monday and Friday from 9 am to 4 pm (last entry at 3 pm).

Kitanomaru-kōen Park (Map 1)

The park itself is fairly average, but it is home to a few museums and the **Budokan**, if you're in the mood to pay homage to the venue at which so many live recordings have been produced over the years. The park is reached most easily from Kudanshita or Takebashi subway stations. Alternatively, if you're walking from the Imperial Palace East Garden, take the Kitahanebashi-mon Gate, turn left and look for Kitanomaru-kōen Park on the other side of the road.

If you continue your walk past the Budokan, look out for the **Science Museum** on your left. There's little in the way of English explanations but the museum does give out an excellent booklet in English when you buy your ticket – Y515. The museum is open Monday to Friday from 9.30 am to 4.50 pm.

Towards the back of the park, facing across from the Imperial East Garden are the **National Museum of Modern Art** (Map 2) and the **Craft Museum**. The National Museum of Modern Art has a collection of Japanese art from the Meiji period onwards. With over 3000 exhibits, it is claimed to be the best collection in the country. Admission is Y360, and it is open Tuesday to Sunday from 10 am to 5 pm. The Craft Museum is actually an annex of the former museum and houses crafts such as ceramics, lacquerware and dolls. Admission is Y360, and it is open Tuesday to Sunday from 10 am to 5 pm.

Yasukuni-jinja Shrine (Map 1)

If you take the Tayasu-mon Gate exit (just past the Budokan) of Kitanomaru-kōen Park and cross the road, to your left is the Yasukuni-jinja Shrine, literally 'Peaceful Country Shrine'. Given that it is actually a memorial to Japan's war dead, enshrining some 2.5 million souls

Saké barrels, Yasukini-jinja Shrine (TW)

who died in combat, among them some class-A war criminals, the very name of the shrine invites controversy.

In the years leading up to and during WW II, Yasukuni was established as Tokyo's chief shrine of state Shintō. Despite a Japanese constitutional commitment to a separation of religion and politics and a renunciation of militarism, in 1979 a group of class-A war criminals were enshrined here. The shrine has also over recent years been treated to visits by leading Liberal Democratic Party (LDP) politicians on the anniversary of Japan's defeat in WW II (15 August).

Whatever your personal feelings about honouring Japanese war dead, it's an interesting shrine to visit. The enormous torii (gates) at the entrance to the shrine are, unusually, made of steel and the second set, of bronze. The inner shrine area is quite beautiful and is laid out in the style of the ancient Ise shrines. One interesting, if not a little disturbing, thing to look out for as you enter the grounds of the shrine are the evil-looking black vans that sometimes make an appearance and broadcast right-wing propaganda from speakers mounted on their roofs.

Next to the shrine is the **Yūshūkan Museum**, with treasures from the Yasukuni-jinja Shrine and other items commemorating Japanese war dead. There are limited English explanations, but an English pamphlet is available. Interesting exhibits include the long torpedo in the large exhibition hall which is actually a *kaiten*, or 'human torpedo', a submarine version of the kamikaze. There are displays of military uniforms, samurai armour and a 'panorama of the Divine Thunderbolt Corps in final attack mode at Okinawa'. Admission is Y200, and the museum is open daily from 9 am to 5 pm.

Tokyo Station Area (Map 2)

This area includes **Tokyo station** itself (a replica of Amsterdam's central station), Nihombashi to the east and Marunouchi, Tokyo's most prestigious office district, to the west. It is not rich in sightseeing possibilities, but it is home to the **Nihombashi Bridge** (the iron pole on its north end indicates the geographical centre of Tokyo), the prestigious **Mitsukoshi department store**, the **Yaesu underground arcade**, with its hundreds of small shops and restaurants, and a couple of art museums.

It is a 10-minute walk from Nihombashi subway station to the **Tokyo Stock Exchange** (☎ 3666-0141). Alternatively you can take the No 10 or 11 exits of Kayabacho subway station. The exchange has a gallery on the second floor from which you can watch all the frenzied activity. There are explanatory videos and stock trading simulation games that add to the excitement. The exchange is open from Monday to Friday from 9 am to 11 am and from 1 pm to 3 pm.

Also close to Nihombashi subway station and just down from the Tōkyū department store is the **Kite Museum** (☎ 3271-2465). It may sound a little obscure but there are some stunning kites here (4000 exhibits on a rotating basis) from all over the world. Take the elevator to the 5th floor from the Taimeiken restaurant. Entrance is Y200, and the museum is open from Monday to Saturday, from 11 am to 5 pm.

A little east of the Kite Museum on the corner of Eitai-dōri is the **Yamatane Museum of Art** (☎ 3669-4056) on the 8th and 9th floors of the Yamatane Securities building. The museum includes an interior garden and a collection of Japanese paintings. Admission is Y600 and it is open Tuesday to Sunday from 10.30 am to 5 pm.

If you walk back west to Chūō-dōri and make a left, on the far left hand side of the intersection with Yaesu-dōri is the **Bridgestone Museum of Art** (☎ 3563-0241). There are a lot of museums featuring French Impressionist art in Tokyo, but those in the know rate this private collection of the founder of the Bridgestone Tire Company quite highly. Examples of Western-style paintings by Japanese artists are also featured. Entrance is

Y500 and the museum is open Tuesday to Sunday from 10 am to 5 pm.

GINZA (Map 2)　銀座

Ginza is the shopping area in Tokyo that *everyone* has heard of. Back in the 1870s, Ginza was one of the first areas to modernise, featuring a large number of novel – for Tokyoites of the time – Western-style brick buildings. Ginza was also home to Tokyo's first department stores and such other Western emblems of modernity as the gas lamp.

Today, other shopping districts rival Ginza in opulence, vitality and popularity, but Ginza retains a distinct snob value. Ginza is still *the* place to be seen exchanging the contents of a bulging wallet or purse for a designer T-shirt or a Gucci handbag. While you are in Ginza make a point of checking out some of the top-notch department stores like **Wako**, **Mitsukoshi** or **Matsuzakaya**. At the very least, the window displays are always a creative treat. Keep a special look out as well for the speciality stores tucked away in the most unlikely places.

Even if you are an impecunious traveller, Ginza remains an interesting area in which to browse. It overflows with small galleries, interesting craft shops and showrooms – and you should at least be able to afford a cup of coffee at one of the discount coffee shops that materialise from among the exclusive boutiques every block or so.

The best starting point for a wander around Ginza is the Sukiyabashi Crossing, a 10-minute walk from the Imperial Palace. Alternatively, take the Sukiyabashi Crossing exit at Ginza subway station.

Showrooms

There are several showrooms for major Japanese manufacturers in Ginza. The main ones are Sony, Toshiba and Panasonic. All three of them feature hands-on displays of their products as well as products which have yet to be released.

Right on the Sukiyabashi Crossing is the **Sony building** (☎ 3573-2371), which has fascinating displays of Sony's many products. You're free to fiddle with many of the items. The building also has a Toyota showroom and a branch of Maxim de Paris with an imported Parisien chef. The showroom is open every day from 11 am to 8 pm.

On Chūō-dōri Ave, next door to the Lion Beer Hall, is **Toshiba Ginza Seven** (☎ 3571-5971), exhibiting, yes, you guessed it, Toshiba products. It includes an AV section with large collections of videos and CDs with which you can test the Toshiba equipment. It is open from 11 am to 7 pm, and closed Wednesday and the 2nd and 4th Tuesday of every month.

Along the same lines, **Tokyo P/N** (☎ 5568-0461), the National Panasonic showroom, down Shōwa-dōri and across the expressway, is even more adventurous in its displays than its rivals in Ginza. It is closed the first Monday of every month.

Galleries

Ginza is overflowing with galleries, many of them so small that they can be viewed in two or three minutes. Many of these feature vanity exhibitions by unknown artists who have hired the exhibition space at their own expense – if they are lucky they will make a few sales and recoup some of the costs. Wander around and visit any galleries that seem particularly interesting. They are scattered throughout Ginza but are concentrated in the area south of Harumi-dōri Ave, between Ginza-dōri Ave and Chūō-dōri Ave.

If you have an interest in ukiyo-e woodblock prints, a few minutes south-west of the Sukiyabashi Crossing, next to the railway tracks, is the **Riccar Art Museum** (☎ 3571-3254). Admission is Y300, and it is open Tuesday to Sunday from 11 am to 6 pm. Do not enter by the Riccar building's main door but through another entrance at the side of the building. The gallery is on the 7th floor.

The **Idemitsu Art Museum** (☎ 3213-9402) holds Japanese and Chinese art exhibitions and is famous for its collection of work by the Zen monk Sengai. It's a five-minute walk from either Hibiya or Yūraku-cho stations, on the 9th floor of the Kokusai building, next door to the Teikoku Gekijō Theatre (the Imperial Theatre). Admission is Y550, and it is open Tuesday to Sunday from 10 am to 5 pm.

Probably the best of the photographic galleries in the area are the **Nikon Gallery** (☎ 3572-5756), the **Contax Gallery** (☎ 3572-1921) and the **Canon Photo House Ginza** (☎ 3573-7821). They are sponsored by the respective camera companies and have free, changing exhibits. The Nikon Gallery is on the 3rd floor of the Matsushima Gankyōten building, opposite the Matsuya department store on Chūō-dōri Ave, and is open Tuesday to Sunday from 10 am to 6 pm. The Contax Gallery is on the 5th floor of the building next door to the Sanai building on Chūō-dōri Ave; there is no English sign at ground level. Admission is free, and it is open Tuesday to Sunday from

10.30 am to 7 pm. The Canon Photo House is on one of the side streets between Chūō-dōri Ave and Shōwa-dōri Ave. It's open Monday to Saturday from 10 am to 6 pm.

Kabuki-za Theatre

To the east, along Harumi-dōri Ave, is the Kabuki-za Theatre (☎ 3541-3131). Even if you don't plan to attend a kabuki performance, it's worth wandering down and taking a look at the building. Performances usually take place twice daily and tickets range from Y2000 to Y14,000, depending on the seat. If you only want to see part of a performance you can ask about a restricted ticket for the 4th floor. For Y600, plus a deposit of Y1000, you can get an earphone guide that explains the kabuki performance in English as you watch it. However, the earphone guide is not available with restricted tickets. For phone bookings, ring at least a day ahead; the theatre won't take bookings for the same day.

World Magazine Gallery

Just around the corner from the Kabuki-za is the World Magazine Gallery (☎ 3545-7227). It's not really a sight but belongs in a category of its own. The gallery stocks around 1200 magazines from around the world, and although loans cannot be made you are free to sit down and read anything you please. Twice a year the gallery sells off its magazines for the previous six months – look out for announcements in the *Japan Times* or the tourist literature.

Hachikan-jinja Shrine

The Hachikan-jinja Shrine is so small that you could stroll past it and not even notice it was there – and that's what makes it interesting. Real-estate values in Ginza have generally forced places of worship elsewhere (or relocated them on the rooftops of Ginza's temples of commerce). This is one small shrine that remains at street level, a feat that was achieved by building over the top of it.

Hibiya-kōen Park

Finally, if all the concrete and razzle dazzle of Ginza has left you yearning for some greenery, it is possible to retrace your steps along Harumi-dōri, back through the Sukiyabashi Crossing to Hibiya-kōen Park. As its name suggests, the park is actually in Hibiya, an area notable for the Imperial Theatre and its cinema complexes, but

Top: Ginza at night (CT)
Bottom: Ginza telephones (CT)

it is only a five to 10-minute walk west of the Sukiyabashi Crossing. It was Tokyo's first Western-style park, and although there is nothing special to see here it makes for a pleasant break after visiting all those galleries and showrooms.

TSUKIJI (Map 2) 築地

Tsukiji is famous of course for its fish market, the largest in Asia, if not the world, but there are several other sights here, including **Hongan-ji Temple**, next to Tsukiji subway station. If you find the curious Indian flavour of the temple a little odd, it was designed this way by its architect as a tribute to the birthplace of Buddhism. Quite a walk from the station is the **Tokyo International Trade Centre**, with over 56,000 sq metres of exhibition space. There are different trade shows running throughout the year. Finally, next to the fish market, is one of Tokyo's most beautiful gardens, the Hama Rikyū Detached Palace Garden.

Tsukiji Fish Market

This is where all that sushi and sashimi turns up after it has been fished out of the sea. The day begins very early, with the arrival of fish and its wholesale auctioning. The wholesale market is not open to the general public, which is probably a blessing, given that you'd have to be there before 5 am to see the action. You are free to visit the outer market and wander around the stalls that are set up by wholesalers and intermediaries to sell directly to restaurants, retail stores and other buyers. It is a fun place to visit, and you don't have to arrive *that* early – as long as you are there sometime before 8 am there'll be something going on. Watch out for your Reeboks – there's a lot of muck and water on the floor.

The done thing is to top off your visit with a sushi breakfast in one of the nearby sushi shops. There are plenty of places on the right as you walk from the market back to Tsukiji subway station, including the main branch of the famous Sushisei chain (see the Places to Eat chapter later in this guide). The market is closed on Sunday and public holidays.

Hama Rikyū Detached Palace Garden

This garden is one of Tokyo's best, featuring a large pond with an island and a pavilion. It was once a shogunal palace, having been the property of the Tokugawa family, and extended into the area now used by the

Tokyo Fish Market. It can be combined either with a visit to Ginza, Tsukiji Fish Market or, via the Sumida-gawa River Cruise, with a visit to Asakusa (see the Asakusa section later in this chapter). Admission is Y200, and it is open Tuesday to Sunday from 9 am to 4.30 pm.

AKIHABARA (Map 1) 秋葉原

Akihabara is Tokyo's discount electrical and electronics centre, with countless shops ranging from tiny specialist stores to electrical department stores. You could go there with no intention of buying anything and within half an hour find half a dozen things that you couldn't possibly live without.

The range of products is mind boggling; but before you rush into making any purchases, remember that most Japanese companies use the domestic market as a testing ground. Many products end their days in Japan without ever making it onto overseas markets. This may pose difficulties if you take something home and later need to have a fault repaired. Also, the voltage for which the product was made may not be the same as that available in your home country. Some larger stores (Laox is a reliable option) have tax-free sections with export models for sale. For audio goods, try Laox or Shintoku Echo, and for TV and video Hirose Musen has a good selection that includes export models.

Many of the prices can be quite competitive with those you are used to at home, though it's unusual to find prices that match those of dealers in Hong Kong or Singapore. You should be able to knock another 10% off the marked prices by bargaining. To find the shops, take the Electric Town exit of Akihabara station. You'll see the sign on the platform if you come in on the JR Yamanote line.

JIMBŌ-CHO (Map 1) 神保町

Jimbō-cho is an area of booksellers, close to some of Tokyo's more prestigious private universities and schools. There is at least one excellent English bookshop here, Kitazawa, with the second floor devoted to used books – don't expect any bargains however. The area can be reached in a 15-minute walk from Akihabara by walking south down Chūō-dōri and turning right into Yasukuni-dōri. Alternatively you can walk down Yasukuni-dōri from Yasukuni-jinja Shrine or catch the subway to Jimbō-cho subway station.

Top: Ueno-kōen Park (TW)
Bottom: Saigō Takamori Statue, Ueno (TW)

UENO (Map 3)　上野

Ueno Hill was the site of a last-ditch defence of the Tokugawa Shogunate by about 2000 Tokugawa loyalists in 1868. They were duly dispatched by the imperial army and afterwards the new Meiji government decreed that Ueno Hill would be transformed into one of Tokyo's first parks.

Today, **Ueno-kōen Park** is Ueno's foremost attraction. The park has a number of museums, galleries and a zoo that, by Asian standards at least, is pretty good. The park is also famous as Tokyo's most popular site for hanami (cherry-blossom viewing) when the blossoms come out in early to mid-April.

Ueno is an interesting area to stroll around. Opposite the station is the Ameyoko-cho Arcade (look for the large romaji sign over the entrance), a market area where you can buy anything from dried fish to imitation Rolex watches. Only two stops away on the Ginza subway line is Kappabashi-dōri Ave, the place to buy up big on some of that mouth-watering plastic food that graces the windows of almost every Tokyo restaurant.

Shitamachi History Museum

Just around the corner from McDonald's, close to Ueno station, is the Shitamachi History Museum. The museum recreates life in Edo's Shitamachi, the plebeian downtown quarters of old Tokyo, through an exhibition of typical Shitamachi buildings. The buildings include a merchant's shop, a sweet shop, the home and business of a copper-boiler maker, and a tenement house. You can take off your shoes and look around inside. Upstairs, the museum has many utensils and items from the daily life of the average Shitamachi resident. You are free to pick many of them up and have a closer look. Admission is Y200, and it is open Tuesday to Sunday from 9 am to 4.30 pm.

Ueno-kōen Park

There are two entrances to Ueno-kōen Park. The main one takes you straight into the museum and art gallery area, a course that is likely to leave you worn out before taking a look at Ueno's temples. Accordingly, it's better to start at the southern entrance between Ueno station and the Keisei Line station and do a little temple viewing on the way to the museums. From Ueno station, take the Keisei station exit and turn right. Just around the corner is a flight of stairs leading up into the park.

Ahead of you and slightly to your right as you reach the top of the stairs is the **Saigō Takamori Statue**. This slightly unusual statue of a samurai walking his dog is a favourite meeting place. Saigō Takamori's history is a little complicated. He started out by joining the imperial forces of the Meiji Restoration and ended his life by committing seppuku after having been frustrated in his attempts to defeat the same imperial forces. The turnabout in his loyalties occurred when the Meiji government withdrew the powers of the military class to which he belonged.

Bear to the far left and follow the wide tree-lined path until you reach the **Kiyōmizu Kannon-dō Temple**. The model for the temple is the Kiyōmizu-dera Temple in Kyoto, not that there's any real comparison. It looks as if the temple has seen better times. Nevertheless, it's definitely worth a browse. Women who wish to conceive a child come here and leave a doll for the *senjū kannon* (thousand-armed goddess of mercy) and the accumulated dolls are burnt ceremoniously once a year on 25 September.

From the temple continue down from the park to the narrow road that follows Shinobazu Pond – almost directly opposite is the **Benzaiten Temple**. It is actually a shrine to Benten, a patron goddess of the arts. Behind the temple it is possible to hire a peddle boat for 30 minutes (Y500) or a row boat for one hour for the same price.

Make your way back to the road that follows Shinobazu Pond and turn left. Where the road begins to curve and leaves the pond behind, there is a stair pathway to the right. Follow the path and take the second turn to the left. This takes you into the grounds of **Tōshō-gū Shrine**. Originally established in 1627 (the present building dates from 1651), this is a shrine which, like its counterpart in Nikkō, was founded in memory of Tokugawa Ieyasu, who unified Japan and who, after his death, was declared a divinity. Miraculously the shrine has survived the myriad of disasters that have befallen Tokyo over the last few hundred years, making it one of the few early Edo structures still in existence. There is a good view of Kanei-ji Temple Pagoda to your right as you take the pathway into the shrine. The pathway itself is fronted by a stone torii (gate) and lined with 200 stone lanterns. Admission to the shrine is Y200 and it is open from 9 am to 5.30 pm, excepting the winter months, when it's open from 9 am to 4.30 pm.

Tokyo Metropolitan Museum of Art

Not far from Tōshō-gū Shrine, the Tokyo Metropolitan Museum

of Art has a number of different galleries that run various displays of contemporary Japanese art. It is worth entering the museum just to see what is on display. Galleries feature both Western-style art such as oil paintings and Japanese-style art such as ink brush and ikebana. The admission charge varies according to the exhibition, but entry to the museum itself is free, and there are often interesting displays with no admission charge. It's open Tuesday to Sunday from 9 am to 5 pm.

Ueno Zoo The zoo is also close by. There's nothing here to get particularly excited about, although on a nice day it can make for a pleasant walk, and watching the big excursions of six year olds in their immaculate school uniforms, all diligently sketching the animals under their teachers' supervision, can be fun. Among the Japanese, the zoo is very popular for its pandas (not on view on Fridays). Admission is Y400, and it is open Tuesday to Sunday from 9.30 am to 4 pm.

Tokyo National Museum This is the one museum in Tokyo that is worth going out of your way to visit. Not only is it Japan's largest museum, it also has the world's largest collection of Japanese art. Only a portion of the museum's huge collection is displayed at any one time. Admission is Y360, and it is open Tuesday to Sunday from 9 am to 4.30 pm.

The museum has four galleries, the most important of which is the Main Gallery. It's straight ahead as you enter, and houses a very impressive collection of Japanese art, from sculpture and swords to lacquerware and calligraphy. The Gallery of Eastern Antiquities, to the right of the ticket booth, has a collection of art and archeological finds from all of Asia east of Egypt. The Hyōkeikan, to the left of the ticket booth, has a collection of Japanese archeological finds. There is a room devoted to artefacts used by the Ainu, the indigenous ethnic people of Japan now living only in Hokkaidō.

Finally, there is the Gallery of Hōryū-ji Treasures, which is only open on Thursday, and then only 'weather permitting'. The exhibits (masks, scrolls, etc) are from the Hōryū-ji Temple in Nara. Because they are more than 1000 years old, the building often remains closed if it's raining or humid.

National Science Museum In many ways, this is a museum that is of more interest to Japanese than to foreigners. As well as a wide range of general scientific displays, there are displays on the origin of the Japanese people, on Japanese technology and so on. Not all the exhibits are labelled in English, but an English pamphlet is available for Y300. Admission is Y360, and it is open Tuesday to Sunday from 9 am to 4 pm.

National Museum of Western Art This museum contains an impressive collection of Western art. The main building was designed by Le Corbusier, and the garden contains originals by Rodin, including *The Thinker*. Inside, there is a special emphasis on the French impressionists, with paintings and sketches by, among others, Renoir and Monet. Loan exhibitions are also often on display here from art museums around the world, although these will require an extra admission charge. Admission is Y360, and it is open Tuesday to Sunday from 9.30 am to 4.30 pm.

Other Attractions Back in the direction of the southern entrance of Ueno-kōen Park is the **Tokyo Metropolitan Festival Hall**, a venue for classical music, and the **Ueno-no-Mori Art Museum**, which has a variety of exhibition spaces for changing exhibits. Admission is free, and it is open Tuesday to Sunday from 10 am to 5 pm.

Ameyoko-cho Arcade

Directly opposite the southern exit to Ueno station is the Ameyoko-cho Arcade. Cross the road and enter beneath the big romaji sign. This is a good area to just take a wander in. There are a multitude of inexpensive restaurants – just drag the staff outside and point to the plastic food in the window if you don't know how to order. There's also a Doutor coffee shop off one of the side streets.

The Ameyoko-cho area was famous as a black-market district in the early years following WW II, and is still a lively shopping area where many bargains can be found. Many of the same tourist items on sale at inflated prices in Ginza sell here at more reasonable rates. Shopkeepers are also much less restrained than those in other shopping areas in Tokyo, hawking their goods loudly to prospective customers in the crowded alleyways. This is a good area in which to take a stroll and get something of the feeling of old Shitamachi.

Around Ueno

Corin-cho Rd Just north of Ueno station is the Corin-cho Rd motorcycle centre, and the interesting motorcycle

Plastic food, Kappabashi-dōri, Ueno (CT)

museum on the 3rd and 4th floor of the clothing shop of Corin Motors. This is a good area to pick up second-hand bikes as well as new ones. Several of the shops also have native English speakers on the staff.

Kappabashi-dōri Ave (Map 4) Just two stops from Ueno subway station on the Ginza line or a 10-minute walk from Sensō-ji Temple in Asakusa is Kappabashi-dōri Ave. This is where you go if you're setting up a restaurant. You can get flags that advertise the food in your restaurant, personalised cushions, crockery and of course, most importantly, all the plastic food you need. Whether you want a plate of bolognese complete with an upright fork, a steak and chips, a lurid pizza or a bowl of rāmen (noodle soup), it's all there. Items aren't particularly cheap, but some of them are very convincing and could make unusual Japanese souvenirs.

Kappabashi-dōri Ave is about five minutes from any of the Tawaramachi subway station's exits. Alternatively, you can walk there in about 10 to 15 minutes from Asakusa.

ASAKUSA (Map 4) 浅草

Asakusa's most famous attraction is the Sensō-ji Temple, also known as the Asakusa Kannon Temple. Like Ueno, though, Asakusa is an interesting area just to look around. It has long been the very heart of Shitamachi. In Edo times, Asakusa was a halfway stop between the city and its most infamous pleasure district, Yoshiwara. In time, however, Asakusa developed into a pleasure quarter in its own right, eventually becoming the centre for that most loved of Edo entertainments, kabuki. In the very shadow of the Sensō-ji Temple a fairground spirit prevailed and a whole range of very secular entertainments were provided, from kabuki theatres to brothels.

When Japan ended its self-imposed isolation with the commencement of the Meiji Restoration, it was in Asakusa that the first cinemas opened and the first music halls appeared, and in Asakusa's Teikoku Gekijo Theatre (Imperial Theatre) that Western opera was first performed before Japanese audiences. It was also in Asakusa that another Western cultural export – the striptease – was introduced. It is said that it almost did not catch on, such was the popularity of a rival form of risqué entertainment – female swordfighting – but that the introduction of a bubble-bath show saved the day. A few clubs still operate in the area.

Unfortunately, Asakusa never quite recovered from the bombing at the end of WW II. Although the Sensō-ji Temple was rebuilt, other areas of Tokyo assumed Asakusa's entertainment functions. Asakusa may be one of the few areas of Tokyo to have retained something of the spirit of Shitamachi, but the bright lights have shifted elsewhere – notably, to Shinjuku.

Sensō-ji Temple

The Sensō-ji Temple enshrines a golden image of the Buddhist Kannon, goddess of mercy, which according to legend was miraculously fished out of the nearby Sumida-gawa River by two fishermen in 628. In time, a temple was built to house the image, which has remained on the spot ever since, through successive rebuildings of the temple.

If you approach the Sensō-ji Temple from Asakusa subway station, you'll enter through the **Kaminari-mon Gate** (Thunder Gate). The gate houses a pair of scowling gods: Fūjin, the god of wind, on the right; and Raijin, the god of thunder, on the left.

Straight ahead through the gate is **Nakamise-dōri Ave**, a shopping street set within the temple precinct. Everything from tourist trinkets to genuine Edo-style crafts is sold here. There's even a shop selling wigs to be worn with a kimono. If you're not in the market for souvenirs, you can at least buy some of the *sembei* (savoury crackers) that a few shops specialise in – you'll have to queue, though, as they are very popular with the Japanese.

Nakamise-dōri Ave leads to the main temple compound, but it's hard to say if the long surviving Kannon image really is inside, as you cannot see it – not that this stops a steady stream of worshippers making their way up the stairs to the temple, where they cast some coins, clap ceremoniously and bow in a gesture of respect. In front of the temple is a large incense cauldron where people go to rub smoke against their bodies to ensure good health. If any part of your body (as far as modesty permits) is giving you trouble, you should give it particular attention when 'applying' the smoke.

The temple itself is a post-1945 concrete reproduction of the original, but the temple is not the reason people go there. It's the sheer energy of the place, with its gaudy, almost fairground atmosphere lingering from Asakusa's past that is the real attraction.

On your left, just before you reach the temple, is **Dempō-in Garden**. Unfortunately it is not open to the public. But this does not stop you from taking a look at what is rated by many as one of Tokyo's most beautiful gardens. It is possible to obtain a ticket by calling into the main office just to the left of the pagoda. The garden contains a pond and a replica of a famous Kyoto tea house.

Behind Sensō-ji, to the right, is **Asakusa-jinja Shrine**. Unlike its Buddhist neighbour Asakusa-jinja is a Shintō shrine, a tribute to the comfortable coexistence of Japan's religions. It was built in honour of the brothers who discovered the Kannon statue. The shrine dates back to 1649 and is the site of one of Tokyo's most important festivals, the Sanja Festival, a three-day extravaganza of costumed parades and lurching mikoshi (portable shrines).

Shitamachi Walking Tour

Unfortunately there's not much material evidence of Shitamachi remaining in Tokyo. What does remain, however, is something of the atmosphere of Shitamachi. If you have already spent a few days in Tokyo, you notice the difference between Asakusa and other parts of Tokyo as soon as you pass into Nakamise-dōri Ave. For the most part, the Japanese vision of the future has swallowed up Tokyo, and for this reason it's worth taking a stroll outside the precincts of Sensō-ji Temple. What you get is not so much an abundance of sights (as in Kyoto) as an alternative to Japan Inc.

To start the walk, exit Sensō-ji Temple the way you entered it – through the Hōzō-mon Gate at the temple end of Nakamise-dōri Ave. Turn right here and follow the road around the perimeter of the temple grounds. Look out for the **Chingo-dō Temple** on your right, next door to the back entrance to Dempō-in Garden. More than anything else it's an interesting oddity. Founded in 1883, the temple was constructed for the 'raccoon dogs'

Sensō-ji Temple, Asakusa (TW)

living on the Sensō-ji Temple precincts. It doesn't seem
to have done them much good, as they are not much in
evidence nowadays. This stretch of road also has a
vague flea market feel about it, as there are often stalls
set up along the outside of the temple precincts. You can
pick up some interesting festival accessories here.

If you follow the road round to the right, you'll pass
an arcade with shops selling traditional items at reasonable prices. Look out for the shops selling *yukata*
(dressing gowns) and kimono. Further along is the
Hanayashiki Amusement Park. It hasn't got a lot to
recommend it, unless you are overcome by a hankering
to risk your life on one of the fairly rickety-looking rides.
The amusement park dates back to 1853, when it was a
botanical garden, and the park pays homage to
Asakusa's past with a Panorama Hall that displays
photographs of old Asakusa. It's open seven days a week
and has an entry charge of Y500 for adults and Y250 for
children.

The area around the amusement park is what's left of
Rokku, Asakusa's old cinema district. It's all kind of
down-at-heel nowadays, and the few remaining
cinemas seem to restrict their screenings almost exclusively to Japanese pornography – at least they all carry
the familiar lurid posters depicting naked women
trussed up like hams, their meek eyes casting plaintive
looks at the tattooed torturers standing over them. It's

worth remembering as you wander through here that this was once the most lively of Tokyo's entertainment districts – how times change. Presiding over the area today, just next door to the Big Boy restaurant, is the **Rox building**, a shopping centre that is notable above all else for its failure to endow Asakusa with an air of cosmopolitan modernity.

Ahead is another arcade. Mostly it is taken up by Japanese restaurants specialising in tempura and so on. However, worth a look are the traditional sembei-making shops. These savoury crackers are very popular with the Japanese, and in the open-fronted shops in the arcade you can watch them being produced.

The arcade takes you back onto Kamanarimon-dōri Ave, which is lined with excellent Japanese-style restaurants (see the Places to Eat chapter later in this guide). Turn right here and cross over Kokusai-dōri Ave. Following the small road that runs to Kappabashi-dōri Ave, to your left is a block that is riddled with temples, most of them quite small. The largest is the **Tokyo Hongan-ji Temple**, which is on your left just before you get to Kappabashi-dōri Ave.

Kappabashi-dōri Ave is Tokyo's wholesale restaurant supplies area. This makes for a more interesting walk than you might think, and can be a better source of souvenirs than the tourist oriented shops of Ginza and Ueno. Kappabashi-dōri Ave is chock-a-block with shops selling plastic food, bamboo cooking utensils, *noren* (the curtains that hang in the front of Japanese restaurants), customised cushions and even the red lanterns *(aka-chōchin)* that light the back alleys of Tokyo by night. Turn right into Kappabashi-dōri and walk up the road a few blocks, before crossing over the road and walking back in the other direction.

The landmark that tells you you've reached the end of your Shitamachi tour and done the rounds of the plastic food shops is the **Niimi building**, crowned with an enormous chef's head – you can't miss it. The Niimi building is on the corner of Asakusa-dōri, and a few minutes down the road to your left is Tawaramachi subway station on the Ginza line.

Sumidagawa River Cruise

Nowadays, 'cruise' is something of an overstatement, but it was not always that way. In its time the Sumidagawa was a picturesque river punctuated by delicate arched bridges and brimming with fish. Today, it may not rate as the most scenic river cruise you've ever taken, but it's a good way of getting to or from Asakusa.

The cruise departs from next to Asakusa's Azuma Bridge and goes to Hama Rikyū Detached Palace Garden, Hinode Pier and Odaiba Seaside Park. Probably the best option is to buy a ticket to Hamarikyū-teien Garden for Y720 (the ticket includes the Y200 entry fee for the garden). After looking around the garden it is possible to walk into Ginza in about 10 to 15 minutes. Boats leave every 20 to 30 minutes during the day and cost Y520 to Hamarikyū-teien Garden, Y560 to Hinode Pier and Y960 to Odaiba Seaside Park.

SHINJUKU (Map 6)　新宿

Shinjuku is a city in itself and without doubt the most vigorous part of Tokyo. If you had only a day in Tokyo and wanted to see the modern Japanese phenomenon in action, Shinjuku would be the place to go. It's an incredible combination of high-class department stores, discount shopping arcades, flashing neon, government offices, stand-up drinking bars, hostess clubs and sleazy strip shows.

Shinjuku is such a huge business, commercial and entertainment centre that the place never seems to stop. It is calculated that up to two million people a day pass through Shinjuku station alone, making it one of the busiest stations in the world. And even if it's not quite *the* world's busiest station, it's commonly regarded by foreign residents and visitors alike as certainly (along with Ikebukuro station) one of the most confusing.

On the western side of the station is Tokyo's highest concentration of skyscrapers, several of which have reasonably interesting interiors, and the new Tokyo Metropolitan Government Offices, which is a sight in itself. It is the eastern side of the station, however, that is far and away the most lively part of Shinjuku to visit.

From Shinjuku station's eastern exit, your first sight will be of the Studio Alta building, with its huge video screen showing advertisements and video clips all day and night. The sheltered area underneath the screen is Shinjuku's most popular meeting place, though like the Almond coffee shop in Roppongi, it has become so popular that finding the person you're meeting is something of an ordeal – gaijin at least stand out in the crowd.

To the right of Studio Alta, about 100 metres up Shinjuku-dōri Ave and on your left, is the Kinokuniya bookshop (see the Bookshops section of the Shopping chapter later in this guide). The sheltered area here is also a popular meeting place. All around Kinokuniya there are shops selling discounted clothes and shoes. There are also some cheap second-hand camera shops on the backstreets. The area abounds in fast-food restaurants, cheap noodle shops, reasonably priced Western food, and some of the best Chinese food in Japan.

West Side

Shinjuku's west side is Tokyo's high-rise centre. Although the city is very prone to earthquakes, those in the know reckon this to be one of the few stable areas around – let's hope they are right. Apart from wandering around straining your neck at all the big buildings, the west side does have some attractions. If you're after camera equipment, it's home to Tokyo's largest camera stores: Yodobashi Camera (☎ 3346-1010) and Sakuraya Camera (☎ 3354-3636. Yodobashi Camera has practically everything you could possibly want that relates to photography, including a huge stock of film, darkroom equipment, tripods, cameras, lenses and other accessories. Its prices are usually very reasonable. Yodobashi even has a limited selection of second-hand photographic equipment. The stores are behind the Keio department store.

West Side Walking Tour The west exit of Shinjuku station leads into an underground mall lined with shops and restaurants. There are some good lunch-time specials to be had here. Follow the mall to the Shinjuku post office exit and take the stairs to the right. Ahead of you is the **Shinjuku Centre building** which, apart from the Toto Super Space, a bathroom and kitchen display venue complete with a 'Toilet Zone', and a free observation port on the 53rd floor, does not have a lot to offer. Next door to the Shinjuku Centre building is the **Kaisai-Kaijo building**. On the 42nd floor is the **Tōgō Seiji Art Museum**. The Museum is notable mainly for its purchase, at more than Y5 billion, of Van Gogh's *Sunflowers*. The museum is, however, mainly a forum for the work of the Japanese artist Tōgō Seiji. Entrance is Y500, and the museum is open Monday to Friday from 9.30 am to 4.30 pm.

The **Shinjuku Mitsui building**, notable mainly for the **Pentax Forum** (☎ 3348-2941), is on the 1st floor. The forum is a must for photography buffs. The exhibition space has changing exhibits by photographers sponsored by Pentax. Undoubtedly, the best part of the Pentax Forum, however, is the vast array of Pentax cameras, lenses and other optical equipment on display. It's completely hands-on – you can snap away with the cameras and use the huge 1000 mm lenses to peer in through the windows of the neighbouring buildings.

Admission is free, and it's open daily from 10.30 am to 7 pm.

On the opposite corner of the intersection is the **Shinjuku Sumitomo building**, which bills itself as 'a building that's actually a city', a concept that the Japanese seem to find particularly appealing (Sunshine City in Ikebukuro is another 'city' building). The Sumitomo building has a hollow core. The ground floor and the basement feature a 'jewel palace' (a jewellery shopping mall) and a general shopping centre. There is a free observation platform on the 51st floor, which is a good deal when you consider the inflated prices being charged by Tokyo Tower and Sunshine City for entry to their observatories.

Shinjuku street scene (TW)

By now you cannot but have noticed the towering **Tokyo Metropolitan Government Offices**. There are three blocks, and the central block is Japan's tallest building. The building itself was designed by Kenzo Tange, and whatever your feelings about its appearance, it is something of a marvel. The aim was to construct a 'people friendly' city hall, but the resulting edifice, with its Ministry of Truth overtones, looks like it's straight off the set from a high-budget production of Orwell's *1984*. The building is open to the public, with yet another observation platform in its higher reaches and a Citizen's Plaza at ground level. The plaza features shops, restaurants, a passport section and, curiously, a blood donation room.

If you're in the mood for a bit of eccentric high-tech, the interior of the **Shinjuku NS building**, just down the road, is hollow, like the Sumitomo building, featuring a 1600 sq metre area from which you can gaze upwards at the transparent roof. Overhead, at 110 metres, is a 'sky bridge'. The square itself features a 29-metre pendulum clock that is listed by the *Guinness Book of Records* as the largest in the world. The 29th and 30th floors have a large number of restaurants, including a branch of the Spaghetti Factory. On the 5th floor, you can browse through the showrooms of the Japanese computer companies in the OA Centre.

At this point you have basically exhausted west Shinjuku's walking possibilities, unless you opt for a stroll in the rather drab **Shinjuku Central Park**. The best option is probably to walk back to Shinjuku station via the underground arcade and grab a bite to eat in one of the restaurants that line it.

East Side

Shinjuku's east side is an area to wander through and gaze at rather than an area in which to search out particular sights. It offers quite a contrast with the the west side. While the former is showy, administrative and planned, Shinjuku's east side is more like something that just happened and is happening still.

East Side Walking Tour From within the bowels of Shinjuku station, follow the east exit or Kabuki-cho exit signs. Once you have passed through the ticket gates, take the My City exit. As you surface, directly ahead of you, is the **Studio Alta building**. You can't miss its enormous video screen. Next door to Studio Alta, on the right, is the **Konika Plaza**, which has a photo gallery on the 4th floor. Some of the exhibitions are quite good, and the exhibition space also includes a small library of photography books and a museum of antique cameras. Admission is free.

Continue walking eastwards down Shinjuku-dōri Ave. This area is good for men's clothing and shoes. It is also possible to come across some good bargain prices here. A little further on is **Kinokuniya bookshop**, with its superb collection of English books (especially books on Japan and Japanese text books) on the 6th floor. Continue walking and you pass the **Mitsukoshi department store** on the right and **Isetan** on the left. Isetan, in particular, is a department store that is worth a browse. It has everything from arts and crafts to fashionable boutiques. There are even art galleries on the upper floor.

Turn left at Isetan and walk down to Yasukuni-dōri Ave. Down a lane on the opposite side of the road is **Hanazono-jinja Shrine**. It is not one of Tokyo's major shrines, but nestled so close to Tokyo's most famous red-light district its clientele can make for some interesting people watching. The shrine has a reputation for bringing success to business ventures, legitimate or otherwise.

Exit Hanazono-jinja Shrine into **Golden Gai**, a tiny warren of alleyways devoted entirely to small stand-up watering holes. Traditionally the haunt of Bohemian Tokyoites, writers and the like, it is a safe area to take a walk through, even by night. You may not, however, be welcome in many of the bars – regulars only. By day it is usually deserted. It is also an area that is said to be gradually being bought up by Seibu – in which case it will probably not be long before we see another department store going up here.

Continue in the same direction along the alleyways that run parallel to Yasukuni-dōri Ave and you reach **Kabuki-cho**, Tokyo's most notorious red-light district. Despite its reputation, Kabuki-cho remains a relatively safe area to stroll around. Most of what goes on is pretty much off limits to foreigners. There are, however, several strip clubs in the area that are frequented by foreigners, and single gaijin males are likely to be approached by touts offering to take them to one. These places will have a straight door charge of around Y4000 and no other hidden costs. Further explorations of Kabuki-cho's seedy delights will require a Japanese escort or exceptional Japanese-language skills.

Kabuki-cho is probably one of the more imaginative red-light areas in the world, with 'soaplands' (massage parlours), love hotels, no-pants coffee shops (it's the waitresses who doff their undies, not the customers), peep shows, so-called pink cabarets ('pink' is the Japanese equivalent of 'blue' in English), porno-video booths and strip shows that involve audience participation. As you walk through streets lined with neon signs and crowded with drunken salarymen, high-pitched female voices wail out invitations to their establishments through distorting sound systems, and Japanese punks earn a few extra yen passing out advertisements for telephone clubs, where young Japanese men pay an hourly fee for a room, a telephone and a list of girls' telephone numbers – if the two like the sound of each other, they can make a date to meet.

Follow the walking tour on Map 6 along the perimeter of the Kabuki-cho area, and look out for the **Tokyo Kaisen Ichiba**, or the fish market, on your right. It's not particularly big as fish markets go, but there's a great restaurant upstairs (see the Places to Eat chapter later in this guide). Turn left here into the area dominated by the enormous **Koma Theatre**. The Koma started its life as a movie theatre but quickly switched to stage performances. It's still host to performances of a more mainstream variety than those in other parts of Kabuki-cho. The square facing the Koma is ringed by cinemas and is also a popular busking spot at night, though the yakuza are usually quick about moving anyone too popular along. Any of the lanes radiating off the square are Kabuki-cho at its best – a great mix of restaurants, porno-video booths, telephone clubs and who knows what else (the *Tokyo Journal* team claim to have stumbled across the Black Hole S&M Club, but I suspect this one's apocryphal).

From this point wander back to Yasukuni-dōri Ave and take one of the lanes that connect it with Shinjuku-dōri Ave. Like much of Shinjuku, all of these lanes are lined with restaurants, shot bars and shops. It's also another area popular with buskers, and one that is good to linger in – look out for the revolving sushi bars – providing the crowds aren't too overwhelming.

Shinjuku-gyoen Gardens

Further east down Shinjuku-dōri Ave, or directly in front of Shinjuku-gyoen-mae subway station, Shinjuku-gyoen Gardens is one of Tokyo's best escapes. It has a Japanese garden, a French garden, a hothouse containing tropical plants and, near the hothouse, a pond containing giant carp. If you're lucky enough to be in Tokyo for the cherry blossom season, this is also a popular place for blossom viewing. Admission is Y200, and it's open Tuesday to Sunday from 9 am to 4.30 pm.

IKEBUKURO (Map 5)　池袋

Come to Ikebukuro and you get a funny feeling that the people who produce enormous shopping complexes and big buildings know something that everybody else doesn't. I mean, how is it that a place like Ikebukuro is home to Asia's largest department store (Tōbu), the second tallest building in Asia (the Sunshine City building – the new Tokyo Metropolitan Government Offices in Shinjuku comes first), the world's largest automobile showroom (Toyota Amlux), the escalator experience of a lifetime (Tokyo Metropolitan Art Space) and the second busiest station in Tokyo? By the time you have this book in your hands, there'll even be a branch of HMV Records in Ikebukuro.

For the time being, don't believe the hype. In many ways, Ikebukuro is like a Shinjuku waiting to happen, but for some reason the bright lights and the revellers are always somewhere else. Ikebukuro's few sights are on the eastern side of the station. The western side is notable only for the Tokyo Metropolitan Art Space, a sleazy red-light area and some discount clothes shops. Over recent years, the west side, with its high concentration of love hotels, has also become a favourite haunt of freelance prostitutes from all over the world. It all seems to be quite open, though how long it will be before there is a clamp down is anyone's guess.

Tokyo Metropolitan Art Space

Part of the 'Tokyo Renaissance' plan launched by the Department of Education, the Art Space has brought a bit of culture to the west side of Ikebukuro. The building is designed mainly for performance art, featuring a large hall, a medium hall and two small halls. For those without a ticket to see anything, it is memorable mainly for its soaring escalator ride – this is about as exciting as it gets on the west side!

Tōbu Department Store

For many years Seibu Ikebukuro was the biggest department store in Japan and, by some counts, the world. All this has changed. But you can breathe a sigh of relief – the honour still goes to good ol' Ikebukuro. As of 10 June 1992, the Tōbu department store, by adding an extra nine floors to the 20 it already had (crafty, that), became the largest department store in Asia. The question on everyone's lips is...will Seibu let them get away with it?

Sunshine City

What a monstrosity! Billed as a city in a building, this 'workers' paradise', as it's referred to in the promotional literature, is basically 60 floors of office space and shopping malls, with a few overpriced cultural and entertainment options thrown in. If you've got Y620 to burn, you can take a lift (apparently the fastest in the world) to the observatory on the 60th floor and gaze out on Tokyo's murky skyline.

Not in the Sunshine City building itself but in the Bunka Kaikan building of Sunshine City is the **Ancient Orient Museum** on the six and seven floors. Admission is Y400. It's open Tuesday to Sunday from 10 am to 5 pm and is strictly for those with a special interest in ancient odds and ends such as coins and beads.

Seibu Department Store

Seibu has branches all over Tokyo, but the Ikebukuro branch is the biggest. You can easily spend an entire afternoon just wandering around the basement food floor sampling the little titbits on offer. The 12th floor has an art museum and the top floor is restaurant city, with something like 50 restaurants, many of them with great lunch specials. Seibu is open daily except Thursday from 10 am to 6 pm.

In the Seibu annex next door is the **Sezon Museum of Art**, which holds high-quality art exhibitions. Across the road from the annex is a **Wave** record shop. There are AV and hi-definition TV exhibitions as well an extensive selection of CDs that make it an excellent place for a browse.

Toyota Amlux

Strictly for automobile aficionados, this automobile showroom is touted as the world's largest. It is on the Sunshine City building in between the Shuto expressway and the road parallel to Sunshine City. You can walk there from Ikebukuro station in 10 minutes. The building is immense and ultra slick.

Around Ikebukuro

Rikugi-en Garden (Map 1) Just three stops from Ikebukuro, near the JR Komagome station on the JR Yamanote line, is the Rikugi-en Garden, a very pleasant place for a walk, with landscaped views unfolding at every turn of the pathways that crisscross the grounds.

The garden is rich in literary associations; its name is taken from the six principles of Japanese *waka* poetry (poems of 31 syllables), and the garden itself recreates in its landscaping, famous scenes from Chinese and Japanese literature (good luck finding them). The garden was established in the late 17th century by Yanagisawa Yoshiyasu, and after falling into disuse was restored by the founder of the Mitsubishi group, Iwasaki Yataro. Admission is Y200, and it is open Tuesday to Sunday from 9 am to 5 pm.

HARAJUKU & AOYAMA (Map 7)
原宿／青山

There's something different about Harajuku and Aoyama. Getting off the train here is like surfacing in another city – it's a far cry from the brashness of Shinjuku, or the ostentation of Ginza. Perhaps it's the tree-lined Omote-sandō, with its Parisien-style cafes and fashionable boutiques, or then again perhaps it's the almost complete absence of noise (apart from Sunday), one of the single most aggravating sources of stress in Tokyo. Whatever the case, a visit to Meiji-jingū Shrine, followed by a leisurely coffee or an ice cream on Omote-sandō and a stroll up to Aoyama's Killer-dōri (not a dangerous place unless you are phobic about spending the contents of your wallet), would have to rate as one of Tokyo's more high-class outings. And of course nearby Yoyogi-kōen Park is host to Tokyo's subcultures on Sunday afternoons – that's if you can face the crowds.

Harajuku

Harajuku is an area to see on any day other than a Sunday, but if you enjoy intimate contact with strangers while being assaulted by the sounds of 40 to 50 rock bands playing simultaneously, a special trip to **Yoyogi-kōen Park** may be in order. Generally the park does not have a lot going for it, but Sunday is the day when Tokyo's subcultures put themselves on public display, performing anything from avant-garde theatre to Sex Pistols-style punk. There's no need to be coy about photographing them; everyone goes there to be seen, and being photographed is like achieving momentary star status.

The activity starts at 1 pm, when the road through the park is closed to traffic. Just five minutes from the park, on **Takeshita-dōri**, are the shops that serve as the source of the bizarre fashions you see in Harajuku. Look out for **Octopus Army**, the shop that has the last say on

Harajuku fashion. The streets may resemble rush hour on the JR Yamanote line, but if you don't mind the push and shove it can be fun. A tip: buy your return ticket when you arrive at Harajuku station. Once things start to quieten down in Yoyogi-kōen Park, the queues for the ticket vending machines get horrendous.

Late on Friday and Saturday nights, you can see another side of Japanese youth culture, when car enthusiasts parade up and down Kōen-dōri between NHK Hall and Shibuya station (Map 8).

Meiji-jingū Shrine Next door to Yoyogi-kōen Park, this is without a doubt Tokyo's, if not Japan's, most splendid Shintō shrine. It is difficult to believe that it is so close to the crowds in Harajuku. Completed in 1920, the shrine was built in honour of Emperor Meiji and Empress Shōken, under whose rule Japan ended its long isolation from the outside world. Unfortunately, like most of Tokyo, the shrine was destroyed in the bombing towards the end of WW II. Rebuilding was completed in 1958.

The Meiji-jingū Shrine might be a reconstruction of the original, but unlike so many of Japan's postwar reconstructions, it has been rebuilt with all the features of a Shintō shrine preserved. The shrine itself was built with Japanese cypress, while the cypress for the huge torii gates came from Ali Shan in Taiwan.

On the grounds of Meiji-jingū Shrine (on the left, before the second set of torii) is **Meiji-jingū-gyoen Park**. The English explanation on the entry ticket to the park points out that this park was originally part of the garden of a 'feudal load' and that the garden itself has 'spots in it'! Don't let this put you off – the park has some very peaceful walks and is almost deserted on weekdays. It's particularly beautiful in June, when the irises are in bloom. Admission is Y300, and it is open daily from 9 am to 4.30 pm.

As you approach the Meiji-jingū Shrine, there are so many signs indicating the way to the **Meiji-jingū Treasure Museum** that you tend to feel obliged to pay it a visit. In fact, the collection of items from the lives of the emperor and empress is not very exciting. It includes official garments, portraits and other imperial odds and ends. Admission is Y200, and it is open daily from 9 am to 4.30 pm, except on the third Friday of each month, when it is closed.

Harajuku Walking Tour It doesn't take that long to take in Harajuku, though the proceedings can be drawn

Top: Hip-hop dudes, Yoyogi-kōen Park (RI'A)
Bottom: Guitar hero, Yoyogi-kōen Park (RI'A)

Top: Reception counter, Meiji-jingū Shrine (CT)
Bottom: Shintō wash basin, Meiji-jingū Shrine (CT)

out by stopping for a coffee or an ice cream somewhere. Opposite the upper exit to Harajuku station is Omote-sandō, a fashionable avenue and the ideal place to start your exploration of Harajuku.

The coffee shops and boutiques start right from the top of the hill opposite Harajuku station. Look out for **Harajuku Quest** on the left-hand side. It's one of those designer spaces housing boutiques and a few restaurants that are so popular in Tokyo. Just a little further down the hill, on a small side street, is the **Ota Memorial Art Museum**. It has an excellent collection of ukiyo-e woodblock prints and offers a good opportunity to see works by Japanese masters of the art, including Hiroshige. The museum is open daily from 10.30 am to 5.30 pm, except from the 25th to the end of the month, when it is closed. Entry is very expensive at Y800.

Continue down Omote-sandō. You'll pass **Stage Y2** on your left, a fashionable coffee shop/restaurant with an open front in warm weather. The first major intersection you come to is Meiji-dōri Ave. If you turn right here you can walk down to Shibuya in about 15 minutes. Leave this for later, if you are up to it, and turn to the left. Here you'll find **Laforet**. Laforet is such a well-known Harajuku landmark that it's worth a special mention. The big face on the front of the building marks it out. Hang around outside and you'll see a fascinating spectrum of trendy types passing in and out of the building. This is also a very popular spot with talent-spotting Japanese photographers. Inside are fashionable boutiques and downstairs a branch of HMV, where you can check out the latest CD releases on the headphones provided. Continue down Meiji-dōri Ave and watch out for a crowded narrow lane on your left. This is Takeshita-dōri, and you can't miss it. Just look for the crowds of trendy Japanese teenagers passing in and out loaded with shopping bags.

Turn into Takeshita-dōri for an interesting diversion. There is a wide variety of shops providing for the subcultural needs of Tokyo's *zoku*, its tribes. Some of the stuff looks like it has come straight out of Madame Lash's private wardrobe and yet, oddly, there's an air of innocence about this area of winding alleys crammed with boutiques. It's all ultimately another facet of the Tokyo consumer phenomenon. One of the biggest shops is on the left hand side about half way up Takeshita-dōri: **Octopus Army**. It's a little bit more mainstream than some of its competitors but it makes for an interesting browse.

Thread your way back through the crowds, turn left from Meiji-dōri Ave back into Omote-sandō and cross the road via the pedestrian bridge. Back towards Meiji-dōri Ave is the popular **Café de Rope**, which has some relatively inexpensive lunch sets – a cool place to hang out and watch the crowds. The little alleys heading off Omote-sandō here are home to scores of fashionable hair salons, coffee shops and design studios. Back on Omote-sandō, don't miss the big **Haagen-Dazs ice-cream shop**. Diagonally opposite is **Time's Café**, where you can get a coffee for Y250 – a bargain in Harajuku.

A little further on you pass the **Oriental Bazaar** (see the Shopping chapter later in this guide), **Genroku**, rated as one of Tokyo's best revolving sushi shops (see the Places to Eat Chapter later in this guide) and a host of boutiques with names like 'Gallerie de Pop' and 'Coccoon'. Perhaps the most famous of Harajuku's boutiques is the **Hanae Mori building**, a building designed by Kenzo Tange, the designer of the Tokyo Metropolitan Government Offices in Shinjuku, among a host of other famous Tokyo landmarks. You can see the designs of Hanae Mori, perhaps Japan's most famous fashion designer, here. There is also an antique bazaar in the basement.

If you continue on from the Hanae Mori Building you reach Aoyama-dōri Ave. To the left is Aoyama. From here you can catch the subway to somewhere else from Omote-sandō subway station, wander down to Aoyama or backtrack to Meiji-dōri Ave and walk down to Shibuya (a worthwhile option on a pleasant day).

Aoyama

Aoyama is not rich in sights, and as such it would be best to take it in as a side-trip from Harajuku. It is only a 15-minute walk. The area is worthwhile mainly for Killer-dōri, with its ultraexpensive boutiques, and for several museums and galleries.

If you arrive from Harajuku down Aoyama-dōri Ave, keep walking until you hit Gaien Nishi-dōri. This is the street that is better known as **Killer-dōri**, so named for its fashionable boutiques. On the corner is the **Japan Traditional Craft Centre**. It has a permanent display of crafts as well as crafts for sale, making for an excellent souvenir-hunting excursion (see the Shopping chapter later in this guide). On the opposite corner is another boutique building, but one that is regarded highly by Tokyoites – **Bell Commons**.

Up Killer-dōri, on the left hand side, is the **Watari Gallerie**. It is an interesting building, with an enormous collection of obscure postcards (all on sale, mostly for around Y150) and an excellent art bookshop in the basement, where there's also a small coffee shop. The building also has exhibition space for young non-mainstream artists.

Back down Killer-dōri, in the other direction and off to the right, is an oddity you might want to check out – the **Sleep Culture Gallery Alpha**. This is one of those eccentric institutions that somehow sum up the quirkiness of Tokyo. The gallery has a library dedicated to sleep, displays devoted to sleep, and a 'relaxation room' where you can, yes, sleep...accompanied by a soothing sound and vision display. What's more, it's all free of charge. The gallery is open Monday to Friday from 10 am to 6 pm.

The **Nezu Fine Art Museum** in Minami Aoyama is a more conventional exhibition space. It has a well established collection of Japanese art that includes paintings, calligraphy and sculpture, as well as Chinese and Korean art exhibits and a teahouse where tea ceremonies are performed. There are around 7000 exhibits here, some of which are designated as 'Important Cultural Properties'. From Omote-sandō subway station, walk down Omote-sandō away from Harajuku. Turn right at the end of the road and look for the museum on the left. Admission is Y550, and it is open Tuesday to Sunday from 9.30 am to 4.30 pm.

SHIBUYA (Map 8) 渋谷

Shibuya is one of the most trendy shopping areas in Tokyo, and its appeal is predominantly to the young – it's one of those areas in Tokyo notable for an absence of old people. It's not an area rich in sights; it's a place to come and have fun.

Shibuya Walking Tour

The first stop on anyone's tour of Shibuya is clearly signposted in Shibuya station. Take the Hachikō exit to see the bronze statue of the dog **Hachikō**. The statue is Shibuya's most popular meeting place although, as with other Tokyo meeting places, its popularity sometimes makes it less than an ideal spot to find a friend. The story goes that Hachikō waited for his master every day at the railway station for 10 years, unable to come to terms with the fact that his master had died one day at work and wouldn't be coming home again...ever. It's a touching tale, and the dog was much admired throughout Japan for its uncompromising loyalty, a quality that still plays a big part in Japanese social life.

Opposite Hachikō, roads radiate in a number of directions. The pedestrian crossing here must be one of the busiest in the world. To get your bearings, look for the silver 109 building pinioned between Bunkamura-dōri, to the right, and Dogen-zaka (*zaka* means 'slope' or 'hill'), to the left. Take Bunkamura-dōri. The 109 building is not worth entering itself, unless you are in the mood for some boutique shopping, but keep your eyes to the left as you pass it for the tiny, ramshackle wooden building that has survived the architectural onslaught of the 20th century. It is actually a popular izakaya restaurant (see the Places to Eat chapter later in this guide) known as Tamakyu that has achieved a legendary reputation for its tenacity in refusing to budge when its ultramodern neighbour went up.

On the other side of the road is the Tokyo branch of **Spike's Joint**, selling Spike Lee products, and a little further on the One-Oh-Nine building, with a branch of HMV records (complete with a resident British DJ) in the basement. At the fork at the top of the hill is the enormous **Tōkyū department store** (another place for some great basement food sampling) and, just around the corner to the left, the **Tōkyū Bunkamura**. The Bunkamura features a couple of halls for performing arts, with world-class acoustics. There are also two cinemas here specialising in art films and a museum in the basement with changing exhibits.

A walk around the Tōkyū complex and back eastwards takes you into the mazelike heart of fashionable Shibuya. From Club Quattro, one of Tokyo's most important live venues, onwards the lanes to the right are a warren of bars, specialist shops, restaurants and all kinds of oddities. Don't just restrict your gaze to street level. Where the road forks, double back on yourself, looking out for the Shibuya branch of the popular teenage fashion shop **Octopus Army** as you do. On your right is **Tōkyū Hands**, a Tokyo institution with a mind-boggling eight floors of do-it-yourself supplies, hobby items, hardware, toys and other bizarre oddments. Also not far away is **Tower Records**, an excellent record shop and the place to pick up imported US CDs.

Up the hill, the second lane on the right runs between Parco I and II. The enormous **Parco I, II,** and **III** complex is touted by some as Tokyo's ultimate shopping experience. The Parco stores even include a couple of art galleries – Parco I has two galleries on the 8th floor (the Clifford Gallery and the Parco Gallery), and on the 6th floor of Parco II is Exposure. All three feature changing exhibits. The upper floors of the Parco stores also provide some great lunch specials. The lane continues down into Spain-dōri; not that there's anything particularly Spanish about it really. Still it's a popular spot with teenage shoppers, and it provides some great people-watching opportunities.

Turn left at the bottom of Spain-dōri and take the second lane on the left. Here you'll find the enormous **Seibu** department store complex. Up the lane is **Loft** and the Shibuya branch of **Wave** records, both of which are also run by Seibu. Loft is a youth-oriented department store – lots of junk and interesting oddments. You can even buy bunny suits here, if you've always wanted to dress up as a bunny and were too embarrassed to ask around where you could buy one. Wave has a great, if somewhat cluttered, collection of CDs with a good 'world music' selection.

If you can't face another department store (very likely), five minutes up Kōen-dōri Ave is the **Tobacco & Salt Museum**, another of those eccentric Tokyo museums. There are diagrams and exhibits explaining the history of tobacco use and production (salt gets the same treatment) and a display of cigarette packets from around the world. There's not much in the way of English explanations, but you get a useful English pamphlet when you pay your Y100 admission fee. And if none of this interests you, there's a cheap coffee shop on the ground floor. The museum is open Tuesday to Sunday from 10 am to 6 pm.

The area around the Tobacco & Salt Museum is rich in fast-food stores, but then again why bother when the upper floors of so many of the nearby department stores are crowded with restaurants offering great lunch-time specials. Alternatively, head back down to the area between Bunkamura-dōri and Spain-dōri and explore the lanes there for a bite to eat and a drink.

Love Hotel Hill

Take Dogenzaka-dōri to the left of the 109 building, and at the top of the hill, on the sidestreets that run off the main road, is a concentration of love hotels catering to all tastes. The buildings alone are interesting, as they represent a broad range of architectural pastiches, from miniature gothic castles to Middle-Eastern temples. It's OK to wander in and take a look. Just inside the entrance there should be a screen with illuminated pictures of the various rooms available. You select a room by pressing the button underneath a room's picture and proceeding to the cashier. This is not an area for cheap love hotels, however. Prices for an all-night stay start at around Y8000.

Tepco Electric Energy Museum

The Tepco Electric Energy Museum is the building on Jingū-dōri with the bulbous silver roof (visible from Hachikō), and it makes for an interesting diversion if you're in the area. There are lots of electrical hands-on exhibits and, importantly, admission is free. It's open Thursday to Tuesday from 10.30 am to 6.30 pm.

National Children's Castle

This place is primarily for kids, but by all accounts the grown-ups have a good time here as well. There's a pool and a large AV selection available freely once you've paid to get in. Entrance is Y410 and the castle is open from 1 to 5.30 pm weekdays, and 10 am to 5.30 pm on weekends.

NHK Tenji Plaza

This is actually a kind of broadcasting museum, with sets from Japanese drama serials and exhibitions demonstrating the behind-the-scenes activity on a broadcasting set. It's not exactly a must see unless you happen to have a special interest in such things, but it's free and reasonably entertaining. The plaza is actually closer to Harajuku station than it is to Shibuya station. It's open 10 am to 4.30 pm and closed one Monday a month.

And Finally...

Hats off to the *Tokyo Journal* team for this unusual find. If you're tired of all that sightseeing and couldn't face another museum, it might be time for something silly. Dr Jeekhan's (☎ 3476-7431) – *jikan* is Japanese for 'time' – offers you a trip to Planet Septon, where you get to don an interplanetary space suit (let's hope they come in Gaijin sizes) and lay waste to hordes of alien monsters with a laser blaster – they shoot back as well. Why bother with the rest of Tokyo when you can have *this* much fun? Dr Jeekhan's has a video game room and a restaurant which gives you what will probably be the first subaqueous dining experience of your life. Buy a Y6000 or Y10,000 'debit card' and use it up as you go along.

AKASAKA (Map 9)　赤坂

Akasaka is the area of Tokyo with the greatest concentration of top-notch hotels. These include the ANA, the New Otani and the Akasaka Prince among others. The major hotels tend to form a ring around an area that is a gastronomic paradise. There may not be much in the way of sights, beside the Hie-jinja Shrine and the occasional museum, but Akasaka is certainly the place to indulge yourself with some of the best culinary treats that Tokyo has to offer...and that's saying something.

Hie-jinja Shrine

The shrine itself is by no means one of Tokyo's major attractions; the impressive part is the walk up to the shrine through a 'tunnel' of orange torii gates. It can be quite an attractive sight on a sunny day, when the sunlight passing through the trees above dapple the gates and bring out their rich colours – don't forget to bring your canvas and paints. If you're wondering about the carved monkey clutching one of her young in the shrine area, she is emblematic of the shrine's ability to offer protection against the risk of a miscarriage.

Suntory Museum of Art

The museum is on the 11th floor of the Suntory building, and offers a pleasant area in which to view its collection of over 2000 traditional artefacts, including lacquerware and pottery. The premises also have a library and a tea room for experiencing the traditional tea ceremony (an extra charge of Y500 is required). Entrance is Y500, and it is open Tuesday to Sunday from 10 am to 4.30 pm.

Laforet Museum

This is really a commercial display area, but you might be lucky and catch an interesting exhibition. The interior of the building is interesting enough in its own right to make it worth a look if you're in the area.

Hotel Sights

Even the hotels themselves in Akasaka deserve a couple of mentions. Notable is the **New Otani** which managed to preserve part of a 400-year-old garden that once belonged to a Tokugawa regent. And another thing – all those tall hotels have got to provide some interesting views of the area. The **Akasaka Prince** and the **ANA** hotels are both touted as providing excellent views from their upper reaches.

Top: Tokyo Tower (CT)
Bottom: Hie-jinja Shrine, Akasaka (CT)

Ark Hills

Ark stands for Akasaka Roppongi knot, as this group of buildings, touted as a subcity in their own right, are pinioned between Akasaka and Roppongi. There are display rooms, banks, restaurants, entertainment and even housing here. It's worth a browse, as much for an insight into how the Japanese see the future as anything else.

Down Aoyama-dōri Ave

Down Aoyama-dōri Ave, in the direction of Aoyama-Itchome subway station, there are a couple of sights you might want to take a look at. About halfway to the station, on the left hand side, is the **Sogetsu Kaikan**, a centre for the Sogetsu school of avant-garde flower arrangement (which has just *got* to be of interest to someone). On the 6th floor is the **Sogetsu Art Museum**, with its bewilderingly eclectic collection of art pieces from across the centuries and the four corners of the world – selections range from Indian Buddhas to works by Matisse. Admission is Y500, and it's open Monday to Saturday from 10 am to 5 pm.

A little further down Aoyama-dōri, beside the Aoyama-Itchome subway station, is the **Honda Welcome Plaza** (☎ 3423-4118), a showroom in which classic Honda Grand Prix motorcycles and Formula I cars are displayed. Displays also include the latest Honda products and a projection room with a 'sonic floor', where you can watch motor races with the sensation that you are actually in the thick of it all.

ROPPONGI (Map 10)　六本木

Playground of the rich, the beautiful and hordes of lecherous off-duty English teachers, Roppongi comes to life with the onset of darkness. There's no reason to come here by day, but by night it's the throbbing disco capital of Tokyo. You may not be a disco kind of person but, let's face it, anyone who spends any time in Tokyo is going to have at least one late night here. There are even a few bars where you can have a quiet drink, not to mention the fantastic restaurants. See the Places to Eat and Entertainment chapters later in this guide for the lowdown on what's happening in Roppongi. In the meantime, there are a few attractions in the area that can be visited before nightfall and the onset of disco fever.

Around Roppongi

Tokyo Tower (Map 1) This Eiffel Tower lookalike is really more impressive from a distance; up close to the 330-metre tower one begins to wonder whether there isn't just a bit too much hype going on here. The Grand Observation Platform (Y750) is only 150 metres high; if you want to peer through the smog at Tokyo's uninspiring skyline from 250 metres up, it will cost you a further Y520 to get to the Special Observation Platform. The tower also features an overpriced aquarium (Y1000), a wax museum (Y750), the Holographic Mystery Zone (Y300) and showrooms.

The tower is a fair trudge from Roppongi: take the Hibiya subway line one stop to Kamiya-cho station. The observation platforms are open daily from 9 am to 6 pm. They close at 8 pm from 16 March to 15 November, except in August, when they are open until 9 pm.

Zōjō-ji Temple (Map 1) Behind the Tokyo Tower is this former funerary temple of the Tokugawas. It has had a calamitous history, even by Tokyo's standards, having been rebuilt three times in recent history, most recently in 1974. Nevertheless, it remains an interesting temple to visit if you're in the vicinity of the tower. The main gates date from 1605 and are included among the nation's 'Important Cultural Properties'. On the grounds there is a large collection of statues of Jizō, the patron saint of travellers and the souls of departed children.

OTHER ATTRACTIONS

Parks & Gardens

Although the Japanese purport to be ardent lovers of nature and see this as one of the qualities that distinguishes them from other races, Tokyo, like many other Japanese cities, is not particularly green and has a shortage of park space. If you've been hitting the bitumen and haven't seen a tree for days, there are two more parks besides the ones already mentioned that you might want to take a look at.

The **Koishikawa Kōraku-en Garden** (Map 1) is next to the Kōraku-en amusement park and baseball stadium and has to be one of the most beautiful and least-visited (by foreigners at least) gardens in Tokyo. Established in the mid-17th century, it incorporates elements of Chinese and Japanese landscaping. Admission is Y200, and it is open Tuesday to Sunday from 9 am to 4.30 pm.

Just north of the Hanzō-mon Gate at the Imperial Palace is a park that often gets neglected: **Chidorigafuchi Park** (Map 2). Among Tokyoites the park is renowned for its migratory birds and its cherry blossoms.

Museums & Galleries

There's an enormous number of museums and galleries in Tokyo. In many cases their exhibits are small and specialised and the admission charges prohibitively expensive for travellers with a limited budget and a tight schedule. For an up-to-date and more complete listing, get hold of the TIC's *Museums & Art Galleries* pamphlet.

A long way from anywhere else, near Monzen Nakacho subway station on the Tōzai Line, is the **Fukagawa Edo Museum** (☎ 3630-8625). The museum recreates old Edo as it was some 150 years ago. This is a museum which receives rave reviews from some visitors.

Close to Ikebukuro is Zoshigaya (one of the few places in Tokyo you can visit by tram – from Ikebukuro), where you can find the **Small Museum of Musical Boxes** (☎ 3941-0008). It has performances at 1.30 and 3 pm. Admission is Y500, and it is open Monday to Saturday from 10.30 am to 4.30 pm.

The Kokugikan Sumō Stadium (Map 1), where the **Sumō Museum** (☎ 3622-0366) is located, is a hop, skip and a jump from Ryōgoku station on the Sobu line. Admission is free, and it is open Monday to Friday from 9.30 am to 4.30 pm.

For corporate warriors with a hankering for Japan's samurai past, the **Sword Museum** has a collection of over 6000 swords. Entry is Y550, and it is open Tuesday to Sunday from 9 am to 4 pm. The nearest station is Sangubashi station on the Odakyū line.

For anyone with a special interest in the tea ceremony, check out the **Hatakeyama Memorial Hall** (☎ 3447-5787), east of Shinagawa station. The extensive collection that includes a great number of 'Important Cultural Properties' is accompanied by a tea-ceremony garden. Admission is Y500, and the hall is open Tuesday to Sunday from 10.30 am to 4 pm.

Temples

A temple that should be included in the sights of Tokyo, less for any intrinsic interest than for the story that surrounds it, is **Sengaku-ji Temple** (Map 1). The story is that of the 47 Rōnin. A rōnin is a masterless samurai, and these particular 47 plotted for two years to have vengeance on the man who caused the death of their master, Lord Asano. The act of vengence was undertaken in the knowledge that they too would have to forfeit their lives. After having brought the head of his enemy to their master's grave, forty-six of them were condemned to commit *harakiri*, or ritual disembowelment, in the samurai fashion (the 47th it seems got off on a technicality). The story, with its themes of the supreme sacrifice in the name of loyalty, has captured the Japanese imagination as no other story has, having been adapted into countless films and plays. The temple is open daily from 9 am to 4.30 pm and is close to Sengaku-ji subway station on the Toei Asakusa line.

Theatre

Tokyo now has it's own **Globe Theatre** (☎ 3360-1151). The London Globe was of course where many of Shakespeare's plays were first performed. Unfortunately, unlike Maxim's de Paris, certain problems have stood in the way of bringing out representatives (including the immortal bard himself) from the original London branch. Perhaps they have heard about the salmon-pink decor. Performances of Shakespeare's work are, nevertheless, held here. The theatre is on the west side of the railway tracks between Shin-Ōkubo and Takadanobaba station on the JR Yamanote line (Map 1).

Showrooms

Beside the showrooms already mentioned in the Ginza section, audiophiles might want to take a look at the **Pioneer Showroom** (☎ 3495-9900), just behind Meguro station on the JR Yamanote Line. Admission is free and it's open every day from 10.30 am to 6.30 pm.

Amusement Parks

Of course, number one on any list of Tokyo amusement parks has to be **Tokyo Disneyland**. Only the Japanese signs reveal that you're a long way from Orange County; Tokyo Disneyland is a near-perfect replica of the Anaheim, California, original. A few rides may be in slightly different locations, but basically you turn left from the entrance to the African Jungle, head straight on to Fantasyland or turn right to Tomorrowland. The latest addition, which is sure to be a hit in Japan, is the Star Tours feature, based on the Star Wars series.

It's open varying hours (usually from 9 am to 7 pm at least, but phone 3366-5600 or inquire at the Disneyland information counter at the Yaesu exit of Tokyo station for details) every day, except for about a dozen days a year (most of them in January) when it is closed all day. A variety of tickets are available, including an all-inclusive 'passport' which gives you unlimited access to all the rides for Y4440 (children aged 12 to 17, Y4000; those aged 4 to 11, Y3000). As at the original Disneyland, there are often long queues at popular rides (30 minutes to one hour is normal). Crowds are usually lighter in the mornings and heavier on weekends and holidays.

To get to Tokyo Disneyland, take the Tōzai subway line to Urayasu station. Follow the 'direct bus to Disneyland 340 m' sign out of the station. A shop-lined laneway leads to the Disneyland bus station. A ticket on this bus costs Y200. Alternatively, take the Yūraku-cho subway line to Shin-kiba station and the JR Keiyo line to Mahihama station, which is right in front of Disneyland's main gate. A variety of shuttle buses also run from Tokyo (Y600), Ueno (Y600) and Yokohama (Y1000) stations, from Narita (Y2000) and Haneda (Y700) airports and from the various nearby Disneyland hotels.

Next to Kōraku-en subway station on the Marunouchi subway line is **Kōraku-en Amusement Park** (Map 1). Some of the rides here are not for the faint hearted. The 'Ultra-Twister', with its 85° slope, is the most popular ride. Admission for adults is Y1100, children Y650 (rides not included), and it's open every day from 10 am to 7 pm.

TOURS

There are tours available for both the Tokyo metropolitan area and for areas further afield. An alternative to these, particularly for those interested in industrial Japan, are factory tours.

For tours of Tokyo, one of the most reliable operators is Hato Bus Tours (☎ 3435-6081). Their Panoramic Tour takes in most of the major sights of Tokyo, although the inclusion of Tokyo Tower is perhaps unwarranted, and costs Y9300. Probably the widest range of Tokyo tours is available from JTB's Sunrise Tours (☎ 3276-7777). Sunrise offers general sightseeing tours such as its morning tours (Y4230) and afternoon tours (Y4670), as well as tours aimed at more specialist interests. These include industrial tours (Y10,560), and a village life and crafts tour (Y11,170).

Night tours are also available from Sunrise and Gray Line (☎ 3433-5745). Sunrise offers a Kabuki Night tour that includes a sukiyaki dinner, kabuki at Ginza's Kabuki-za and a geisha show for Y13,240. An alternative to this dose of high culture is the nudge-nudge, wink-

wink 'adults only' Fascinating Night tour, with its kushiage dinner, geisha show and topless review at the Shogun. The tour costs Y11,310. Gray Line has similar deals for its Shogun Night tour (Y13,900) and its Samurai Night tour (Y11,000), both of which include kabuki and a live review at the Crystal Room in Akasaka. The former includes a sukiyaki dinner.

All of these tours pick up their guests at various major hotels around town.

The Hato Bus Industrial tour is worthwhile for those who want to see another side of Tokyo. Gray Line's Tuesday tour includes a trip to the Tokyo Stock Exchange followed by lunch and a visit to one of Isuzu Motor's factories. Alternatively, it is possible to contact Nissan Motors (☎ 5565-2149), who operate tours of one of their factories with an English-speaking guide.

If you happen to be in Tokyo for May or September, you might want to join the sumō tour offered by Tōbu Travel (☎ 3281-6622). The cost for the tour is Y12,500.

Finally, see the Excursions chapter for information on some of the tours available for areas outside Tokyo.

Places to Stay

Types of Accommodation

Most accommodation you are likely to encounter in Tokyo will provide no surprises for the uninitiated, particularly for those on an up-market visit to the city. In the lower reaches of the accommodation market, however, there are some forms of lodging that are peculiarly Japanese and may take a little getting used to. Perhaps the most famous of these is the capsule hotel. Measuring around two metres by one metre by one metre (about the size of a coffin the morbid will remark), this small area packs in a bed, reading light, TV, alarm clock and one insensate human body. Despite their small size, capsule hotels are not the accommodation bargain you might suppose. Prices for an overnight stay range from Y3500 up to Y4800, mainly depending on the services available.

In a similar quirky category is the love hotel. Rooms in a love hotel are generally rented out two hours at a time, but after 10 pm there will usually be fairly reasonable all-night rates available (around Y7000 on average). Of course prices can soar if you request the all-leather S&M deluxe suite with the African safari theme decor – don't say we didn't warn you.

Another form of accommodation mainly used by budget travellers in Tokyo is the ryokan, or guesthouse. Ryokan in Tokyo are a reasonably inexpensive form of accommodation as well as offering those who stay in them an opportunity to enjoy a more traditional Japanese experience. Shoes are taken off before entering the ryokan and are exchanged for a pair of slippers. These in turn are to be taken off before stepping onto the tatami (straw matting) floor of your room. Baths are generally available at fixed times during the day. Remember that you are supposed to wash and lather up with soap before you get into the bath and have a soak. Rarely will you find a shower. Ryokan in Tokyo are generally more accustomed to foreigners than their counterparts in more remote parts of Japan, and the rules tend to be a bit more relaxed as a result.

An even less expensive category of accommodation than the ryokan is the gaijin house. Many of these are private houses or apartments that have been partitioned off into rooms and rented out to foreigners. In general, gaijin houses are not an option for the short-term visitor to Tokyo. But for those planning on an extended stay, a gaijin house may initially be the only affordable option.

A form of mid-range accommodation that you come across a lot in Tokyo is the business hotel. Basically these are economical and practical places geared to the single traveller, though many in Tokyo will also take couples. In Tokyo, a room in a business hotel will have a pay TV and a small bathroom, and will cost around Y6000. Many business hotels will also add a 10% service charge to this. You will usually be required to book out at 10 or 11 am and check in around 3 or 4 pm.

Where to Stay

If you are not on a budget, areas such as Akasaka and Ginza (Central Tokyo) are ideal places to be based. There are even some mid-range hotels in this part of town, though you won't find anything under Y7500 for a single room. From this point prices spiral ever upwards as you move into the giddy heights of opulent indulgence offered by hotels of international renown, such as the Hotel Ōkura and the Imperial Hotel. If your budget doesn't reach five-star levels you can find cheaper accommodation with easy access to central Tokyo by staying somewhere on the JR Yamanote line.

Around the JR Yamanote line, business and entertainment districts like Shinjuku or Ikebukuro will have capsule hotels from around Y4000 per night or business-hotel singles from Y6000 to Y7500 per night. For the same price, a couple could even find a room in a love hotel from 10 or 11 pm. (Normally you will be required to check out at around 9 to 10 am the next day.) Shinjuku, which is also a very convenient area to be based in, also has some international-class hotels, mainly concentrated on the west side of the station. Both Ikebukuro and Ueno have some particularly good deals in the business-hotel category.

Most of the more reasonably priced accommodation such as ryokan are slightly less conveniently situated. Nevertheless, areas such as Ueno and Ikebukuro, both of which have a number of budget accommodation options, have the advantage of being on the JR Yamanote line and being within easy striking distance of central Tokyo. Asakusa is another area with a number of ryokan used by foreigners. It's two stops out from Ueno on the Asakusa subway line, a line which runs into Ginza and then on to Shibuya.

As a general rule of thumb, gaijin houses are usually further out on obscure suburban rail lines. Even if they were available as a short-term accommodation option, they would usually not be very convenient for seeing Tokyo.

PLACES TO STAY – BOTTOM END

The accommodation situation in Tokyo is not what it is in other cities around Asia. If you're happy spending from Y6000 to Y7000 or more a night for a single room, there's no shortage of accommodation, but things are definitely harder if you are travelling on a budget.

The problem for shoestring travellers is not only astronomical real-estate prices but also Tokyo's reputation as a city whose streets are paved with gold. The last five or six years has seen increasing numbers of travellers arriving in pursuit of yen with which to finance further travels. They frequently get stuck in Tokyo for quite some time. Add to this the popularity of Japanese studies and the large numbers of students arriving from around the world and you have an extremely high demand for budget accommodation indeed. Unfortunately for genuine travellers, this influx of long-term gaijin means that a lot of Tokyo's budget accommodation is booked out for weeks or even months at a time.

The best advice to anyone flying into Tokyo on a budget is to book your accommodation at least a month ahead. Popular budget options such as the Kimi Ryokan and the Asia Centre of Japan are often booked ahead for as long as six weeks.

Youth Hostels

The cheapest short-term accommodation options in Tokyo are the youth hostels in Iidabashi and Yoyogi. The only drawbacks are the usual youth-hostel restrictions – you have to be out of the building between 10 am and 3 pm (10 am and 5 pm at Yoyogi) and you have to be home by 10 pm in the evening – a real drag in a city like Tokyo. Finally, there's a three-night limit to your stay and the hostels can often be booked right out during peak holiday periods.

If you can handle these drawbacks, the common consensus is that the Yoyogi Youth Hostel is the better option of the two. The Tokyo International Youth Hostel (Iidabashi) might be a showcase for Japan's youth hostels (it's on the 18th floor of a towering office block, giving you great views of Tokyo), but there's a business-like atmosphere and the staff are more officious.

The *Tokyo International Youth Hostel* (☎ 3235-1107; Map 1) in Iidabashi doesn't require that you be a member but does ask that you book ahead and provide some identification (a passport will do) when you arrive. To get there, exit from Iidabashi station (either JR or subway) and look for the tallest building in sight (it's long, slender and glass fronted). There is a basic charge of Y2650 per person per night, or Y3850 with two meals, and a sleeping sheet costs Y150 for three nights. The Narita Airport TIC has a step-by-step instruction sheet on the cheapest means to get to the hostel from the airport.

The *Yoyogi Youth Hostel* (☎ 3467-9163) requires that you be a youth hostel member to stay, but will accept nonmembers upon payment of a Y600 'one welcome stamp'. There are no meals available, but there are cooking facilities. There is a charge of Y2000 per person per night. To get there, take the Odakyū line to Sangubashi station and walk towards the Meiji-jingū Shrine gardens. The hostel is enclosed in a fenced compound – not a former prison camp but the National Olympics Memorial Youth Centre – in building No 14. Staff may let you exceed the three-night limit if it is not crowded.

Ryokan & Other Budget Accommodation

The *Kimi Ryokan* (☎ 3971-3766; Map 5) deserves a special mention in any listing of Tokyo's budget accommodation. The Kimi is in Ikebukuro, which isn't a bad location from which to see Tokyo; it's 10 minutes from Shinjuku and 20 minutes from Ginza. The rooms are relatively inexpensive by Tokyo standards, nicely designed in Japanese style (tatami mats and futons) and the place is friendly, clean and relaxed about the hours you keep – just remember to take your room key with you if you're going to be out after 11.30 pm.

The Kimi lounge area is a good meeting place, with an excellent notice board; the Kimi bulletin board has metamorphosed into the nearby Kimi Information Centre. Some of the people who come to the lounge are actually staying elsewhere, but the Kimi lounge is still a popular place in which to hang out and discover what's new in town. If you're planning to stay at the Kimi, phone and book a month or so ahead, as there's nearly always a waiting list. Alternatively, arrive early in the morning and hope there's a cancellation.

To get to the Kimi, leave from the west exit of Ikebukuro station and follow Map 5 or go to the police box on the west side and say 'Kimi Ryokan' to the policeman on duty. He'll give you a map. Prices range from Y3500 to Y4300 for singles, from Y7000 to Y8000 for doubles and Y7500 for twins.

Also in Ikebukuro, and also booked out for long stretches at a time is *House Ikebukuro* (☎ 3984-3399; Map 5). It's popular with Chinese tourists on a budget, but Westerners can stay there too. It's not that far from the Kimi, so if you can't get in at the latter, try giving House Ikebukuro a call. It has singles/doubles/triples for Y4120/6180/7725.

The *Asia Centre of Japan* (☎ 3402-6111), near Aoyama-Itchome subway station on the Ginza line, is a popular option in the upper-budget category. This is another place that attracts many long-term stayers, and even though it's a lot bigger than the Kimi, it's still often fully booked. The station is under the easily recognisable Aoyama Twin Tower building on Aoyama-dōri Ave. Walk past the building towards Akasaka-Mitsuke, turn right (towards Roppongi) and the Asia Centre is a short walk up the third street on the left. Rooms have pay TVs, and singles cost Y4500, or Y6200 with bathroom. Twins cost from Y6000, or Y9600 with bathroom. Doubles cost from Y7100 to Y8500 with bathroom. Triples cost from Y9720 to Y12,000.

There's a lot to be said for being based in Shinjuku if you can stand the hustle and bustle. On the east side, the seventh street on the left of Yasukuni-dōri once you've passed through the Gyoen-dōri intersection, is the *Inabaso Ryokan* (☎ 3341-9581; Map 6). It has singles/doubles/triples for Y5000/8800/11,500.

Close to the JR Gotanda station on the JR Yamanote line is the *Ryokan Sansuisō* (☎ 3441-7475). This is not the greatest of locations, but it's only a few stops from Shibuya, the nearest main railway terminus. Take the exit furthest away from Shibuya and exit on the left-hand

Signposting (CT)

side. Turn right, take the first right after the big Tōkyū department store and then the first left. Turn left and then right, walk past the bowling centre and look for the sign on the right directing you down the sideroad to the ryokan. Prices for singles/doubles are Y4700/8000; triples cost Y11,000.

In Ueno, which is a good place to be based for sightseeing, even if it is a bit of a trek from the bright lights, there are several budget ryokan. The cheapest is *Sawanoya Ryokan* (☎ 3822-2251; Map 3) – Nezu subway station on the Chiyoda line is the closest station. Take the Nezu Crossing exit and turn right into Kototoi-dōri Ave. Turn left at the fourth street on your left – the Sawanoya Ryokan is a couple of minutes down the road on your right. If you're coming from Narita International Airport, it would probably be easier and just as cheap if there are more than one of you to catch a taxi from Ueno station. Singles/doubles cost Y4200/7800; triples cost Y10,500.

A bit closer to Ueno station is *Ryokan Katsutaro* (☎ 3821-9808; Map 3). If you follow the road that runs alongside Shinobazu Pond for about 10 minutes, you'll see the ryokan on the right. Singles/doubles/triples cost Y4200/7800/10,500. On the left, before you get to Ryokan Katsutaro, is the larger *Suigetsu Hotel* (☎ 3822-9611; Map 3), which has a launderette and rooms with private bathrooms. You can also change money there. Singles/doubles cost Y6000/10,500; triples cost Y10,800.

One stop away from Ueno on the JR Yamanote line (Uguisudani station) is the *Sakura Ryokan* (☎ 3876-8118). Take the southern exit and turn left. Pass the Iriya subway station exits on the left – the Sakura Ryokan is on the right-hand side of the second street on your left. If you're exiting from Iriya subway station on the Hibiya line, take the No 1 exit and turn left. Singles/doubles cost Y5000/9000; triples cost from Y12,000 to Y13,500.

Three stops away from Ueno on the Ginza line is Asakusa, which also has a few reasonably priced ryokan. *Ryokan Mikawaya Bekkan* (☎ 3843-2345; Map 4) is in an interesting area, just around the corner from the Sensō-ji Temple. It's on a sidestreet off the shop-lined street leading into the temple. From the Kaminari-mon Gate, the street is a few streets up on the left – there's a toy shop and a shoe shop on the corner. The ryokan is on the left-hand side of the road. Singles/doubles/ triples cost Y5700/10,400/15,300.

Just outside the Sensō-ji Temple precinct is the *Sukeroku-no-yado Sadachiyo Bekkan* (☎ 3842-6431; Map 4). Singles/doubles/triples with private bathrooms and air-con cost Y5500/9000/12000.

In Nishi Asakusa (near Tawaramachi subway station, which is one stop away on the Ginza line from Asakusa station) is the *Kikuya Ryokan* (☎ 3841-6404; Map 4). It's just off Kappabashi-dōri Ave and prices are Y4300/7500 for singles/doubles; triples cost Y10,000.

There are several other budget alternatives worth checking out, although they are popular with long-term visitors and often full. Near Kotake-Mukaihara subway station, a few stops out of Ikebukuro on the Yūraku-cho line, is the *Rikkō Kaikan Guest Room* (☎ 3972-1151) with singles/doubles from Y3605/7210. Near Shin-Nakano subway station on the Marunouchi line is the *Shin-Nakano Lodge* (☎ 3381-4886), which has singles/doubles for Y4000/Y7000.

The *YMCA Asia Youth Centre* (☎ 3233-0611) takes both men and women. It's halfway between Suidobashi and Jimbō-cho subway stations. Rooms with bathroom cost Y6500/11,000 for singles/doubles; triples cost Y15,000. The *Japan YWCA Hostel* (☎ 3264-0661) is a bit cheaper but only accepts women. It's a few minutes from the Kudan exit of Ichigaya subway station and costs Y4738 per person. The *Tokyo YWCA Sadohara Hostel* (☎ 3268-4451), near the Ichigaya exit of Ichigaya subway station, accepts couples and is cheaper, but it closes its doors at 11 pm. Singles/doubles with toilet cost from Y5360/10,300.

Capsule Hotels

Capsule hotels are a strictly male domain and you find them wherever there are large numbers of salarymen, bars, hostess clubs and other drains for company expense accounts. Close to the western exit of Ikebukuro station is the *Ikebukuro Plaza* (☎ 3590-7770; Map 5), which costs Y3800 per night. Even cheaper in Ikebukuro is the *Capsule Kimeya Hotel* (☎ 3971-8751; Map 5), over on the east side, not far from the Sunshine City building. It's open from 4 pm to 10 am and a capsule is only Y3000.

Right in Shinjuku's sleazy Kabiku-cho is the *Shinjuku-ku Capsule Hotel* (☎ 3232-1110; Map 6), open from 5 pm to 10 am at Y4100 per night. Also in Shinjuku, over towards Shinjuku-gyoen Park is the *Winning Inn Shinjuku* (☎ 3350-0601; Map 6), open from 5 pm to 10 am for Y3500 per night. Just down the road from the Prince Hotel on Shinjuku's east side is *Green Plaza Shinjuku* (☎ 3207-5411; Map 6). It's open from 5 pm to 10 am, and your own personal capsule is Y4100.

In Ueno there is a branch of the *Ueno Capsule Kimeya Hotel* (☎ 3833-1924; Map 3). It's open from 2 pm to 10 am, and it is Y3000 per night.

In Akasaka, not far from Akasaka station, is the *Capsule Inn Akasaka* (☎ 3588-1811; Map 9). It's open from 5 pm to 10 am and costs Y4000 per night. Closer to Akasaka Mitsuke Station is an up-market capsule hotel, *Capsule Hotel Fontaine Akasaka* (☎ 3583-6554; Map 9). An overnight stay here will set you back Y4800.

A Night in Capsuleland

My one experience of a capsule hotel was, like much else in Japan, initially a little bewildering. Shoes were left at the entrance, just like in a traditional Japanese inn, but there the similarity ended. There was no space to take anything (apart from myself) into the capsule – a locker room was available for clothes and personal effects and, at the entrance, larger secondary lockers for bigger bags.

In the locker was a pair of pyjamas, emblazoned with the hotel's logo. Most of the other inmates seemed to wear their pyjamas all the time both in the hotel and outside in the neighbouring streets. (When I returned to the hotel later in the evening I realised I was getting close when, still a block or two away, I began to see men in blue and yellow short pyjamas!)

The hotel had a coffee bar, restaurant, TV lounge, sauna, massage room, toilets, washing facilities and a large communal bath. The capsules didn't lock (all my valuables were supposedly in the locker), and there was just a screen to pull down at the entrance. The capsule was exactly the length and width of the mattress but, also squeezed in, was a small shelf, a light, controls for a radio, alarm and the air-con and, mounted on the 'ceiling' of the capsule, a TV set complete with the obligatory porno channel. The capsules were stacked two high but were surprisingly quiet and, since the lighting was all artificial and there was no way of telling day from night, I slept way past my normal waking time.

Tony Wheeler

Gaijin Houses

Although a few gaijin houses quote daily or weekly rates, they are generally not an option for short-term visitors. If you are planning a long stay, a gaijin house may be the only affordable option, but the shortage of cheap accommodation means they often have long waiting lists. Typically prices range from Y35,000 for a single to Y70,000 a month for a bed in a shared room, with no deposits or key money required.

While you wait for a room to become available, you may have to book into a cheap ryokan or a youth hostel.

There have been reports of travellers paying nearly
Y1000 a night for the privilege of sleeping in a car parked
outside a gaijin house. The proprietors had the nerve to
class it as one of their rooms.

Gaijin house conditions often leave much to be
desired. Rooms are usually very small and chances are
you're going to be sharing one to keep expenses down.
Facilities are often pretty limited – one shower and toilet
for 40 people is a typical shock-horror story. This kind of
thing is OK for a while, but if you're going to be based
in Tokyo for an extended period, you'll probably want
to start looking for something better.

The Tourist Information Centre used to give out information to travellers on gaijin houses in Tokyo. They no
longer do so, after investigations found many of them to
be 'illegal'. What this means is that nowadays gaijin
houses rely on word of mouth for most of their business.
The *Tokyo Journal* also has listings of gaijin houses with
vacancies.

If you ring a gaijin house, there is always someone
who speaks English. Generally someone will be able to
meet you at the station and take you to the house. The
following list only provides some of the more permanent
gaijin houses. There are many, many more scattered
around Tokyo, with new ones opening as quickly as the
old ones close down. If you want to find them you'll have
to keep an ear to the ground. Unless otherwise indicated,
the prices given here are per person per month.

ABC House –share one week Y7000; private one week Y16,000;
three minutes from Kamata station on the Keihin Tōhoku
line (☎ 3736-2311)

At the Palace of Confucius – singles from Y62,000; doubles from
Y70,000 (☎ 3728-7061)

Big World – doubles Y43,000; dorm Y33,000; five-minute walk
from Higashi-Koganei station (☎ 0423-87-7701)

Bilingual House – share from Y38,000 to Y40,000; private from
Y43,000 to Y60,000; three houses – near the Seibu Shinjuku
line, the Keio line and the JR line (☎ 3200-7082)

Friendship House – Higashi Kōenji (☎ 3314-7441)

Guesthouse – twins Y47,000 to Y50,000; per day Y1700 (☎ 3366-
7209)

ITC House – 'ladies only'; share rooms Y30,000; singles Y40,000
(☎ 3792-0749)

Japan House – share from Y45,000; two locations – near
Senkawa subway station on the Yūraku-cho line, and
Kamata station on the Keihin Tōhoku line (☎ 3962-2495)

Lily House Mansion – share Y50,000; private Y70,000; near
Kawaguchi station on the Keihin Tōhoku line (☎ 0482-23-
8205)

Marui House – near Ikebukuro station and not far from Kimi Ryokan; daily doubles Y3800; singles Y2600; cheaper monthly rates (☎ 3962-4979)

New Gaijin House – singles Y50,000 (☎ 0424-23-4162)

Taihei House III – shared room from Y25,000; singles from Y35,000 (☎ 3940-4705)

Tokyo English Centre – shared room Y1900 per day; Y47,000 per month (☎ 5370-8440)

Villa Paradiso – singles/doubles Y69,000/88,000 (☎ 045-911-1184)

PLACES TO STAY – MIDDLE

Hotels

The middle price bracket in Tokyo principally comprises business hotels. There's very little to distinguish one from another, and their main attraction is usually convenience. Every district in Tokyo has numerous business hotels with singles/doubles from about Y6000/10,000. Generally, each room will have a built-in bathroom with shower, bath and toilet, a telephone, pay TV and other features like disposable toothbrushes and shaving equipment.

An interesting late-night alternative is a love hotel. There are plenty of these in any of Tokyo's entertainment districts but particularly in Shinjuku, Shibuya, Roppongi and Ikebukuro. All-night rooms range in price from about Y6000 to Y7000, but 'all night' doesn't start until 10 or 11 pm, when the regular hour-by-hour customers have run out of energy.

Although the following is a very selective list of mid-range hotels, most of them at least have English-speaking staff. As a general rule of thumb, the lower the price of rooms in a business hotel, the less likely the staff are accustomed to dealing with foreigners. They won't turn you away though. In some cases room prices are listed with consumption tax included – where a round price is given for a room, you can expect an additional 3% consumption tax to be added.

An interesting alternative to the list of mainly business hotels included here is the *Gajoen Kankō Hotel* (☎ 3491-0111) in Meguro. The hotel is actually a Japanese-style ryokan decorated with ukiyo-e woodblock prints and wall hangings, and features an enormous bathing area. Singles range from Y10,197 and twins from Y16,695. The hotel is about five minutes south-west of Meguro station on the JR Yamanote line.

The hotels listed here are divided by area, and in as many cases as possible they are indicated on the appropriate area maps.

Central Tokyo Any hotels in this area (Map 2) tend to be expensive, simply because real estate values are so high. Nevertheless, there are a few mid-range places.

Hotel Atamisō – singles Y9800; twins Y19,000; two minutes from Higashi-Ginza subway station (☎ 3541-3621)

Business Hotel Heimat – singles/doubles Y7000/9000; across from the Marunouchi exit of Tokyo station (☎ 3273-9411)

Centre Hotel Tokyo – singles/doubles Y7700/9900; close to Nihombashi subway station (☎ 3667-2711)

Ginza Capitol Hotel – singles Y8300; twins Y13,800; two minutes from Tsukiji subway station (☎ 3543-8211)

Ginza Capitol Hotel Annex – singles Y8500; doubles Y15,000; three minutes from Tsukiji subway station (☎ 3543-7888)

Hotel Ginza Dai-ei – singles Y10,000; doubles or twins Y16,000; one minute from Higashi-Ginza subway station (☎ 3545-1111)

Ginza International Hotel – singles/doubles Y14,729/19,261; twins Y21,527; two minutes from Shimbashi station (☎ 3574-1121)

Ginza Marunouchi Hotel – singles from Y10,000 to Y15,000; doubles from Y19,000 to Y24,000; two minutes from Higashi-Ginza subway station (☎ 3543-5431)

Hotel Ginza Ocean – singles from Y8000 to Y9000; doubles from Y14,000 to Y15,000; five minutes from Higashi-Ginza subway station (☎ 3545-1221)

Ginza Nikkō Hotel – singles/doubles Y19,588/33,580; four minutes from Shimbashi station (☎ 3571-4911)

Hotel Kokusai Kankō – singles/doubles Y14,000/21,5000; two minutes from the Marunouchi exit of Tokyo station (☎ 3215-3281)

Mitsui Urban Hotel – singles/doubles Y15,669/22,660; one minute from Shimbashi station (☎ 3572-4131)

Sun Hotel Shimbashi – singles Y7500; twins Y12,600; three minutes from Shimbashi station (☎ 3591-3351)

Tokyo City Hotel – singles/doubles Y8034/11,845; twins Y13,805; two minutes from Mitsukoshi-mae subway station (☎ 3270-7671)

Tokyo Station Hotel – singles Y7930; doubles or twins Y13,590; in the JR Tokyo station (☎ 3231-2511)

Yaesu Fujiya Hotel – singles/doubles Y12,500/Y16,000; five minutes from Tokyo station (☎ 3273-2111)

Yaesu Terminal Hotel – singles/doubles Y9700/15,500; one minute from the JR Tokyo station (☎ 3281-3771)

Ueno & Asakusa The cheaper ryokan in the Ueno and Asakusa area are better value, but if they're all full, the business hotels there are generally cheaper than those in other areas around Tokyo.

Asakusa Plaza Hotel – singles/doubles Y6700/10,500 (☎ 3862-7551; Map 4)

Ikenohata Bunka Centre – singles Y5665; twins Y11,330; three
minutes from Yushima subway station (☎ 3822-0151)

Kinuya Hotel – singles without bath Y5300; with bath Y6700;
doubles Y10,800; next to Keisei Ueno station (☎ 3833-1911;
Map 3)

Hotel New Ueno – singles/doubles Y8000/13,000; next to Ueno
station (☎ 3841-3221; Map 3)

Hotel Ohgasio – singles/doubles Y7000/12,000; next to Ueno
Zoo (☎ 3822-4611; Map 3)

Hotel Parkside – singles/doubles Y9300/16,500; near Ueno's
Shinobazu Pond (☎ 3836-3459; Map 3)

Hotel Pine Hill Ueno – singles Y7500; doubles and twins
Y14,000; 10 minutes from Ueno station (☎ 3836-5111; Map
3)

Hotel Top Asakusa – singles/doubles Y8500/9500; five minutes
from Asakusa subway station (☎ 3847-2222; Map 4)

Ueno Terminal Hotel – singles/doubles Y7500/15,000; five
minutes from Ueno station (☎ 3831-1110; Map 3)

Shinjuku Shinjuku (Map 6) is a good hunting ground for business hotels that cater to foreigners.

Business Hotel Shinjuku Inn – singles Y7200; doubles or twins
Y11,000; five minutes north of Shinjuku-gyoen-mae
subway station (☎ 3341-0131)

Central Hotel – singles/doubles Y9000/14,000; two minutes
from the east exit of Shinjuku station (☎ 3354-6611)

Shinjuku New City Hotel – singles/doubles Y9700/19,000;
twins Y13,600; 10 minutes from the west exit of Shinjuku
station (☎ 3375-6511)

Shinjuku Palace Hotel – singles/doubles Y6800/9600; 10
minutes from the east exit of Shinjuku station (☎ 3209-
1231)

Shinjuku Park Hotel – singles Y6800; twins Y11,800; seven
minutes from Shinjuku station in the direction of
Shinjuku-gyoen Park (☎ 3356-0241)

Shinjuku Sun Park Hotel – singles/doubles Y6490/8760; five
minutes from Shin-Okubo and Okubo stations (☎ 3362-
7101)

Shinjuku Washington Hotel – singles/doubles Y12,000/17,500;
10 minutes from the south exit of Shinjuku station, close
to the NS building (☎ 3343-3111)

Star Hotel Tokyo – singles/doubles Y9000/17,300; three
minutes from Shinjuku station (☎ 3361-1111)

Hotel Sun Lite – singles/doubles Y7700/11,000; ten minutes
from the east exit of Shinjuku station (☎ 3356-0391)

Hotel Sun Route Tokyo – singles/doubles Y9500/14,000; five
minutes from the south exit of Shinjuku station (☎ 3375-
3211)

Taisho Central Hotel – singles/doubles Y6180/14,420; twins
Y11,330; two minutes from Takadanobaba station
(☎ 3232-0101)

Ikebukuro There are innumerable business and love hotels in the Ikebukuro area (Map 5).

Business Hotel Ikebukuro – singles/doubles Y7000/10,000; close to the west exit of Ikebukuro station (☎ 3982-8989)

Hotel Grand Business – singles Y7700; twins Y12,800; five minutes from the east exit of Ikebukuro station (☎ 3984-5121)

Plaza Inn Ikebukuro – singles/doubles Y8000/12,500; five minutes from the west exit of Ikebukuro station (☎ 3985-0121)

Hotel Sun City Ikebukuro – singles/doubles Y6500/9500; across from the north exit of Ikebukuro station (☎ 3986-1101)

Hotel Sun Route Ikebukuro – singles/doubles Y7500/12,500; close to the east exit of Ikebukuro station (☎ 3988-2261)

Hotel Star Plaza Ikebukuro – singles/doubles Y7500/10,000; five minutes from the west exit of Ikebukuro station (☎ 3590-0005)

Shibuya Shibuya (Map 8) is another expensive area that has few genuine mid-range hotels. Those listed here are definitely in the high end of the middle category. Still, Shibuya is a good area to be based in, and some of the hotels, such as Hotel Ivy Flat, are in very pleasant locations.

Aoyama Shanpia Hotel – singles/doubles Y11,220/16,5000; five minutes from the south exit of Shibuya station (☎ 3407-8866)

Hotel Ivy Flat – singles Y10,500; twins Y16,000; five minutes from Shibuya station (☎ 3770-1122)

Shibuya Business Hotel – singles/doubles Y8600/11,400; two minutes from Shibuya station (☎ 3409-9300)

Shibuya Tōbu Hotel – singles/doubles Y11,400/13,600; up past the Parco department stores (☎ 3476-0111)

Shibuya Tōkyū Inn – singles Y13,800; doubles or twins Y19,200; one minute from Shibuya station (☎ 3498-0109)

Hotel Sun Route Shibuya – singles/doubles Y7200/14,200; five minutes from Shibuya station (☎ 3464-4611)

Akasaka & Roppongi This is a good area to be based in if you want access to central Tokyo and a lively nightlife. Akasaka is an area with a concentration of top-end hotels, and Roppongi too is a notoriously expensive area.

Akasaka Shanpia Hotel – singles Y9780; twins Y16,480; four minutes from Akasaka subway station (☎ 3583-1001)

Hotel Ibis – singles/doubles Y13,000/20,000; two minutes from Roppongi subway station (☎ 3403-4411; Map 10)

Marroad Inn Akasaka – singles/doubles Y9600/10,600; five minutes from Akasaka subway station (☎ 3585-7611; Map 9)

Hotel Tōkyū Kankō – singles/doubles Y7364/14,729; seven minutes from Akasaka subway station (☎ 3583-4741)

Tōshi Centre Hotel – singles Y7200; twins Y11,600; seven minutes from Akasaka-Mitsuke subway station (☎ 3265-8211)

Hotel Yōkō Akasaka – singles/doubles Y8900/13,000; 3 minutes from Akasaka subway station (☎ 3586-4050; Map 9)

Shinagawa & Hammamatsu-cho This is an area that does not have a lot to recommend it, except its easy access to Haneda Airport – handy for those early flights out of Tokyo.

Shinagawa Prince Hotel – singles from Y8900; doubles from Y14,000; close to Shinagawa station (☎ 3440-1111)

Tokyo Grand Hotel – singles/doubles Y12,500/16,000; close to Shiba station (☎ 3456-2222)

Saké barrels (RS)

PLACES TO STAY – TOP END

Although Tokyo is one of the world's most expensive cities, its top-end hotels are usually no more expensive than similar hotels anywhere else, and you get Japan's legendary high standard of service.

Areas such as Ginza, Akasaka, Roppongi and Shinjuku (mainly the west side) have the highest concentration of top-end hotels. Any of these areas would make convenient locations to be based, though Ginza and Akasaka are somewhat classier than Shinjuku.

Tokyo has no shortage of hotels with internationally acclaimed standards of service. As you would expect, great attention is given to interior design and to the comfort of the guests. Moreover, there is enough competition to keep everyone on their toes.

In central Tokyo the *Imperial Hotel* has a reputation as being one of Tokyo's best hotels. The hotel features a vast array of services and has views of the Imperial Palace. On a less grand scale and with an emphasis on personal service, the *Seiyo Ginza* provides each of its guests with a personal secretary – a service which, as you might expect, really bumps up the price of your stay. Big hotels like the *Ginza Dai-Ichi* and its annex combine reasonable top-end rates with a reputation for good service and an ideal location. The same is true of the *Ginza Tōbu Hotel*. The *Palace Hotel* also has a great location right across from the Imperial Palace.

Alternatively, for some up-market comforts at lower rates in a slightly less convenient location, try the *Hotel Metropolitan* in Ikebukuro or the *Asakusa View Hotel* in Asakusa.

The *Roppongi Prince* would be a good option for anyone whose primary interest is the bright lights of Roppongi, just up the hill.

In Akasaka the *Hotel Okura* has built up a prestigious reputation for itself with its exemplary service and features such as a Japanese garden and tasteful decor. The *Akasaka Prince Hotel* is another of the Japanese architect Kenzo Tange's creations and is something of a landmark. The rooms provide excellent views and attention has been given to providing guests with a feeling of spaciousness, a commodity in short supply in Tokyo. The *ANA Hotel Tokyo*, also in Akasaka, is rated highly for the tastefulness of its interior design and its attention to detail.

The *Capitol Tokyū Hotel* is a favourite among business people and is rated highly for its views and friendly service. The *New Otani Hotel*, not far from the Akasaka Prince, is renowned most of all for its Japanese garden around which the hotel was constructed (see the Akasaka section of the Things to See & Do chapter earlier in this guide). The hotel itself is massive, with an enormous guest capacity, giving it something of an impersonal feeling.

In Shinjuku, the *Century Hyatt Tokyo* features a 'penthouse' swimming pool on its 28th floor and has spacious Western and Japanese style rooms. The 47-storey *Keio Plaza Inter-Continental Hotel* provides guests with excellent views of the area.

The rates given in the following list of top-end hotels will almost invariably be subject to government taxes of up to 6% and a service charge of 10%. Bear this in mind when you're budgeting your trip.

Akasaka Prince Hotel – singles from Y24,000; doubles Y34,000; twins from Y32,000; next to Nagata-cho subway station (☎ 3234-1111; Map 9)

Akasaka Tōkyū Hotel – singles from Y20,000; doubles from Y29,500; twins from Y29,000; next to Nagata-cho subway station (☎ 3580-2311; Map 9)

ANA Hotel Tokyo – singles from Y26,000; doubles from Y34,000; twins Y34,000; near Akasaka subway station (☎ 3505-1111; Map 9)

Asakusa View Hotel – singles from Y15,000; doubles from Y21,000; twins from Y28,000; behind Sensō-ji Temple, Asakusa (☎ 3847-1111; Map 2)

Capitol Tōkyū Hotel – singles from Y24,500; doubles from Y33,500; twins from Y33,500; near Nagata-cho subway station (☎ 3581-4511; Map 9)

Century Hyatt Tokyo – singles from Y22,000; doubles from Y29,000 twins from Y32,000; near Shinjuku station (☎ 3349-0111; Map 6)

Ginza Dai-Ichi Hotel – singles from Y19,000; doubles from Y27,000; twins from Y24,000; near Higashi-Ginza and Shimbashi stations (☎ 3542-5311; Map 2)

Dai-Ichi Hotel Annex – singles from Y25,000; close to Shimbashi station (☎ 3503-5611)

Ginza Tōbu Hotel – singles from Y17,000; doubles from Y31,000; twins from Y31,000; close to Higashi-Ginza subway station (☎ 3546-0111)

Ginza Tōkyū Hotel – singles from Y17,000; doubles from Y38,500; twins from Y28,500; near Higashi-Ginza subway station (☎ 3541-2411)

Imperial Hotel – singles from Y33,000; doubles from Y38,000; twins from Y38,000; five minutes from Yūraku-cho station (☎ 3504-1111; Map 2)

Keio Plaza Inter-Continental Hotel – singles from Y22,000; doubles from Y27,000; twins from Y27,000; near the west exit of Shinjuku station (☎ 3344-0111; Map 6)

New Takanawa Prince Hotel – singles from Y21,000; doubles from Y28,000; twins from Y28,000; close to Shinagawa station (☎ 3442-1111)

Hotel Metropolitan – singles from Y16,000; doubles from Y20,500; twins from Y21,000; five minutes from the west exit of Ikebukuro station (☎ 3980-1111; Map 5)

Hotel New Otani – singles from Y27,500; doubles from Y33,500; twins from Y32,500; near Akasaka-Mitsuke subway station (☎ 3265-1111; Map 9)

Hotel Okura – singles from Y28,500; doubles from Y38,000; twins from Y38,500; near Kamiya-cho subway station (☎ 3582-0111; Map 9)

Hotel Pacific Meridian – singles from Y21,000; doubles from Y25,000; twins from Y25,000; near Shinagawa station (☎ 3445-6711)

Palace Hotel – singles from Y23,000; doubles from Y32,000; twins from Y28,000; near Tokyo station (☎ 3211-5211; Map 2)

Roppongi Prince Hotel – singles from Y19,500; doubles from Y23,500; twins from Y22,000; 10 minutes from Roppongi subway station (☎ 3587-1111; Map 10)

Hotel Seiyo Ginza – singles from Y45,000; twins from Y62,000; 10 minutes from Higashi-Ginza subway station (☎ 3535-1111; Map 2)

Shinjuku Prince Hotel – singles from Y15,000; doubles from Y28,000; twins from Y26,000; close to Seibu-Shinjuku station (☎ 3205-1111; Map 6)

Takanawa Prince Hotel – singles from Y20,000; doubles from Y24,000; twins from Y24,000; near Shinagawa station (☎ 3447-1111)

Tokyo Hilton International – singles from Y27,000; doubles from Y34,000; twins from Y34,000; near Shinjuku station (☎ 3344-5111; Map 6)

Tokyo Prince Hotel – singles from Y24,000; doubles from Y25,000; twins from Y25,000; near Onarimon subway station (☎ 3432-1111)

LONG TERM

Those looking to rent an apartment in Tokyo will usually have to fork out a lot of money up front. This is due to a variety of legalised forms of extortion that have become common practice in the housing rental business. First of all, unless you are very lucky, you will have to find your apartment via a real-estate agency. The fee for the agent's work (generally going through a list and ringing your potential landlord to ask discreetly whether he or she is prepared to rent to a gaijin) is a month's rent. Secondly, and this is the one that really hurts, you will have to pay a bribe (known politely as 'key money', or *reikin*) to your landlord. Key money is usually two to three months' rent and will usually be required again after two years. You never see it again. After this, there is the deposit, which might be one or two months' rent and an up-front payment of one or two months' rent. If you imagine

abound in small Japanese and Chinese noodle bars, though Ikebukuro also has a few up-market alternatives including a French and an Italian restaurant or two. Another good eating area is Roppongi, which is also Tokyo's centre for nightclubs.

For a serious restaurant crawl get Rick Kennedy's *Good Tokyo Restaurants*. Many of the places recommended are too expensive for travellers on a budget, but if you feel like splurging or are planning a longer stay the book is definitely a worthwhile investment.

The following cuisine guide first describes restaurants serving Japanese food by area. Places serving international cuisine are listed in the Other Cuisines section.

JAPANESE

Many Japanese restaurants specialise in a particular type of food. At one extreme, the simple neighbourhood okonomiyaki and yakitori places found on every corner are often very economical. At the other extreme there are very exclusive restaurants with high prices; you may not even get in without an introduction. For those on a real budget, you still have the opportunity to sample Japanese food via the revolving sushi shops and fast-food chains such as Yoshinoya, with their good beef and rice (*gyūdon*) and katsudon dishes. *Hokaben*, the stalls and hole-in-the-wall outlets selling bentō (take-away lunch sets), are also a very economical alternative – it's usually easy to recognise them by the photographed dishes displayed outside.

The following recommendations include both economical gastronomic excursions as well as more serious assaults on your savings. Just remember, in Tokyo, cheap doesn't necessarily mean poor quality, and in a lot of the expensive restaurants, while the food may be delicious, a lot of your yen is going on the ambience and service. Even if you have the money to spend, it's worth going down-market sometimes.

Central Tokyo & Ginza (Map 2)

Restaurants in the central area are not all aimed at the company expense account. There are some great lunch-time bargains in department stores and plenty of small night-time food stalls. *Restaurant City* on the 8th floor of the Matsuya department store has a wide variety of restaurants with not too outrageous prices. *Tsunahachi*, with its excellent tempura dishes, is recommended. Matsuya, conveniently close to the centre of Ginza on

Ginza-dōri Ave, is open until 9 pm every day except Thursdays. The store itself closes at 6 pm but the restaurant floor has its own elevator.

Another floor of restaurants can be found in the 2nd basement level of the Matsuzakaya department store, also on Ginza-dōri Ave but just the other side of Harumi-dōri Ave. A little further along Ginza-dōri is the *Lion Beer Hall*, where you'll find beer and cheap food.

Also just south of Harumi-dōri Ave is *New Torigin*, hidden away down a very narrow back alley but signposted in English and quite easy to find. There's a menu in English and this authentic, very popular little place does excellent food including yakitori at Y120 to Y200 per stick and the steamed rice dish known as kamameshi at Y700. A complete meal with a beer costs about Y1500. Just around the corner from New Torigin is *Anjyu*, a superior rāmen shop, with dishes ranging from Y750.

South of Yūraku-cho station, beneath the railway tracks, is the *Funachu* restaurant, which gives you the opportunity to try a mini-kaiseki for Y2400. They also have yakitori, and large beers are only Y680.

North of Harumi-dōri is *Kawa* (☎ 3564-6984), a small restaurant serving delicious tonkatsu (pork cutlets) and katsudon at prices ranging from Y800. In the small lane

Yakitori bar, Yūraku-cho Station (CT)

beside Kawa are a couple of expensive Edo-style restaurants with cheaper lunch-time specials. *Kamogawa* (☎ 3561-0550) serves very expensive kaiseki (the traditional Japanese high cuisine).

Almost behind the TIC office, in the shadow of the elevated expressway and railway lines, is a host of popular and budget priced little yakitori stalls. A few doors down from the TIC office is *Dondo*, which has an excellent selection of udon dishes from Y750 up. *Chichibu Nishiki* (☎ 3541-477) is a traditional *nomiya* (saké pub) with good cheap food in a very authentic setting. It's tucked away behind the Kabuki-za theatre.

Of course, Ginza is also one of the best places in Tokyo to sample Japanese food at its best. For sushi, try *Kyubei* (☎ 3571-6523). It's just up the road from the Mitsui Urban Hotel, and it has lunch specials for Y6000. Equally renowned and just as expensive is *Ginza Ten-Ichi* (☎ 3571-1272), which has Tempura sets from Y7000. *Suehiro* (☎ 3571-9271) has branches all over Tokyo, and serves a host of beef dishes, including the popular favourites, sukiyaki and shabu-shabu. Be warned, however, the Ginza branch is particularly expensive (courses from Y5000) – the branch in Harajuku has cheaper lunch-time specials.

Tsukiji (Map 2)

Of course, if you make that early morning trip to the Tsukiji market, you have to do it properly – and a sushi breakfast is *de rigueur*. Actually there are quite a few sushi shops close to the market. But the word out on the streets is that *Sushi-sei* (☎ 3541-7720), the main branch of the chain that has spread its fishy tentacles throughout the city, is *the* place to start your day with some raw fish. Sushi-sei opens at 8 am and its prices are very reasonable (Y100 to Y300 a piece).

Ueno & Asakusa (Maps 3 & 4)

In these older areas, the Shitamachi or 'low' city of pre-Meiji Tokyo, you find fewer foreign restaurants and more traditional Japanese food. The Ameyoko shopping area near the station is packed with small Japanese places, including *Irohazushi* (Map 3), a very reasonably priced sushi shop. It's just on the left as you enter the arcade. Just a little down the arcade is *Uroya* (Map 3), with inexpensive and tasty curry rice dishes. Further down on one of the lanes that runs off from the right fork of the arcade is another popular cut-price sushi restaurant – *Kappazushi* (Map 3).

South of Shinobazu Pond, near the Hotel Parkside, is *Menja* (Map 3), a high-class udon restaurant, with prices ranging from around Y1000. Just a few doors down is *Yoshibei*, which has very good sushi sets at fairly reasonable prices.

If you manage to get lost in the bowels of Ueno station (a common occurrence, rest assured), look out for the restaurants in underground walkways that connect the JR station with the subway station. Some of them look like they are competing for a place in the annual monster-size rāmen awards – very reasonable prices too.

Asakusa is an area teeming with Japanese restaurants. The best hunting ground is Kaminarimon-dōri Ave. *Tonkyu*, to the right of the entranceway to the Sensō-ji Temple (Map 4), is a small family-run restaurant with good lunch-time prices. Tonkatsu (pork cutlets) are the speciality. The restaurant is closed on Thursday. To the left of the gates is a branch of *Yoshinoya*, where a rice and beef dish (gyūdon) is only Y400. Walking away from the gates down Kaminarimon-dōri Ave, watch out for *Naowariya* (Map 4; no English sign, so look for the plastic soba dishes in the window), a classy soba restaurant with dishes ranging from Y1100. A little further down again is *Tendon* (Map 4), a tendon shop with dishes from Y460 served in a pleasant atmosphere.

Back in the other direction, it's worth taking a look at the lane running parallel to Nakamise-dōri. *Rāmen House Asakusa* (Map 4) is highly recommended for its inventive rāmen dishes ('sausage rāmen' and 'beef patty rāmen', to name a couple) and the English descriptions that come with them. Prices for a rāmen dish range from Y750. On the same lane, *Tatsumiya* (☎ 3842-7373; Map 4) is an old-fashioned looking place where you can try kaiseki ryōri (the traditional Japanese high cuisine) without breaking the bank. *Edokko* (Map 4) is a tempura restaurant with a traditional atmosphere. It's just on the perimeter of Sensō-ji Temple, and has meal sets from Y1800. Just around the corner from Edokko is a stand-up noodle bar simply displaying the hiragana for rāmen. A bowl of noodles is only Y280 – you don't get much more economical than that!

Finally, right across from Asakusa station is *Kamiya* (☎ 3841-5400; Map 4), claimed to be the oldest bar in Japan. There's a beer hall on the ground floor where you order and pay for beer and food as you enter. The bar is also renowned for a cocktail of its own concoction: denki bran. The *bran* stands for brandy, and the cocktail itself comes in two varieties: 60 proof and 80 proof. Upstairs, both Western and Japanese food are served. The Kamiya is closed on Tuesday.

Ikebukuro (Map 5)

Ikebukuro is not an area that you would want to visit especially for its Japanese cuisine, but there are a few surprises here.

Close to Kimi Ryokan on the west side is *Sushi Kazo*, a sushi restaurant that stays open late and has sets from Y1200. Around the corner is a restaurant that deserves a mention for its popularity among both locals and foreigners staying in the area – *Fushin*. The yakiniku-men noodles (Y580) are recommended in this Japanese/Chinese rāmen shop.

It is also worth exploring the slightly sleazy area behind the Rosa Cinema for places to eat. *Toneria* is a busy izakaya with friendly staff who are used to the occasional gaijin calling in. Prices are reasonable, but watch out because they add up quickly – especially if you include a few drinks. Look out for all the empty saké bottles piled up outside.

Over on the east side, there's a revolving sushi shop across from Seibu called *Taiyuzushi*. It's not bad, but if you're really hankering for some cheap sushi it's worth walking a little further to *Komazushi*, a popular place with a friendly atmosphere. In the same area as Komazushi are a number of aka-chōchin (worker's pub) bars that you might want to try out. They all seem very popular. Also not far away is *Men*, a superior rāmen restaurant with an extensive menu illustrated with photographs for easy ordering. Prices start from Y650.

Finally, don't forget that Ikebukuro is home to some of the biggest department stores in Tokyo. Seibu, Tōbu and Marui, to name a few, all have restaurant floors in their upper reaches – Seibu alone has around 50 restaurants, many of them specialising in various Japanese cuisines. The dishes are all on display in plastic outside, so there's no problem ordering. We're not giving any recommendations – just do a little exploring.

Shinjuku (Map 6)

Shinjuku is the busiest and most energetic commuter junction in Tokyo, and there are a vast number of restaurants around the station and in the raucous entertainment area.

A number of restaurants in Shinjuku specialise in sukiyaki and shabu-shabu. *Ibuki* has great sukiyaki and shabu-shabu starting at around Y1500 per head. Next door is a pleasant sushi restaurant. Both are just around the corner from the Studio Alta building – unfortunately the sign for Ibuki is in kanji only.

Just west of the station *Tori-jun* and *Volga* are two popular yakitoris, on the same little block. Tori-jun has good tempura and an English menu.

Also on the east side, *Funabashiya* (☎ 3354-2751) has great tempura, with courses ranging from Y1100. It's a popular place where the wait is worth a seat at the counter. Close by is another tempura restaurant: *Tsunahachi* (☎ 3352-1012). It's more expensive than Funahachi, but is a renowned Tokyo restaurant. Tempura sets start at Y2000. Not far away is the rowdy *Daikokuya* (☎ 3352-2671), with its all-you-can eat yakiniku (Y1700), shabu-shabu (Y2300) and sukiyaki (Y2300) courses (add Y1000 and it's all-you-can drink too). Daikokuya is popular with students, and can be a good place to meet young Japanese, whose inhibitions start to dissolve with a few beers.

Kappabashi-dōri, Asakusa (TW)

Also in the same area is a kushiage (food on skewers) restaurant, *Tatsukichi*, where the food comes to your table – no ordering required. Count on Y150 per stick. *Suehiro* (☎ 3356-4656), the expensive Japanese steak and sukiyaki restaurant chain, also has a branch in the vicinity.

On the road that runs between Seibu-Shinjuku station and Kabukicho is *Negishi* (☎ 3232-8020), which is touted as a Japanese health-food restaurant. Meals here are not cheap, but it has a wonderful ambience of old-time Edo. Back up on Yasukuni-dōri Ave, on the 6th floor of the Piccadilly movie house, is *Irohanihoheto* (☎ 3359-1682), a big lively izakaya with affordable prices.

There are some good-value eating places in department stores and hotels at lunch time. The NS building is on the west side of the station, and the top two floors are entirely devoted to restaurants. The Tokyo Hilton International, also on the west side, has a bargain weekday lunch-time curry and salad buffet in its *St George's Bar*. There are also many restaurants underground, along the 1½ km of shopping streets which run from around the station.

Harajuku & Aoyama (Map 7)

Many of the Japanese restaurants in Harajuku and Aoyama tend to be fairly expensive and deal in nouvelle Japanese creations. If you're in the area during the day, you would probably be better off taking lunch at one of the cafes that allow you to watch the fashionable set do the catwalk down Ōmote-sandō. Still, if you're in the mood for something Japanese, you need not go away disappointed.

Genroku (☎ 3498-3968) is worth a special mention as a revolving sushi shop in a league of its own. Prices are very affordable, starting at Y120 per plate. For an expensive experiment in nouvelle Japanese cuisine, *Yuzen* (☎ 3486-0206) is a Japanese restaurant with a Gallic influence. *Suehiro* (☎ 3401-4101), a branch of the famous Ginza steak restaurant, is a bit expensive but provides sukiyaki and shabu-shabu as well as steak dishes in a classy environment.

On the other side of the road, a little further down after crossing Meiji-dōri Ave, is a great noodle shop: *Gojinhasero*. The sign is only in Japanese, but you can find it in the basement next door to the Body Shop. Noodle dishes (the servings are large) start at Y700.

Another good place for a reasonable lunch special is *Shūtarō* (☎ 3402-7366) on Takeshita-dōri. It specialises in tonkatsu and katsudon and most of its dishes cost Y1000.

Shibuya (Map 8)

Some of the best and most economical Japanese food to be found in Shibuya is on the restaurant floors of the department stores such as Parco and Seibu. *Shaburi* (☎ 3464-4711), on the 7th floor of Parco I, for example, has an all-you-can-eat shabu-shabu deal for Y3200. The 8th floor of the One Oh Nine building has a kaiseki restaurant with a mini-kaiseki sampler that costs Y3800. Alternatively, there's *Junikagetsu* ('12 months' for all you students of Japanese) or the restaurant building. There are a wide range of restaurants here, including those offering Japanese food – none of them are particularly cheap, however.

A restaurant that perhaps is really a sight can be found next to the 109 building. *Tamakyu* is an izakaya restaurant housed in a rickety old wooden building nestled in the heart of hi-tech Shibuya. Affectionately known as the 'restaurant that refused to budge', it did just that – refused to budge – when Tōkyū were constructing their 109 building. The food inside is reportedly not bad either.

Akasaka & Roppongi (Maps 9 & 10)

The Akasaka/Roppongi area is a gourmet paradise, but as might be expected most of the restaurants are fairly up-market. Still, even in expensive Roppongi, there are a host of small yakitori and soba bars which offer good food for reasonable prices. Akasaka, on the other hand, offers an enormous range of fast-food alternatives to the ritzy designer cuisine restaurants that abound in the area. The Akasaka and Roppongi area is also a happy hunting ground for a huge variety of non-Japanese restaurants and bars (check the following Other Cuisines section).

In Akasaka, the side streets running off and parallel to Sotobori-dōri Ave, opposite the Tōkyū Plaza, are almost completely devoted to restaurants. Wander in and take your pick – there's something for everyone here. In the basement of the Tōkyū Plaza itself, there are a couple of top-end Japanese restaurants – *Tenichi* (Map 9) has expensive tempura (sets from Y6500) in opulent surroundings, and *Kabuto* (Map 9) specialises in shabu-shabu. On the side streets is a branch of the famous sushi chain, *Sushi-sei* (☎ 3582-9503; Map 9). Also in the same area, you can find a branch of *Suehiro* (☎ 3585-9855; Map 9), with sukiyaki, shabu-shabu and steak sets ranging from Y1300.

Close to Akasaka subway station, next door to a Vietnamese restaurant, is *Yakitori Luis* (☎ 3585-4197; Map 9), a lively yakitori place with prices ranging from Y200.

Roppongi is a late-night area, and accordingly there are a number of restaurants that stay open late. *Tsubohachi* (☎ 3470-4488; Map 10) is an inexpensive little yakitori bar where even some English is spoken; what's more it's open until 5 am. Another inexpensive place that's open late is *Bikkuri Sushi* (Map 10), a revolving sushi shop that sits amid a group of bars that are popular with the gaijin set. Roppongi also offers the opportunity to try eel inexpensively. *Shojikiya* (☎ 3401-8333; Map 10), opposite the Hotel Ibis, specialises in eel.

Of course, Roppongi would not be Roppongi if there were not a few places to eat Japanese in style. Just across from the Square building is *Seryna* (☎ 3403-6211; Map 10), Roppongi's most well-known Japanese restaurant. The menu here is extensive, ranging across the Japanese culinary spectrum – be prepared for an expensive night out. Take the second road to the left after the Wave building (Map 10) and on the right-hand side a little down the road is another branch of *Sushi-sei* (☎ 3401-0578), part of a celebrated chain of sushi restaurants. Delicious sushi sets range from Y1500. Not far from Roppongi crossing is *Tsunahachi* (☎ 3404-1813; Map 10), a tempura restaurant with good meal sets starting at Y1300. Yakitori at affordable prices is the speciality at *Ajiro* (☎ 3475-5755; Map 10), and likewise, *Kushisuke* (Map 10) has big yakitori sets for Y2600.

OTHER CUISINES

One of the best things about Tokyo, apart from the Japanese restaurants, is the way that Tokyoites have taken to foreign cuisines. All the standards are solidly represented in Tokyo, as well as some obscure ethnic alternatives, nouvelle experiments and quirky little places that are hard to categorise, such as crossover cuisines and theme restaurants – garlic restaurants for example. French and Italian restaurants are perhaps most in abundance, but Tokyo also has some great Thai and Indian restaurants. The big surprise is that in many cases international cuisines in Tokyo are not necessarily that expensive. Many restaurants serve excellent lunch sets for between Y700 and Y1000. Even an evening meal in most of the restaurants recommended here won't set you back more than Y1500 per head (add a few extra yen for your drinks).

African

African restaurants are not exactly thick on the ground in the Tokyo, so *Rose de Sahara* (☎ 3379-6427; Map 6) in Shinjuku has cornered the market and charges accordingly. Nevertheless, with its African decor and sounds, this place creates a good atmosphere – try the guinea fowl in orange sauce. Courses range from ¥3500.

American

A much overlooked cuisine in many parts of the world, Tokyo has a few restaurant chains devoted to bringing out the best in US food. *Victoria Station*, with its great salads, has branches in Roppongi, Shibuya and Akasaka. *Tony Roma's* has branches in Roppongi and Akasaka. And of course in Shibuya there's *Chicago Dog* (Map 8), a small operation that does one thing and does it well: the humble hot dog.

British

British-style pubs are a popular import and Tokyo has no shortage of them. The *1066* (☎ 3719-9059) in Naka-Meguro has hearty English food (roast lunch on Sunday) and British beer on tap. There is also live folk music regularly – the entrance fee includes a banquet. In Roppongi *Hub* (☎ 3478-0414; Map 10) has traditional English food and beer on tap at reasonable prices.

Cambodian

There's not much else to do in Yoyogi by night (one stop from the JR Shinjuku station on the Yamanote line), but it's worth a special trip to visit *Angkor Wat* (☎ 3370-3019). This place has been around for some time, and despite a move to more spacious (but less atmospheric) quarters, the food is as good as ever. The staff are friendly and speak Japanese, Mandarin, Khmer and some English, so there should be someone who can help you with the Japanese menu.

The food has much in common with Thai cuisine, including spicy salads and great coconut-based curries. To get to Angkor Wat, take the Yamanote line to the JR Yoyogi station. Walk in the opposite direction to Shinjuku station to the end of the platform, exit the station on the left-hand side, cross the road, walk straight ahead and after about 100 metres look for Angkor Wat is a lane on your right.

Chinese & Taiwanese

Just as the food has been modified to suit Western tastes in Chinatowns all over the world, similarly most Chinese food in Japan has been changed to suit Japanese tastes. Fortunately, there are still a number of places in Tokyo where you can find genuine Chinese food.

Some of the most authentic Chinese food you're likely to come across (there's no sweet & sour pork here) outside China or Taiwan is at the Taiwanese restaurant *Tainan Taami*. There are branches in Roppongi (☎ 3408-2111), Suidobashi (☎ 3263-4530), Ginza (☎ 3571-3624), Shinjuku (☎ 3232-8839) and Shibuya (☎ 3464-7544), but the pick of them is the Shinjuku branch (Map 6). The menu is complete with photographs of the dishes to make ordering easy. Most of the dishes are small serves ranging in price from Y300 to Y600 – try as much as possible and whatever you do, don't order rice. If you want rice, the restaurant is famous for its zongzi – sticky rice, pork and other oddments wrapped in a lotus leaf and steamed.

Just two doors down from Tainan Taami in Shinjuku is *Pekin* (☎ 3208-8252; Map 6), a very down-to-earth Chinese noodle shop that is always crowded with Chinese. The décor may leave a lot to be desired and the staff may be surly, but you can get a good bowl of noodles here for around Y650. Unfortunately, there's no English sign, so look for the glass front window through which you can see the chefs at work.

On the same road in the other direction, away from the Seibu Shinjuku station, is a unique Chinese restaurant known as the *Tokyo Kaisen Ichiba* (☎ 35273-8301), literally the 'Seafood Market'. You can't miss the building, a girder and glass construction with a fish market downstairs. Upstairs you get to eat the fish. The prices are slightly up-market but simply picking the cheapest things on the menu at random (around Y1200 per serve) will provide some delicious surprises. Nowadays, it has even got an English menu. A late-night visit makes for some great people watching.

For yum cha or dim sum, one of the few possibilities in Tokyo is at the multistorey (12 floors) *Tokyo Dai Hanten* (☎ 3202-0121; Map 6) in Shinjuku. Most of the food is overpriced and not particularly special, but the yum cha service is not bad, if a bit more expensive than in other parts of the world. This is one of the few places in Tokyo where correct yum cha form is observed by bringing the snacks around on trolleys. Another option for yum cha is Ginza's *Ying Kee Tea House* (☎ 3289-2312) on the 6th floor of the Sanai building.

In Ikebukuro, on the west side, is *Pekintei* (Map 5), a reasonably authentic Chinese restaurant. Dishes start at Y800. Harajuku is home to *Ryunoko* (☎ 3402-9419; Map 7), a small unpretentious Sichuan-style restaurant, with some pretty good food. Look out for the two little sea horses outside. Finally, in Shibuya, *Chef's Gallery* (☎ 3476-0899; Map 8) prepares Chinese food with a Gallic touch. This small homey restaurant is decorated with numerous *objet d'art* and has chefs from Hong Kong, Shanghai and Beijing. Private rooms are available, and courses start at Y6000.

French

Tokyo is awash with French restaurants, but unfortunately many of them are shockingly expensive. In some cases they are probably worth the expense; in others it's difficult not to get the feeling that there's been a wholesale cashing in on the snob value of French cuisine. Be that as it may, one place that gets a thumbs up from reviewers is *Maxim de Paris* (☎ 3572-3621) in the basement of Ginza's Sony building (Map 2). Those in the know say that the interior and the menu are dead ringers for the originals in Paris. Lunch sets start at Y6000 and dinner courses from Y20,000.

Even Ikebukuro has a French restaurant or two nowadays. Recommended is *Chez Kibeau* (Map 5), run by Kibo (get it?), the manager of the Kimi Ryokan. The restaurant has a homey atmosphere and excellent French homestyle cooking. Courses start at Y3500. To get there, walk past the Marui department store in the direction of the Tokyo Metropolitan Art Space and take the third street on your right. Look out for the restaurant in the basement – the sign outside is in katakana – just before you get to a small park.

In Harajuku's Hanae Mori building (5th floor), *L'Orangerie* (☎ 3407-7461; Map 7) is acclaimed by the *Tokyo Journal* team (among others) as Tokyo's best Sunday brunch buffet. Take a look if you're a Sunday brunch buffet kind of person, but be warned, at Y3965 it won't be the cheapest brunch you've ever had. It runs from 11.30 am to 3.30 pm seven days a week.

Roppongi is the kind of area you would expect to have a few classy ultraexpensive French restaurants, and it does. Unexpectedly, however, it also has a very reasonably priced French restaurant in a kind of rustic setting – you'll see what I mean. *Shunsai* (☎ 3405-4501; Map 10) is worth a little trudge up the road away from Roppongi Crossing. It has main courses from Y1800. If it was a classy ultraexpensive French restaurant that you wanted

all along, there's *Aux Six Arbre* (☎ 3479-2888; Map 10) –
Roppongi means 'six trees' – not far away. The latter has
been around for many years and is highly rated by locals.

Finally, another affordable surprise is *Pas A Pas*
(☎ 3357-7888), a tiny, informal place that resembles a
living room more than a restaurant; it has a great atmosphere and great food. You can order any combination
of starter, main course and dessert for Y3000. To get there,
take the Marunouchi line to Yotsuya-Sanchome subway
station, take the Yotsuya-Sanchome exit, turn right, walk
past the Marusho bookshop, cross the road and take the
second street on the left. Pas A Pas is a few doors down
on the left on the 2nd floor.

German

You're most likely to come across German food in a beer
house setting in Tokyo. Two that are worth checking out,
more for the liveliness of their clientele than for the
quality of the food, are the *Hofbraühaus Beer Hall* (☎ 3207-
7591; Map 6) in Shinjuku and *München* (Map 5) in
Ikebukuro. Prices in the former are not that cheap, and
you have to add a Y500 table charge and an overall 15%
service charge. Ikebukuro's München has much more
reasonable food and drink prices, with large beers
costing Y520. It's a popular place with the student crowd.

Indian

Ginza has a couple of good Indian restaurants. *Maharaja*
(☎ 3572-7196; Map 2), which has branches all over Tokyo,
is a bit pricey in the evening, but it has good lunch-time
specials from Y800 and an excellent tandoori mixed grill
for Y1300. Maharaja is in a basement location, so look for
the plastic sample dishes in a glass cabinet at floor level.
The Shibuya branch is on the 8th floor of the 109 building
(Map 8).

Nair's (☎ 3541-8246; Map 2) is a Tokyo institution.
Unfortunately, the lunch-time queues can be horrendous, but dinner is also good value. The curries are very
reasonably priced and made to Nair's unique recipe. It's
closed on Thursday.

Moti has one branch in Roppongi (☎ 3479-1939; Map
10) and two in Akasaka (☎ 3582-3620, 3584-6640; Map 9).
It's almost universally applauded as the best affordable
Indian restaurant in Tokyo, and although the Roppongi
branch is the most popular, the food is great in all three.
The only problem is that you often have to queue for up
to half an hour to get a seat – a common feature of
popular Tokyo restaurants. The food and atmosphere

make the wait worthwhile. You can expect to pay about Y2000 per head.

Directly opposite Moti in Roppongi is *Raja* (☎ 3408-6175; Map 10). Although it doesn't match the standards set by Moti, it's an alternative if you can't face the long queues there. Like Moti, Raja seems to attract a sizeable Indian clientele and has an English menu.

Another Indian restaurant with several branches is *Samrat*. If you're sightseeing in the Ueno area, Samrat (☎ 3568-3226; Map 3) has a good lunch-time special of chicken, mutton or vegetable curry with rice and nan for Y850. Other branches are in Shibuya (☎ 3770-7275; Map 8) and Roppongi (☎ 3478-5877). Main courses average Y1500.

There is a branch of *Taj* (☎ 3352-1111) on the 7th floor of Isetan Park City (Map 6) in Shinjuku and another in Akasaka (☎ 3586-6606). Both branches are a little more expensive than Moti or Samrat. Also in Akasaka is *Mughal* (☎ 3582-9940; Map 9), with main courses ranging from Y1500.

Indonesian

Bengawan Solo (☎ 3403-3031; Map 10) in Roppongi is deservedly the most popular of Tokyo's Indonesian restaurants. The atmosphere is great, and the food is delicious and not particularly expensive. You can find Bengawan Solo across the road from the Wave building.

If you're in the Shibuya area, see if you can find *Warung 1* (☎ 3464-9795; Map 8), a mid-range Balinese restaurant – the sign at least is in English, but it's still easy to miss.

Italian

Tokyo abounds in Italian restaurants. The top floor of almost every department store has one, and every shopping district has a myriad of places serving up spaghettis and pizzas. Of course, what you get in the cheaper places may not be quite the real thing, but they still manage to get some tasty results – most of the time.

The Sony building (Map 2) in Ginza has a few excellent restaurants, including two very different Italian restaurants. *Cartoccio* (☎ 3571-8817) is a very small restaurant with inexpensive pasta dishes. *Sabatini de Firenze* (☎ 3573-0013), on the 7th floor, offers an altogether up-market alternative to its inexpensive neighbour. This is high-class Italian fare with prices to match.

Ikebukuro is home to a couple of affordable Italian restaurants. The *Spaghetteria Ricco Tomieno* (☎ 3985-2222;

Map 5), on the west side near McDonald's, has great lunch sets from Y800 to Y1000. There's no English menu, but the bolognese is recommended. On the east side of Ikebukuro is *Café Presto* (Map 5), with coffee at Y200 and pasta dishes from Y800. In the evenings it becomes a fairly boisterous pub – particularly on Thursday evenings, when it's inexplicably overrun by off-duty English teachers from about 9 pm onwards.

Just around the corner from Killer-dōri in Aoyama-dōri is *Pizzeria Romana* (Map 7), which has an English menu and a good selection of slightly up-market pizza and pasta dishes.

Akasaka has a host of Italian places. One of the most authentic is *Granata* (☎ 3582-3241), with its Italian atmosphere and Italian chef. It's an expensive restaurant, with evening courses starting at Y6000. You can get a lunch set here from Y1000, however. *Chapter One* (☎ 3583-6643; Map 9) offers 'new Italian' fare which appears to the untrained eye and palate just like the old stuff. Still, there are good lunch specials here from Y1000, and there's a rustic ambience that's helped along by the wooden floors and tables. Also in Akasaka, and great value for money, is *Pizzeria Marumo* (☎ 3585-5371; Map 9), with its pizza displays outside. On the street parallel is *Trattoria Marumo* (☎ 3586-6918; Map 9), where you can dig into some inexpensive pasta. Both restaurants have English menus.

An old favourite in Roppongi is *Sicilia* (☎ 3405-4653; Map 10). Look out for it in the basement near Roppongi Crossing – the queue generally snakes out onto the sidewalk.

For great cheap Italian food in a lively atmosphere, try the *Capricciosa* restaurants (there are 12 branches in the

No Littering! (TW)

Tokyo region). They are very popular with students and young people in general and a good alternative to the run-of-the-mill Italian places. It's easy to order too much, as the food comes in enormous servings that are enough for two or three people. If there are three of you, two dishes at about Y1300 will be more than enough. To get to the Roppongi branch (☎ 3423-1171), turn right just before the Hard Rock Café and look for the restaurant on your left. Other branches are in Shimokitazawa (☎ 3487-0461) – a popular area with students – and Shibuya (☎ 3407-9482).

Korean

Korean restaurants are very popular in Japan, and Tokyo is full of them. A lot of the Korean barbecue restaurants that you find on every second street corner are great places at which to have a few beers and eat with friends. If you want to go somewhere a little up-market, there's a huge (nine floors) Korean restaurant on Yasukuni-dōri Ave in Shinjuku called *Tōkaien* (☎ 3200-2924; Map 6). The staff are experienced in giving the uninitiated a few tips on etiquette and procedure. Mandarin is spoken as well as Japanese and Korean, but not much English. Reckon on about Y1500 per head on any of the first four floors. Ask about the Y2500 all-you-can-eat deal. The upper floors have banquets and are more exclusive.

Malaysian

This is easy. *Only Malaysia* (☎ 3496-1177; Map 8) in Shibuya derives its name from the fact that it *is* the only Malaysian restaurant in town. It's upstairs and easy to miss from the street, so look carefully. The food is inexpensive and deliciously authentic.

Mexican

Mexican food has become quite popular in Tokyo. An old standard is *El Borracho* (☎ 3354-7046; Map 6) in Shinjuku. This is another place that often requires a bit of a wait. The Latin American theme décor is not over-done, and the graffiti scrawled everywhere adds to the interest of the place. Figure on spending around Y2500 per head here.

Nepalese

It happens to all of us – the rush hour crowds, the endless subway tunnels and all that rushing about in the shadow of Tokyo's high-rises sets off a hankering for Kathmandu!

Well, about as close as you're going to get to the Himalayan kingdom of Nepal in Tokyo is *Kantipur* (☎ 3770-5358; Map 8), a small friendly Nepalese place with good value meals and a pleasant atmosphere.

Pakistani

Gandhara (☎ 3574-9289; Map 2) in Ginza claims to bring you the 'peculiar world-famous delicious taste of Pakistan'. Actually the food isn't *that* peculiar, but the management do take great pains to distance their cuisine from that of their great neighbour on the subcontinent, maintaining that Pakistani food is quite different and is the 'choice of billions all over the world'. Bold claims for such a small restaurant. Gandhara is a good place for a Y800 lunch-time set meal; the dinner menu is pretty reasonable too. Look out for the sign at ground level; the restaurant is upstairs.

Thai

The Thai restaurant phenomenon has come to Tokyo. Often their trendiness puts them out of the reach of the average traveller, but there are a number of reasonably priced ones around. One of the most popular is *Ban Thai* (☎ 3207-0068; Map 6) in Shinjuku. The food is excellent, but as usual you're going to have to wait for it – the queues can be very long. The menu has pictures to help you order, and there's a very good banquet, although it's rather expensive at Y3500 per person. The restaurant lies in the heart of Shinjuku's Kabuki-cho red-light area, on the 3rd floor of the Dai-Ichi Metro building.

Ginza's *Lemon Grass* (☎ 3289-7154; Map 2) has Thai royal cuisine at reasonably affordable prices – around Y3000 per head for an evening meal. The *Siam Thai Restaurant* (☎ 3770-0550; Map 8) in Shibuya is not a particularly big place, but it's nicely laid out, with rough-hewn wooden tables and chairs. The food's comparable with that of Ban Thai and the meals are a bit less expensive. There's a good lunch-time set menu for Y850.

Roppongi is also home to a couple of Thai restaurants. A favourite among resident foreigners and Japanese alike is *Sabai* (☎ 3470-4110; Map 10), which, while a little expensive, has the advantage of being open until 2 am. Cheaper Thai food can be found close to Gaijin Zone (see the Entertainment chapter later in this guide) at *Bangkok* (☎ 3408-8722; Map 10), a small relaxed place in the heart of all the Roppongi action.

Turkish

Past Isetan in Shinjuku is *Istanbul* (☎ 3226-5929; Map 6), a great little Turkish restaurant. It can be difficult to locate this hole-in-the-wall, but there's an English menu and you can sample a few different dishes for around Y1500. Take the eastern exit at Shinjuku station, walk along Shinjuku-dōri Ave past the Isetan department store, cross the main road that intersects Shinjuku-dōri Ave at Isetan and take the second lane on your left. The Istanbul is a few doors down on your right.

Vegetarian

Eating out in Japan can be a hassle for strict vegetarians. Most people working in Japanese restaurants won't really understand the concept of vegetarianism – simply taking the meat out of a dish that has been cooked in a meat stock is the standard response to customers who profess to be noncarnivorous. There are some vegetarian restaurants springing up around town, however, and there are always Indian restaurants that are used to catering for vegetarians. For those who find this to be a particular problem, the TIC has a list of Tokyo's natural food restaurants that includes some vegetarian possibilities.

Vietnamese

Close to the TIC in Ginza (in the same building as the American Pharmacy) is *Saigon* (☎ 3271-3833; Map 2), a small nondescript restaurant with fairly good Vietnamese and Chinese dishes. Prices are not prohibitive (around Y2000 per head for an evening meal) and there are lunch-time specials for around Y800. In Akasaka, *Aozai* (☎ 3583-0234; Map 9) is a Vietnamese restaurant that has built up quite a following. Courses for evening meals start at Y3500. *Bougainvillea* (☎ 3496-5537; Map 8) is a Vietnamese restaurant in Shibuya that is also very popular. It has a Y3000 set course that allows you to sample a cross-section of Vietnamese cuisine.

Other Restaurants

Tokyo has some great restaurants which defy categorisation. A particular kind of restaurant that has become popular over recent years is the garlic restaurant. Generally the food is drawn from cuisines worldwide, and the dishes share one feature alone – liberal dollops of mashed garlic. Keep your distance from friends the next day. There are garlic restaurants in, among other places, Shibuya, Roppongi and Ebisu.

Ninnikuya (☎ 3476-5391; Map 8) in Shibuya is a small basement den in which the air is thick with the aroma of garlic. There's a great range of dishes and an English menu. *Ninniku Dokoro* (☎ 3403-3667; Map 10) is a very small restaurant with a good range of garlic dishes close to Roppongi crossing. Finally, *Ninnikuya* (☎ 3446-5887) in Ebisu is a very popular place with a lively atmosphere. Ring the restaurant from Ebisu station for instructions on how to get there (there are English speakers on the premises) and be prepared to queue for half an hour or more.

The kanji outside *Sunda* (☎ 3465-8858; Map 8) in Shibuya says mukokuseki ryōri, or 'no nationality cuisine'. The food is an interesting fusion of Thai, Indonesian, Chinese, French and Italian cuisines. The interior is quite incredible, featuring slate floors, muted colours, ambient music and a gurgling stream that runs through the centre of the restaurant. Count on spending around Y4000 per person for a starter, main course and dessert. Nowadays it also has live ethnic music performances as an added bonus.

Sunda's main drawback is the difficulty of finding the place. From the Hachikō exit of Shibuya station, take the shopping street with the arched entrance between the 109 building and the Seibu department store. Continue walking up this road until you leave the shops behind and the road dwindles down to the size of a laneway. Keep walking, passing children's swings (you're in the suburbs now) until the lane forms a V with another lane that flows into it. Sunda is straight ahead on the right – be careful or you'll mistake it for a house. If you have problems with this route, ring them up; they'll be only too happy to help.

Fast Food

Most of the budget-priced Japanese and Chinese restaurants serve their food just as quickly and often more cheaply than the fast-food chain places, but if you simply can't do without a Big Mac or a Shakey's pizza, you can rest assured that Tokyo won't deprive you of the pleasure: these places can be found all over the city.

It seems that almost all the major fast-food chains in the world are trying to muscle in on the lucrative Japanese market. *Shakey's Pizza, Kentucky Fried Chicken* and *McDonald's* seem to have a branch next to every railway station in Tokyo. Others, such as *El Polo Loco*, also have a shop here and there. In another interesting move, the

TOKYO RESTAURANT GUIDE

CENTRAL TOKYO & GINZA (Map 2)

Chinese	Tainan Taami, Ying Kee Tea House
French	Maxim de Paris
Italian	Cartoccio, Sabatini de Firenze
Indian	Maharaja, Nair's
Pakistani	Gandhara
Thai	Lemon Grass
Vietnamese	Saigon

UENO & ASAKUSA (Maps 3 & 4)

Indian	Samrat, Maharaja

IKEBUKURO (Map 5)

Chinese	Pekintei
French	Chez Kibeau
German	München
Italian	Spaghetteria Ricco Tomieno, Café Presto, Shakey's Pizza

SHINJUKU (Map 6)

African	Rose de Sahara
Cambodian	Angkor Wat (in Yoyogi)
Chinese	Tainan Taami, Tokyo Kaisen Ichiba, Tokyo Dai Hanten, Pekin
German	Hofbräuhaus Beer Hall
Indian	Taj
Korean	Tōkaien
Mexican	El Borracho
Thai	Ban Thai
Turkish	Istanbul

HARAJUKU & AOYAMA (Map 7)

Cafés	Bamboo Café , Café de Rope, Café Haus Veiben, Studio V
Chinese	Ryunoko
French	L'Orangerie
Italian	Pizzeria Romana

SHIBUYA (Map 8)

American	Chicago Dog, Victoria Station
Balinese	Warung 1
Chinese	Chef's Gallery, Tainan Taami
Indian	Samrat, Maharaja
International	Sunda, Ninnikuya
Italian	Capricciosa
Malaysian	Only Malaysia
Nepalese	Kantipur
Thai	Siam Thai
Vietnamese	Bougainvillea

AKASAKA	(Map 9)
American	Tony Roma's, Victoria Station, Subway
French	Tate-Vin
Indian	Moti (two branches), Mughal, Taj
Italian	Chapter One, Pizzeria Marumo, Trattoria Marumo, Granata
Vietnamese	Aozai

ROPPONGI	(Map 10)
American	Hard Rock Café, Tony Roma's, Victoria Station, Spago's
British	Hub
Chinese	Tainan Taami
French	Shunsai, Aux Six Arbres
Indian	Moti, Raja, Samrat
Indonesian	Bengawan Solo
Italian	Capricciosa, Sicilia
Thai	Bangkok, Sabai

McDonald's phenomenon has spawned some Japanese variations on the same theme: *Mos Burger*, *Lotteria* and *Love Burger*, to name a few.

The fast-food places are particularly popular with teenagers, so eating in them may mean being squeezed onto a table with a contingent of giggling high-school kids. Some of the chains offer pretty good lunch-time specials – Y600 for all the Shakey's pizza you can eat is an example.

The budget-priced coffee shop, of which there is an ever-increasing number, is one good fast-food option. The major chain is *Doutor* (look for the big yellow and brown signs). Doutor sells coffee for Y180 and German hot dogs for Y190. You can put together a good lunch, including a Y150 piece of cake, for around Y500 – not bad in Tokyo. Providing a little competition to Doutor is *Pronto*, with their roomier interiors and much better cakes. The *Mister Donut* places are good for an economical donut, orange juice and coffee breakfast.

It's also worth looking out for chains like the *Jack & Betty Club*, with their huge selection of cheap Western dishes, and *Victoria Station*, with their acclaimed salads. Finally, for the simply ravenous, there is always the *Capricciosa* chain, with its monster servings of excellent Italian food – unless you're in training for the next Sumō championship, you'll be hard pressed to finish your order.

Coffee Shops, Cakes & Ice Creams

Tokyo is a wonderful city for indulging a sweet tooth. There are good bakeries all over the place, and while the coffee is usually expensive there are usually cheap alternatives (see the previous Fast Food section).

Probably the best area for coffee shops, cakes and ice creams is Harajuku (Map 7). Check out some of the coffee shops on Omote-sandō. *Café de Rope* (☎ 3406-6845) is a great place to hang out and sip on a wine or a coffee. It has some good cakes as well. A little further down Omote-sandō and off to the right is *Bamboo Café* (☎ 3407-8427), with its wonderful patio areas – great on a sunny day. If you're in the mood for an ice cream, you couldn't do better than *Haagen Dazs* (☎ 3404-5513), which has expanded its operations and has seating outside as well as inside.

Entertainment

AFTER DARK

Tokyo is a fascinating city by night, and many of the memories that are likely to stay with you longest will be of the bright lights, neon kanji, street-front video screens and the glowing red lanterns strung up in front of bustling backstreet watering holes. Many of Tokyo's nightlife options tend to be more expensive than those in most Western countries. Nevertheless, even in up-market entertainment areas like Roppongi there are always a few a clubs you can walk into without being hit with an outrageous cover charge.

Music

There's a lot of live music in Tokyo, ranging from big international acts to lesser known performers from the West who end up playing in clubs and other small venues. And, of course, there are many local bands. On any night there are hundreds of performances around town.

Live music in Tokyo has its drawbacks. Apart from some of the more alternative 'live houses', entry charges and drink prices are very high. Another catch is that the quality of the local music often leaves a lot to be desired. Like many other aspects of popular culture, music is almost completely dominated by the mainstream. Nevertheless, Tokyo is a big enough city to be able to provide alternatives to the blandness of the mainstream.

Look for information about what's happening in the mainstream music scene in *Pia*, a weekly what's-on-in-Tokyo Japanese-language magazine, or in the *Tokyo Journal*, the English-language magazine. Both have information on all the high-culture happenings (operas, philharmonics, etc) as well as details about jazz and rock. *Tokyo Journal* is a good place to look for alternative music information.

Live Houses

A number of live houses have reasonable entry and drink charges and provide good opportunities to hear interesting live music. The crowds in these places tend to be a mixture of local foreign residents and eccentric Japanese. Unfortunately, some very interesting local bands are supported far more by gaijin living in Tokyo than they are by the local Japanese.

A place that should be high on any list of live houses in Tokyo is *Lazy Ways* (☎ 3336-5841). It's fairly roomy by Tokyo standards and usually has something interesting happening on Saturday nights. The club is next to Kōenji station on the Chūō line. Facing in the direction of Shinjuku, exit on the left side of the station and make a sharp right. Follow the road beside the railway tracks for about 50 metres and then cross the road. Lazy Ways is opposite the railway tracks, next to Nippon Rent-a-Car, in the basement.

Also in Kōenji, not far from Lazy Ways, is a very special bar, *Inaoiza* (☎ 3336-4480), with a small stage for live music. The people who run the bar are musicians and often, if no-one is booked to perform, there'll just be an impromptu jam session. Live music has to stop at 10.30 pm because of the neighbours, but the action continues with lots of local English teachers, hostesses and out-of-the-ordinary Japanese dropping in after work for a few drinks. Inaoiza also has good food – ask for their menu – and a great, friendly atmosphere. The only problem is finding it. Your best bet is to ask someone at Lazy Ways, as most of that crowd also frequent Inaoiza. You really need someone to lead you by the hand the first time you go.

In Harajuku, *Crocodile* (☎ 3499-5205; Map 7) has something happening seven nights a week. To get there from the JR Harajuku station, walk down Omote-sandō and turn right at Meiji-dōri Ave. Cross the road and continue straight ahead, passing an overhead walkway. Crocodile is on your left, in the basement of the New Sekiguchi building.

Shibuya (Map 8) has a few interesting live music venues. Three clubs, *The Cave* (☎ 3780-0715), *Club Circuit* (☎ 3477-0755) and *Club Quattro* (☎ 3477-8750), are venues for high quality international and local acts, and have dance floors as well. Entry for all three is around Y3000 to Y4000. Check the *Tokyo Journal* for a look at who's performing where. Also in Shibuya, usually featuring local performers at more reasonable entry rates, are *Eggman* (☎ 3496-1461) and *La Mama* (☎ 3464-0801). Finally, for Shibuya country and western buffs, *Aspen Glow* (☎ 3496-9709) has a collection of 8000 records and has live music every night of the week except Sundays. Food is Y600 to Y1200 and drinks range from Y150. There's a cover of between Y1000 to Y2000, depending on who's performing.

Another good live house is *Rock Mother* (☎ 3460-1479) in Shimokitazawa. The whole area around there is worth a look: it's a kind of down-market Harajuku or a youth-oriented Shinjuku with lots of cheap places to eat and drink – very popular with students. To get to Rock Mother, take the Odakyū line to Shimokitazawa station and exit via the southern exit (Minami-guchi). After you leave the station, turn left, then right, and then left again. Follow the road around to the right and look for the club on your left.

Jazz

Jazz is very big in Tokyo, although some places seem to take it rather too seriously. Quiet, solemn audiences hang on the musicians' every note – that's the Japanese for you, a serious lot when it comes to enjoying themselves. Still, if you're interested in jazz, there are a lot of places to try, and all the big names who are visiting Tokyo will have listings in the *Tokyo Journal*.

An old standard is the *Shinjuku Pit Inn* (☎ 3354-2024; Map 6). The cost of the cover charge depends on who's playing, but it should include a drink.

In Roppongi, there's another *Pit Inn* (☎ 3585-1063), where the music is reportedly less traditional than that played at its Shinjuku counterpart. Walking away from Roppongi subway station, turn right at Almond (Map 10), cross over the road and look for the Pit Inn on your left, about 100 metres down the road.

Another Roppongi jazz club is *Birdland* (☎ 3478-3456; Map 10), in the basement of the Square building, the hub of all the disco activity in Roppongi. Admission is around Y3000. Cross the intersection at Almond, continue walking away from Roppongi subway station, take the second right turn and you'll bump into the Square building. Look for all the beautiful people lounging around outside waiting to see where the happening spot is tonight.

Harajuku has a couple of well-known jazz clubs. Right across from Harajuku station is the *Keystone Korner Tokyo* (☎ 5232-1980; Map 7). All acts performing here are international, and the club itself is very classy. Entry to most acts is around Y8000. The *Blue Note Tokyo* (☎ 3407-5781) is also host to many internationally renowned jazz acts. It's an expensive club, so it's probably best to leave it for that one show you'd hate to miss.

Discos

Information on some discos is included in the Harajuku & Aoyama and the Roppongi areas of the following Other Nightlife section. Some other happening places that aren't included there are: *Droopy Drawers* (☎ 3423-6028; Map 10) in Roppongi, with it's rough and ready interior and soul sounds; *MZMZ* (☎ 3423-3066) and *Zipang* (☎ 3586-0006), also in Roppongi – house and reggae (Y4000 cover). In Roppongi, buildings such as the Square building, the Roppongi Plaza building and the Nittaku building all have a number of discos. The Nittaku building's *Cipango* (☎ 3478-0039) and *Lollipop* (☎ 3478-0028), which is a relatively cheaper option at Y1500, both get good reports.

Down in the bay area of Shibaura, an area that's starting to house a few clubs, is *Gold* (☎ 3453-3545), a converted warehouse with an emphasis on house music – there's a Y5000 cover in the form of a card that allows you to buy drinks and food.

Other Nightlife

There's so much happening that it's difficult to make specific recommendations. Most people seem to find their own favourite watering holes wherever they happen to be, but some areas have high concentrations of pubs, clubs and discos which are popular among both foreigners and Japanese. At bars that have gained some notoriety as the hang-outs of wild and crazy gaijin, there will always be a fair sprinkling of Japanese who come along for the thrill.

Shinjuku (Map 6) Shinjuku's nightlife opportunities are underrated by many of Tokyo's residents. There's actually plenty there, but you have to know where to look for it. Just promenading under the bright lights of Kabuki-cho and ducking into one of the revolving sushi shops or one of the yakitori bars for a bite to eat is a good prelude to a night of debauchery.

Most of the action happens on the east side of the station, but the west side does have *Charlie's Not Here* (☎ 3344-3191), a disco that gives itself frequent designer face lifts and which is rated highly by some foreign residents. It has the usual disco cover charge of around Y4000 with two drinks and something to eat.

If you'd like to have a few drinks and some yakitori to the accompaniment of karaoke in slightly claustrophobic but atmospheric surroundings, try *Yamagoya*, just down the road from the Rolling Stone. Feel free to put in a karaoke performance but don't worry, no-one's going to drag you on stage. You enter Yamagoya by a narrow flight of stairs and end up in what seems like the hull of an old wooden ship. Huge wooden beams, every inch of them carved with names and graffiti, crisscross

'What's Happening' posters, Harajuku (CT)

overhead, and wooden stairs continue down two more levels. The bottom level is the gloomiest and most dungeon-like and definitely the most fun. Look out for the kanji sign outside and the rickety flight of stairs descending into the bar.

The *Rolling Stone* (☎ 3354-7347) has been around for years but is definitely not for the faint-hearted. The music is rock & roll from the '70s onwards (with a heavy emphasis on Stones material), and it's a hang-out for Tokyo's heavy metal kids – lots of leather jackets, outrageous hairdos and cool posing. It's fairly quiet on weekdays but really hots up on Friday and Saturday nights, when things often get a little out of control. There's a Y200 cover charge and it's Y800 for a bottle of beer. Look out for it in the basement next door to a soapland.

Another interesting place that does not seem to have been discovered by the gaijin set as yet is *Milo's Garage* (☎ 3207-6953). It's in an interesting location, to the right of the lane that leads into Hanozono-jinja Shrine. Milo's has different musical happenings every night of the week. Friday is house music, and it attracts a reasonable crowd of young devotees. Cover charge varies from Y1000 to Y2000, which includes a drink.

Finally there's *Java Bay* (☎ 3352-2805), a Jamaican-style disco that's mainly popular with Japanese, making it possibly a good place to dance with friends away from the gaijin congestion of Roppongi.

Ikebukuro (Map 5) Your nightlife options in Ikebukuro are on the whole limited to karaoke and seedy nightclubs that won't be all that hospitable to gaijin. Nevertheless, *One Lucky* (☎ 3985-0069) is a favourite among foreign residents and guests of the nearby Kimi Ryokan. 'One Rucky', as it's affectionately called by its Japanese patrons, is a one-man show where the master-san prepares all the food (a delicious set-menu dinner for Y700), pours the drinks (a beer is Y500) and, most importantly, takes a photograph of everyone who visits his establishment. There's a bookcase of photo albums containing the master's social shots, dated so that you can see how you looked when you last visited.

One Lucky is quite close to Kaname-cho subway station – turn left into the lane next to the park on Yamate-dōri Ave and look for it on the right after the second bridge. From the Kimi Ryokan, turn left, left again and then right. Follow this road straight ahead for about 10 minutes (you'll pass a bakery on the right) until you come to a brick-paved road. Turn left there and look for One Lucky on the left – take it slowly; it's easy to miss.

If you walk to One Lucky from the Kimi, you'll pass *Rum Bullion*, or the Reggae Bar, on the left. It's a cosy bar, if a little claustrophobic, that's open until 5 am, making it a popular place with locals at the Kimi and Marui House to drop into after things at One Lucky have wound down.

Also in Ikebukuro is the *Winners Bar*, with reasonably priced drinks and food. Eat here and you get a chance to be a winner – we won't spoil the fun by telling you what happens. Winners also has a good record collection, and everyone gets a request slip. Just down the road, in the basement, is *Reggae Bar Kingston*, with dancing. There's a Y2000 cover charge, and there's definitely 'no looking' first.

Over on Ikebukuro's east side is *Café Presto*, which turns into a bar by night. Thursday nights are rowdy, when the bar is overrun by off-duty English teachers. It is a good place for meeting people – it was very friendly when I was there.

Harajuku & Aoyama (Map 7) Harajuku is one of those rare areas in Tokyo that is more active by day than by night. *Oh God* (☎ 3406-3206) is popular with foreign residents; in fact some people rave about it. It has a bar, pool tables and movie screenings every night, and the food gets very good reports. Walk down Omote-sandō and take the first lane on the right after Meiji-dōri Ave. Oh God is in the basement of the building at the end of the lane. Practically next door to Oh God is *Zest* (☎ 3499-0976), another popular pub with food. *AKA* (☎ 3478-3047), a small reggae bar, is in an obscure location, but is a cozy place with good music and reasonable prices.

Up in Aoyama is the popular disco complex *King & Queen Maharaja Saloon*. Count on a Y4000 entry tab, which will also include a couple of drinks. It's a place to watch the beautiful people watching each other. Back down Aoyama-dōri in the direction of Shibuya is *Cay* (☎ 3498-5790), a trendy bar that combines Thai food with live music. It's a popular place and can be found in the Spiral Building (an interesting sight in itself). Thai food and the live-music charge should cost between Y7000 and Y10,000.

Shibuya (Map 8) Apart from the three clubs mentioned in the previous Live Houses section, Shibuya has a number of shot bars and quiet places to have a drink. Probably the best bet for some dancing is *The Cave*, where house and reggae music is featured. Otherwise, you can take in a beer at either *Pronto* or the *Suntory Shot Bar* close to the station. *Hub*, in the basement almost directly opposite Pronto, is a popular place with a laser-disk jukebox.

Akasaka (Map 9) Being the kind of area it is, there are a lot of company expense account bars in Akasaka. Nevertheless, there are still a few places you might want to check out. Always a sound option for a quiet drink in a colonial-style atmosphere is *Henry Africa* (☎ 3585-0149). There are also branches in Ginza and Roppongi. There's a happy hour from 7.30 to 9 pm, with all Japanese beers at Y300 and free nibbles provided.

Goose (☎ 3582-7924) is a little more down at heel, but it's a sort of funky happening place that doesn't seem to belong in ritzy Akasaka – it has good music too. Look out for the glowing goose outside. Perhaps a little more what you'd expect in Akasaka is the *Rondo Club* (☎ 3589-6707), an up-market disco popular with the fashionable set. It's not that cheap either – Y5000 cover charge. Akasaka also has its own 'oldies but goodies' rock & roll club at *Rock 'n Roll Alba* (☎ 3585-2398). The pricing here is slightly confusing. Basically the deal is entry and all you can drink (for 90 minutes) for Y2960.

Roppongi (Map 10) Roppongi is undoubtedly the nightlife capital of Tokyo. It's where the beautiful people go, and in order to ensure that they keep going, many of the discos let anyone who claims to be a model in for free. (Your looks are going to have to back up this little fib.) Roppongi is one place in Tokyo other than the English-language classrooms where Japanese make a point of mingling with foreigners – often with a degree of intimacy that would not go down well in most English classes.

Not everyone has a negative reaction to Roppongi, and it is worth seeing by night. Most of the action centres around discos, but there are also a few interesting bars and clubs featuring live dance music.

The main point of orientation is the Roppongi Crossing, with the Almond Coffee Shop – a favourite meeting spot – on the corner. Follow the road under the metropolitan expressway in the opposite direction to the Wave building, take the second turn to the right and on the first corner on the right is the Square building, which has eight floors of discos. They all charge Y3000 to Y4000 (Y500 less for women) for entry and a couple of drinks. Most discos ban males unaccompanied by representatives of the opposite sex, but this is rarely enforced as long as there isn't a big crowd of you. It makes little difference which disco you choose, although the most popular is *Java Jive* (☎ 3478-0087), where a reggae band is alternated with recorded music throughout the night.

In the basement, just around the corner from the Square building, is the *Lexington Queen* (☎ 3401-1661), a disco for name-droppers and high-society voyeurs. Reactions about the place are mixed – depending perhaps on whether the person in question was allowed in or not – but without a doubt it's a Roppongi institution.

Not in the same high-class league as the Lexington, on the right if you walk in the direction of Tokyo Tower, is *Hot Co-Rocket* (☎ 3583-9409), with a cover charge of around Y3000 and live reggae music. It can be pretty dead during the week but it hots up on Friday and Saturday nights.

Déjà Vu Bar, Roppongi (CT)

Heading back in the other direction, towards Roppongi Crossing, are a few more bars with much more casual standards. *Henry Africa* (☎ 3405-9868) is a popular spot with both foreigners and Japanese, where a beer and some popcorn will set you back Y800. There's also a great happy hour deal from 7.30 to 9 pm; Japanese beers are Y300 and free food is provided. Opposite Henry Africa is *Gas Panic*, a bar that's hard to describe. Take a look on a Friday or Saturday night – this is Roppongi at its Boschean worst, or best, depending on how you look at it.

Just around the corner to the right, on the left side, is *Déjà Vu* (☎ 3403-8777), one of the liveliest bars in Roppongi. It's very popular and drinkers spill out of the open-fronted entrance into the street. An interesting feature is the seats that vibrate to the rhythm of the music playing.

In the building next door to Déjà Vu, up on the 4th floor, is *Bogey's Bar* (☎ 3478-1997), which is modelled on Rick's Café from the film *Casablanca*. It's a perfect spot for a quiet drink. Opposite Mister Donut, back on the main road, is *Pip's* (☎ 3470-0857). This place is in the basement and entry is free. With a disco juke box and a few pin-ball machines, it's a bit of a dive; not that this prevents it getting fairly rowdy by the time the last train has chuffed off in the evening. Look out for the sign on the big bottle outside, 'Extra cozy pub – contain human dreams bottled in a tropical island'; it's curious what too many late nights in Roppongi can do to the thought processes.

A tour of late-night hang-outs can be completed with a visit to the *Charleston* (☎ 3402-0372), labelled as Tokyo's 'best sleaze pick-up bar' in the book *The Best of Tokyo*, and to *Gaijin Zone*. The Charleston is rapidly losing its legendary status in the pick-up/sleaze stakes to the nearby Déjà Vu and Gas Panic, but if you turn up late on a Saturday night you won't be disappointed. Gaijin Zone is a free dance venue, which is something of a rarity in Tokyo, not to mention Roppongi. As the name suggests, most of its customers are gaijin and of course Japanese who like to let loose with foreigners. Also in the vicinity, and definitely not in the pick-up/sleaze stakes, is *Maggie's Revenge* (☎ 3479-1096), a small Australian-style pub with live music. It's been around for a long time and is still going strong.

Of course, you might take one look at Déjà Vu or Gas Panic and decide you want something a bit more whole-some. A good alternative to the Roppongi pick-up joints is *Kento's* (☎ 3401-5755), a live club devoted exclusively to 'oldies but goodies'. It's actually a great place to visit. The Japanese band playing '50s hits is just part of the fun. The audience, with the girls in their bobby socks and the boys with their hair slicked back, all grooving away on the dance floor, is a treat to see. There's a cover charge of Y1300 – you pay at the end of the night when you settle the bill.

Finally, Tokyo has its own *Hard Rock Café* (☎ 3408-7018), with a ready supply of hamburgers, rock music and expensive cocktails. You can't miss the King Kong figure clambering up its exterior, near Roppongi Cross-ing, in a lane beside the Roy building.

Hangovers

In Japan, just as in the West, hangovers *(futsukayoi)* have their popular remedies. Salted plums *(umeboshi)* in green tea *(sencha)* are one tip for the morning after. Tea made from boiled cloves is also used. Another herbal cure, recommended in rural Tōhoku, requires a handful of *senburi* (a herb) to be steeped for three hours in a cup of hot water – the resulting brew is revoltingly bitter. Less punishing options are a bowl of *rāmen* noodles, rice soup *(ochazuké)* or persimmons *(kaki)*.

Finally, if herbal cures don't help, you can always try evoking sympathy from the Japanese by cradling your head in your hands and moaning 'Kino o nomisugimashita' (Yesterday, I drank too much)!

Robert Strauss

CINEMA

Foreign movies are screened with their original soundtracks and Japanese subtitles. There is usually an excellent selection of alternative movies playing around town.

Japanese cinemas have a bad reputation for doing things like letting the audience for the next screening into the cinema 10 minutes before the end so that they can claim the good seats. Fortunately, things are steadily improving, although even now it is common only to dim the house lights, not to turn them off – maybe it's to discourage members of the audience from misbehaving. If things like this matter, stick to the art-house cinemas, where a lot more attention is paid to these kinds of details. Tickets average Y1700.

One thing to bear in mind, if you can plan ahead a little, is that tickets can be bought at certain outlets at discounted prices. Typically, a Y1700 ticket will cost Y1300 or even less this way, which is not a bad saving, especially if you're buying a couple of tickets. Outlets can be found at: the basement of the Tokyo Kōtsū Kaikan building (Map 2) in Ginza; the 5th floor of Shinjuku's Studio Alta building (Map 6); the 2nd floor of Shibuya's 109 building (Map 8); and the 1st floor of Harajuku's Laforet building (Map 7).

Pia, the weekly Japanese-language Tokyo guide, and the English-language *Tokyo Journal* list what's playing where, complete with maps showing you how to find the cinemas.

TRADITIONAL ENTERTAINMENT

Bunraku

Osaka is the bunraku centre, but performances do take place in Tokyo in February, May, September and December every year at the *Kokuritsu Gekijō Theatre* (☎ 3265-7411; Map 1). Check with the TIC or the theatre for information.

Kabuki

The best place to see kabuki in Tokyo is the *Kabuki-za Theatre* (☎ 3541-3131; Map 2) in Ginza. Performances and times vary from month to month, so you'll need to check with the TIC or with the theatre directly for programme information. Earphone guides providing 'comments and explanations' in English are available at Y600 (Y1000 deposit) for those who would like know what all those people in colourful costumes are doing on stage. Prices for tickets vary from Y2000 to Y14,000, depending on how keen you are to see the stage. One distraction you may encounter is a large group of school children on a school outing – the excitement of the proceedings gives rise to a lot of chatting and giggling.

Kabuki performances can be quite a marathon, lasting from 4½ to five hours. If you're not up to it, you can get tickets for the gallery on the 4th floor for between Y500 to Y1200 and watch just one act. Unfortunately, earphone guides are not available in these seats. Fourth-floor tickets can be bought on the day of the performance. There are generally two performances daily, starting at around 11 am and 4 pm.

Japan's national theatre, *Kokuritsu Gekijō Theatre* (☎ 3265-7411; Map 1), also has kabuki performances, with seat prices ranging from Y1300 to Y7800. Again, earphone guides are available. Check with the TIC or the theatre for performance times.

Nō

Nō performances are held at various locations around Tokyo. Tickets will cost between Y3000 and Y10,000, and it's best to get them at the theatre itself. Check with the TIC or the appropriate theatre for times.

The *Kanze Nō-gakudō Theatre* (☎ 3469-6241; Map 8) is a 10 to 15-minute walk from Shibuya station. From the Hachikō exit, turn right at the 109 building and follow the road straight ahead past the Tōkyū department store. The theatre is on the right, a couple of minutes down the third street on the left after Tōkyū.

The *Ginza Nō-gakudō* (☎ 3571-0197) is about a 10-minute walk from Ginza subway station. Turn right into Sotobori-dōri Ave at the Sukiyabashi Crossing and look for the theatre on the left.

The *Kokuritsu Nō-gakudō* (☎ 3423-1331), or National Nō Theatre, is in Sendagaya. Exit Sendagaya station in the direction of Shinjuku on the left and follow the road which hugs the railway tracks; the theatre is on the left.

Sumō

Sumō may not be in the same league, culturally speaking, as the preceding entries, but there are definite connections – sumō is actually a highly ritualised and quite fascinating event that is as much a spectacle as it is a sport. The actual jostling in the ring can be over very quickly and great importance is attached to the pomp that precedes and follows the action.

Sumō tournaments at Tokyo's *Ryōgoku Kokugikan Stadium* (☎ 3866-8700) in Ryōgoku take place in January, May and September, and last 15 days. The best seats are all bought up by those with the right connections, but upstairs seats are usually available from Y2300 to Y7000. Nonreserved seats at the back sell for Y1500. If you don't mind standing, you can get in for around Y500. Tickets can be bought up to a month prior to the tournament, or simply turn up on the day. The ticket office opens at 9 am, and it's advisable to get there early. The stadium is adjacent to Ryōgoku station on the northern side of the railway tracks.

An interesting outing is to visit a sumō 'stable' and watch the sumō in training. There are several of these stables in the vicinity of the Kokugikan Sumō Stadium (Map 1). The most popular among foreigner visitors is the Azumazeki Stable, a couple of minutes from Honjo-Azumabashi subway station on the Toei Asakusa line.

Tea Ceremony

A few hotels in Tokyo hold tea ceremonies which you can observe and occasionally participate in for a fee of about Y1000. The *Hotel New Otani* (☎ 3265-1111; Map 9) in Akasaka has ceremonies on its 7th floor on Thursday, Friday and Saturday from 11 am to noon and 1 to 4 pm. Ring them before you go to make sure the show hasn't been booked out. The *Hotel Okura* (☎ 3582-0111; Map 9) in Akasaka and the *Imperial Hotel* (☎ 3504-1111; Map 2) also hold daily tea ceremonies.

SPORTS

There are numerous places in Tokyo for both watching sports and for being actively involved in them. If you're staying in one of the five-star hotels, you'll probably have access to plenty of sporting facilities and will not need to go traipsing around looking for them.

Baseball

Baseball is Japan's most popular sport, and six of Japan's 12 pro-baseball teams are based in Tokyo. Probably the best place to catch a game is the Tokyo Dome (☎ 5800-9999), affectionately known as the Big Egg, close to Korakuen and Suidobashi subway stations. The dome is the home ground of Japan's most popular team, the Yomiuri Giants.

Horse Racing

Yes, I found it hard to believe too but there are actually two racing tracks in the Tokyo area, and you can even make bets. Races are generally held on weekends from 11 am to 4 pm.

Tokyo Keibajo – Fuchu Keibajo Nishinomae station on the Keio line (☎ 0423-63-3141)
Oi Keibajo – Oi Keibajo-mae station on the monorail from Hammamatsu-cho (☎ 3763-2151)

Swimming

Like everything else, taking a swim in Tokyo can be costly. Some of pools have some very odd rules too. For example, no wandering around with a towel wrapped around your waist. Why? Well, you might have nothing on underneath! Usually it's everyone out of the pool once every hour to make sure there are no dead bodies laying on the bottom. And if you don't linger long enough under those showers on your way out of the changing rooms, uniformed pool custodians are likely to come after you furiously blowing their little whistles. Have a good time.

Yoyogi National Stadium – close to Harajuku station; open daily from noon to 4 pm; Y460 for the whole day (☎ 3468-1171)
Big Box Seibu Plaza – next to Takadanobaba station; only open Sundays from noon to 10 pm; Y1545 for the day (☎ 3208-7171)

Squash

If you're a short-term visitor, forget it. Squash hasn't caught on in Japan, and the only viable option is to join a club, many of which have hefty admission and membership fees. Figures quoted ranged from Y30,000 to Y200,000 to join up.

Tennis

On the surface of things, there are a lot of tennis courts in Tokyo. But given the enormous population of the city there are just not enough to go round. This has pushed prices up and created a situation where reservations are sometimes needed up to a month in advance. If you're just in Tokyo on a short stay, I'd advise not to bother. You might try the following places if you're really set on a game, however.

Hibiya-kōen Park – open daily from 9 am to 9 pm; Y1300 per hour (☎ 3501-6428)

National Stadium Tennis Court – close to Gaien-mae subway station; open daily from 9 am to 4.30 pm; Y700 per person per hour in the mornings, and Y900 per person per hour in the afternoons (☎ 3408-4495)

Shopping

Even more so than its Asian neighbours, Hong Kong and Singapore, Tokyo is the shopper's city *par excellence*. There is something about consumer culture in Tokyo that is definitive of the city itself; as if, for the average Tokyoite, it is a matter of 'I shop therefore I am'. The halls of worship in contemporary Tokyo are the enormous, opulent *depātos*, or department stores as we call them. They are usually open six days a week until at least 7.30 pm, and always crowded with shoppers. Service standards are very high and products are usually presented quite strikingly. With so many things to buy and such excellent service (none of the rudeness you encounter in Hong Kong and Singapore) it is very easy to get infected with the shopping syndrome. It is not easy to leave Tokyo without having bought *something*.

The good news is that, although Tokyo is an expensive city, certain things can be considerably cheaper than other countries. Many electrical items, for example, can be very reasonably priced – check the Akihabara section of the Things to See & Do chapter earlier in this guide for more information. The same applies for camera accessories. There are also numerous shops around selling second-hand cameras and lenses (especially in Ginza and Shinjuku).

For souvenir items, almost all the big department stores in Tokyo have good selections of traditional crafts such as Japanese dolls, ceramics, lacquerware, fans, etc. Just bear in mind that the department stores often sell their goods at inflated prices, unless you are lucky enough to be around during a sale. You're likely to find less glamorous but possibly more interesting souvenirs in Tokyo's flea markets, where you can buy Japanese antiques and curiosities.

WHERE TO SHOP

If you don't have a hectic schedule, before doing any shopping yourself, it can be an interesting experience to go and watch the Japanese shop. Some of Tokyo's major department stores are experiences in themselves, and the energy levels inside run very high. Ikebukuro has a couple of the largest department stores in Japan, if not the world. It is possible to spend an entire day exploring the Ikebukuro branches of either Seibu or Tōbu (Map 5).

For a total shopping experience, I'd recommend a visit
to Shibuya. The Parco I, II and III (Map 8) stores are
quite remarkable, featuring the latest in fashion, traditional Japanese items, art galleries and restaurant floors.
There is also a branch of Seibu (Map 8) in Shibuya, with
one building for women's clothing and another for
men's. Other Shibuya (Map 8) high points include the
Seibu Seed building (boutiques), the 109 building
(fashion), Loft (indescribable youth-oriented items –
great browsing), Tōkyū Plaza (boutiques), HMV
Records and Tower Records, and last but not least
Tōkyū Hands, perhaps the biggest do-it-yourself shop
in the world.

Laforet building, Harajuku (CT)

It's something of a cliché that Tokyo is a city of villages. But, with regard to shopping at least, it's a cliché that holds true. While areas like Shinjuku and Ikebukuro tend to be home to the whole range of shopping possibilities, in most other areas there is a tendency to specialisation. Shibuya, for example, has a high-fashion orientation but is dominated by the large department stores. Harajuku and Aoyama, on the other hand, are also fashion centres but the emphasis is on boutiques or collections of boutiques, as in the Laforet building (Map 7). Akihabara is an area given over almost entirely to cut-price electrical stores; Jimbō-cho is an area of bookshops; Kappabashi (see the Ueno section of the Things to See & Do chapter earlier in this guide) is where you buy the mouth-watering plastic food that graces restaurant window displays; Ueno is the place for motorcycles; and Asakusabashi is well known for its traditional Japanese dolls.

You ask – what about Ginza? Well, it's true Ginza is the most famous of Tokyo shopping districts, and it's still recommended for a browse. It's worth remembering though that Ginza is about prestige, respectability and having the money to spend there. Check the prices elsewhere before you do any shopping in Ginza, but certainly don't scrub it off your agenda.

WHAT TO BUY

If there's any market for it whatsoever, you can buy it in Tokyo. The question comes down to whether the price that's being asked for it is reasonable or not.

Arts, Crafts & Antiques

As much for the convenience of being able to look at a wide range of traditional arts and crafts in one location as anything else, it's worth checking out some of the big department stores. Isetan (Map 6) in Shinjuku and Seibu (Map 5) in Ikebukuro have impressive collections of all kinds of exquisite traditional items, from pottery to dolls and kimonos. There are often sale bins in the department stores, especially for Japanese-style dining ware.

For genuine antiques, there are a few places in Harajuku and Aoyama (Map 7) that you should visit. One of the best is the basement of the Hanae Mori building (☎ 3406-1021) in Harajuku, where there are more than 30 antique shops, open daily. Not far from the Hanae Mori building, the Oriental Bazaar (☎ 3400-3933) is open every day except Thursday and is an interesting shop to visit even if you can't afford to buy anything. It has a wide range of antiques and souvenirs including fans, folding screens, pottery, etc. On the corner of Killer-dōri and Aoyama-dōri Ave is the Japan traditional Craft Center. The centre has changing displays of Japanese crafts as well as items for sale. Finally, also in Aoyama, is the so-called Antique Street in a side street to the left of Aoyama-dōri moving in the direction of Shibuya. Hidden among the boutiques are some 30 antique shops.

Akasaka's Inachu Lacquerware (☎ 3582-4451; Map 9) is a renowned lacquerware shop, but it's strictly for those who want the genuine item and are prepared to pay for it.

Not far from Ikebukuro station's eastern exit, on the 1st floor of the Satomi building (☎ 3980-8228), there are more than 30 antique dealers. They are open Friday to Wednesday from 10 am to 7 pm.

Strictly along more touristy lines, there's the International Arcade in Ginza (Map 2). Also in Ginza are a couple of small shops with high-quality Japanese souvenirs. Takumi (☎ 3571-2017) has been around for some 60 years and has an elegant selection of traditional crafts from around Japan. Close to the International Arcade is the Taiko Festival Shop, a small retailer with a beautiful selection of Japanese festival souvenirs.

Also worth taking a look at is Nakamise-dōri at Sensō-ji Temple in Asakusa (Map 4). Among the items on sale here are traditional wigs, combs, fans and dolls.

Another possibility for picking up traditional souvenirs is to try out some of the flea markets and antique fairs that are held around Tokyo. The following is a list of some of the bigger flea markets around town.

Tōgō-jinja Shrine – from 4 am to 4 pm on the first and second Sundays of each month; Harajuku station – turn left and take the next right after Takeshita-dōri.

Nogi-jinja Shrine – from dawn to dusk on the second Sunday of each month; Nogi-zaka subway station on the Chiyoda line – the shrine is on the other side of Gaien-higashi-dōri.

Sunshine City (Map 5) – in the Alpa shopping arcade; from 8 am to 10 pm on the third Saturday and Sunday of each month; five minutes from the western exit of Ikebukuro station.

Ramura building plaza – from 6 am to sunset on the first Saturday of each month; next to Iidabashi subway station.

Roppongi Antique Fair – in front of the Roy building (Map 10); from 8 am to 8 pm on the fourth Thursday and Friday of every month.

Finally, the Tokyo Antique Fair takes place three times a year and brings together more than 200 antique dealers.

Top: Sumō for sale (CT)
Bottom: Tokyo shop window (CT)

The schedule for this event changes annually, but for information on this year's schedule you can ring Mr Iwasaki (☎ 3950-0871) – he speaks English.

Audio

Japanese recordings are renowned for their high fidelity, and Tokyo has numerous music stores with enormous collections of discs and tapes to sift through. Some of the best places to check out are the Virgin Megastore in Shinjuku, HMV Records in Harajuku, Shibuya and Ikebukuro, Wave in Roppongi, Shibuya and Ikebukuro, and Tower Records in Shibuya. Wave, in particular, is notable for its AV displays (including hi-definition TV) and extensive audio selections

Cameras & Film

Check the Shinjuku section of the Things to See & Do chapter for information on the big camera stores there. Many places deal in second-hand photographic equipment; foreign-made large-format equipment is usually ridiculously expensive, but Japanese equipment can often be bought at very good prices. One of the best places to look, surprisingly, is in Ginza (Map 2). If you walk along Harumi-dōri Ave, there's a place opposite the Sony building on the Sukiyabashi Crossing. On the same side as the Sony building, towards the Kabuki-za Theatre, there are a couple more places. They're all on ground level and the windows are full of cameras and lenses.

Photographic film and processing in Japan are very expensive. It's advisable to bring your own and process it after you leave if possible. Otherwise, you might try Bic Camera (Map 5) on the east side of Ikebukuro, where there are big bargain bins of film that is approaching its expiry date – usually no problem. As a general point of interest, Bic Camera in Ikebukuro claims to be the cheapest camera store in Japan and will refund the difference if you come across the same product you have bought at a cheaper price elsewhere. The big camera shops on the west side of Shinjuku station (see the Shinjuku section of the Things to See & Do chapter earlier in this guide) also have enormous selections of film, some at cut-rate prices.

Clothes & Shoes

Tokyo is a very fashionable city and the range of clothes and shoes available is enormous. Where you shop, however, depends on your budget. Areas like Shinjuku, Ikebukuro and Ueno are good areas for for picking up either clothes or shoes at discounted prices. Areas like Harajuku, Aoyama, Shibuya and Ginza are good for boutique browsing and making quality purchases.

Reasonably priced clothing stores are scattered all over the east side of Shinjuku – there are quite a few around the Kinokuniya bookshop (Map 6). In Harajuku, Omote-sandō and Takeshita-dōri make good hunting grounds, although the market here is very youth oriented; take a look at Octopus Army on Takeshita-dōri and the Chicago Thrift Shop (Map 7), with its large collection of good quality second-hand clothes, on Omote-Sandō. These are also both good areas for buying shoes. In Ikebukuro, around the western exit of the station, there is a large number of discount fashion shops. Another area to take a look at is Ueno's Ameyoko-cho market (Map 3). It has a number of shops selling clothes and shoes at cheaper prices than other parts of Tokyo.

If you want to make a fashion statement and not shop cheap, head for the boutiques of Harajuku or the department stores of Shibuya. The Laforet building (Map 7) of Harajuku houses a number of designer boutiques in one building. Cushioned between Kiddyland and the Oriental Bazaar in Harajuku is Vivre 21 (Map 7), another fashion forum. One of the more famous of Aoyama's boutique buildings is Bell Commons (Map 7), right on the corner of Killer-dōri. In Shibuya (Map 8), the Parco stores, Seibu, Seibu Seed and the 109 building are all rated highly by shoppers with style.

The prohibitively high prices asked for new kimono and other traditional Japanese clothing items make second-hand shops the best option. The Oriental Bazaar and the basement of the Hanae Mori building (Map 7) in Harajuku are good places to look. (See the preceding Arts, Crafts & Antiques section for more information.) If you've got money to burn and are set on getting a new kimono or a similar item, check the big department stores like Isetan and Seibu. In March and September, there are big sales of rental kimono at Daimaru.

Computers

Tokyo is not a good place to buy computers. Prices tend to be higher than they are in Hong Kong, Taiwan or Singapore – and higher even than in the West. If you remain determined or are stuck in Tokyo, try giving Linc Computer (☎ 3409-6510) in Shibuya a ring. English is spoken here and they have a wide range of computers, both Apple and IBM varieties, and software.

Electronics

Ideally you should have an idea of prices back home or in other places on your travel agenda before you buy any electronic goods in Tokyo. Nevertheless, there are some good bargains to be had. See the Akihabara section of the Things to See & Do chapter for more information on Tokyo's discount centre for electronics. Don't forget to bargain!

Ideas

Inside Shinjuku station, close to the My City department store exit on the east side, on the left just before the steps that go down to the Marunouchi line, is Osano no Idea, which means literally 'king-like ideas'. It's a tiny hole-in-the-wall that sells variations on the better mouse trap. Do you need a fold-up ironing board complete with a miniature water-resistant video screen? This is the place to get it. All items on display come with a Japanese explanation, and there are always quite a number of people in here browsing.

Japanese Dolls

Edo-dōri Ave, next to Asakusabashi station, is the place to go if you're interested in Japanese dolls. Both sides of the road have large numbers of shops specialising in traditional Japanese dolls as well as their contemporary counterparts. This is actually an area for retailers to buy their goods in, so the prices should be substantially lower than buying in the department stores. It's also acceptable to bargain a little.

One shop you should visit if you're in the area is Akasaka Sakuradō (Map 9) in Akasaka. It's only a small shop, but the dolls here are all beautifully hand crafted in innovative designs. It's possible to buy a smaller piece for around Y1500. For the larger ones? I saw one with a price tag of Y300,000.

Kids' Stuff

They're an inventive lot, the Japanese, and consequently Tokyo can be a wonderful place to pick-up toys and games. Loft (Map 8) in Shibuya has a great selection of wacky kids' stuff, and in Harajuku there's Kiddyland (☎ 3409-3431; Map 7), with five floors of products that your children would probably be better off not knowing about. Along similar lines is Hakuhinkan Toy Park (☎ 3571-8008; Map 2) in Ginza. It claims to be the biggest toy shop in Japan, and even has a theatre and restaurants on its higher floors.

Pearls

It was in Japan that cultured pearls were first developed, and pearls are still cheaper here than in many other parts of the world. Ginza's Mikimoto Pearl (☎ 3535-5511), perhaps the most famous of Tokyo's pearl shops, was founded by the man who first developed the cultured pearl, Mikimoto Kokichi, and has been running since 1899. Another store worth checking out is Takasaki Shinju (☎ 5561-8880) in Akasaka.

Stationery

I know, it's an odd kind of category but Ito-ya (☎ 3561-8311; Map 2) in Ginza has nine floors of every kind of stationery item you could possibly think of. What's more, if you're in the market for *washi*, or traditional Japanese hand-made paper, this is the place to come. It's open from 9.30 am to 7 pm Monday to Saturday, and closes at 6 pm on Sunday.

Wrapping it up

So where do you get all these goodies wrapped up to give to the folks back home? In Shibuya the Tsutsumu Factory (☎ 5478-1330; tsutsumu means to wrap in Japanese) is three floors devoted entirely to wrapping things up. Choose your materials and they'll do the wrapping for you.

Excursions

Tokyo itself may be a tangle of expressways and railway lines and an ugly sprawl of office buildings and housing estates, but an hour or so away by train are some of Japan's most interesting travel destinations. All the places in this chapter can be visited as day trips from Tokyo although in several cases it would be worth staying away overnight.

Foremost among the attractions around Tokyo are Kamakura and Nikkō, two important historical sites. Hakone and the Mt Fuji region, on the other hand, provide magnificent views of Mt Fuji if the weather is favourable.

Most other destinations around Tokyo are less interesting to short-term visitors, despite heavy promotion by the Tourist Information Centre (TIC). For long-term residents, places like the Izu-hantō Peninsula and Dogashima are pleasant retreats from Tokyo, but they are geared to Japanese tourists – many of the sights have entry fees, roped walkways and orderly queues.

There are numerous tours operating out of Tokyo to nearby sightseeing areas. Some examples include:

Mt Fuji & Hakone
    Gray Line tours; Y15,900 with lunch (☎ 3433-5745)
Nikkō
    Imperial Coachman tours; Y16,600 with lunch (☎ 3573-1417)
Kamakura & Hakone
    Sunrise tours; Y18,900 (☎ 3276-7777)

There are even day tours operating to Kyoto, but with so much to see there and so much time spent commuting (seven hours round trip), you'd probably be better off seeing some of the sights closer to Tokyo at a more leisurely pace. If you are interested, both Imperial Coachman and Sunrise tours offer a Kyoto deal at around Y47,000 for the day.

The following guide to the sights around Tokyo moves in westerly direction and then takes in Nikkō and Mashiko to the north.

KAWASAKI

Kawasaki (population one million) is a fairly uninteresting industrial city. However, it does have the colourful

Horinouchi entertainment district, an interesting enclave of love hotels and the **Nihon Minka-en Garden**. The garden is an open-air museum with 22 traditional Japanese buildings collected from the surrounding country and reassembled on one sight to give visitors a glimpse of traditional Japan. It's open Tuesday to Sunday from 9.30 am to 4 pm, except over New Year, when it is closed. Admission is Y300. The garden is about a 10-minute walk from Mukōgaoka-yuen station on the Odakyū line.

Getting There & Away

Take the Odakyū line from Tokyo's Shinjuku station to Mukōgaoka-yuen station. From the southern exit, look for the start of the monorail and follow the line until it bears left, when you must bear right. The Nihon Minka-en is up the hill and on the right-hand side, opposite a parking lot.

YOKOHAMA

Yokohama (population three million), Japan's second largest city, is in many ways a dull extension of Tokyo, lacking the bright lights, historical sites and vibrant, international-city atmosphere of the capital. Yokohama has always had a relatively large foreign population, including a sizeable Chinese community, but the city's only real attractions are a fairly uninteresting harbour, an unexceptional Chinatown and the Sankei-en Garden.

For more information on Yokohama, the Yokohama International Tourist Association (☎ 045-641-5824) and the Kanagawa Prefectural Tourist Association (☎ 045-681-0007) are both next door to the Silk Museum in Yokohama.

Things to See

Foremost among Yokohama's attractions is the **Sankei-en Garden**. It's beautifully landscaped, featuring a three-storey pagoda that is 500 years old. The garden is open daily from 9 am to 4.30 pm. The No 8 bus, from the road running parallel to the harbour behind the Marine Tower, operates with less than commendable frequency. If one does happen along, ask for the Sankei-en-mae bus stop.

Some of Yokohama's other sights include the **Marine Tower**, which has a viewing platform for Y600; **Chinatown**, which, with its gaudy colours and good Chinese food, provides a welcome respite from the rest of Yokohama; the **Silk Museum**, which deals with every possible aspect of silk and silk production with characteristic Japanese thoroughness (entry is Y300 and it's closed on Mondays); and the harbourfront **Yamashita-kōen Park**. Moored in the harbour next to the park is the *Hikawa Maru*, a passenger liner that you can board and explore. In summer, the boat stays open until 9 pm and has a beer garden. Admission is Y700.

Harbour cruises operate from the pier next to the *Hikawa Maru* and take from 40 minutes (Y750) to 1½ hours (Y2000). Close to the Marine Tower is the **Yokohama Doll Museum**, which has 1200 dolls from around the world. Admission is Y300 and it is open from 10 am to 5 pm. Just beyond the expressway is the **Harbour View Park** and the nearby **Foreigner's Cemetery**, containing the graves of more than 4000 foreigners.

Places to Stay

The *Kanagawa Youth Hostel* (☎ 045-241-6503) costs Y2300. From Sakuragi-cho station, exit on the opposite side to the harbour, turn right and follow the road alongside the railway tracks. Cross the main road, turn left into the steep street with a bridge and a cobblestoned section and the youth hostel is up the road on the right.

Most other accommodation in Yokohama is aimed at business travellers. The *Yokohama International Seamen's Hall* (☎ 045-681-2358) has singles/doubles for Y5100/ Y10,800. The expensive *Hotel Yokohama* (☎ 045-662-1321) is an up-market option by the waterfront, offering doubles and twins from Y19,500 to Y23,500. The cheaper *Hotel New Grand* (☎ 045-681-1841) has singles/doubles for Y8500/18,000.

Places to Eat

Chinatown is undoubtedly the place for a meal in Yokohama. Front window displays are common in the many restaurants, and long queues of patient Japanese pinpoint the best places.

Getting There & Away

There are numerous trains from Tokyo, the cheapest being the Tōkyū Toyoko line from Shibuya station to Yokohama station for Y230. The trip takes 40 minutes and continues from Yokohama station to Sakuragi-cho station, a bit closer to the harbour area.

The Keihin Tōhoku line from Tokyo station is a bit more convenient, going through to Kannai station, but at Y610 it's considerably more expensive. If you only want to go as far as Yokohama station, take the Tōkaidō line from Tokyo station or Shinagawa station; the 30-minute trip costs Y530.

It is convenient to continue on to Kamakura on the Yokosuka line from Yokohama station. There is also a shinkansen (bullet train) connection for those continuing to the Kansai region.

KAMAKURA

Kamakura once had a spell of glory as the nation's capital from 1192 to 1333. The Minamoto clan and later the Hōjo clan ruled Japan from Kamakura for more than a century, until finally in 1333, weakened by the cost of maintaining defences against threats of attack from Kublai Khan in China, the Hōjo clan fell from power at the hands of the forces of Emperor Go-daigo. Though the restoration of imperial authority was somewhat illusory, real power reverting to another of Japan's clans, the capital nevertheless shifted back to Kyoto and Kamakura disappeared from the history books.

Today, Kamakura may not have as much to offer historically as Kyoto or Nara, but a wealth of notable Buddhist temples and Shintō shrines make it one of Tokyo's most interesting day trips. The town has some relaxing walks and a peacefulness that is hard to come by in Kyoto, where there are so many tourists.

Things to See

The best way to see Kamakura is to start at Kita-Kamakura station and visit the temples between there and Kamakura on foot. There are vendors as you exit the station selling maps with points of interest marked in both English and Japanese.

The **Engaku-ji Temple** is on the left as you exit Kita-Kamakura station. It is one of the five main Rinzai Zen temples in Kamakura, and dates from 1282. Rinzai is distinguished from the other major school of Zen Buddhism in Japan, Sōtō, by its use among other things of riddles and stories concerning the lives of Zen masters, and formal question-and-answer drills as aids to attaining enlightenment. The temple has a Y200 entry fee and is open daily from 8 am to 4 pm.

Across the railway tracks from Engaku-ji Temple is **Tōkei-ji Temple**, notable for its grounds as much as for the temple itself. On weekdays, when visitors are few, it can be a pleasantly relaxing place. Walk up to the cemetery and wander around. In years past women were

Souvenir Nakasandō hats (RS)

officially recognised as divorced if they spent three years as nuns in the temple precinct. It's open daily from 8.30 am to 5 pm; entry is Y50.

A couple of minutes further on from Tōkei-ji Temple is **Jōchi-ji Temple**, another temple with tranquil environs. Founded in 1283, this is considered one of Kamakura's five great Zen temples. It is open daily from 9 am to 4.30 pm, and admission is Y100.

The **Kenchō-ji Temple** is about a 10-minute walk beyond Jōchi-ji Temple. It is on the left after you pass through a tunnel. This is not only Kamakura's most important Zen temple but something of a showcase generally. The grounds and the buildings are well maintained and still in use. The first of the main buildings you come to, the Buddha Hall, was moved to its present site and reassembled in 1647. The second building, the Hall of Law, is used for Zazen meditation. Further back is the

Dragon King Hall, a Chinese-style building with a garden to its rear. The temple bell, the second largest in Kamakura, has been designated a 'national treasure'. The temple is open daily from 9 am to 4.30 pm and admission is Y200.

Across the road from Kenchō-ji Temple is **Ennō-ji Temple**, distinguished primarily by its collection of statues depicting the judges of hell. The temple is open daily from 10 am to 4 pm.

Further down the road is **Hachiman-gū Shrine**. Hachiman, the deity to whom the shrine is dedicated, is both the god of war and the guardian deity of the Minamoto clan. The shrine offers a dramatic contrast to the quiet repose of the Zen temples clustered around Kita-Kamakura station. Look out for the gingko tree at the foot of the stairs leading to the square. It is said that a famous political assassination was carried out beneath it in 1219, making the tree very old indeed. Nearby is a dancing platform, and look out for the arched bridge, which in times past was reserved for the passage of the shogun alone. Its inclination must have made every crossing a formidable test of shogunate athletic prowess.

To the left of the dancing platform is the **National Treasure Museum**. This is one museum which is recommended, as it provides a unique opportunity to see Kamakuran art, most of which is cloistered away in the temples. The museum is open Tuesday to Sunday from 9 am to 4 pm, and admission is Y150.

Kamakura Station Area Apart from Hachiman-gū Shrine, there are no sites of historic importance in the immediate vicinity of the station; most places require a short bus trip from one of the bus stops in front of the station. The most worthwhile trip you could make is to the **Great Buddha**.

The Daibutsu (Great Buddha) was completed in 1252 and is Kamakura's most famous sight. Once housed in a huge hall, the statue today sits in the open, its home having been washed away by a tsunami in 1495. Cast in bronze and weighing close to 850 tonnes, the statue is 11.4 metres tall. Its construction is said to have been inspired by the even bigger Daibutsu in Nara. Nara's Great Buddha may be bigger, but it is commonly agreed that Kamakura's is artistically superior.

To get to the Great Buddha, take a bus from the No 7 bus stop in front of Kamakura station and get off at the Daibutsu-mae bus stop. The Great Buddha can be seen daily from 7 am to 5.30 pm, and admission is Y120.

If you walk back towards Kamakura station and turn right at the intersection where the bus goes left, this small street will take you to **Hase-dera Temple**, also known as Hase Kannon Temple. The grounds have a garden and an interesting collection of statues of Jizō, the patron saint of travellers and souls of departed children. The main point of interest in the grounds, however, is the **Kannon statue**.

Kannon, the goddess of mercy, is a Bodhisattva – a Buddha who has put off enlightenment in order to help others along the same path. Kannon is considered compassionate and is often called upon by those with troubles. The nine-metre wooden carved *jūichimen* (11 faced Kannon) is believed to be very ancient, dating from the 8th century. The 11 faces actually comprise one major face and 10 minor faces, the latter representing 10 stages of enlightenment. From October to February, Hase-dera Temple is open from 7 am to 4.40 pm. During the rest of the year it closes at 5.40 pm. Admission is Y200.

Places to Stay

The *Kamakura Kagetsuen Youth Hostel* (☎ 0467-25-1238) has beds at Y3250 for members and Y5500 for nonmembers (including two meals). You can walk to the hostel from Hase-dera Temple.

Just around the corner from Kamakura station is the *Ryokan Ushio* (☎ 0467-22-7016), which has singles from Y4200. Follow the road next to McDonald's parallel to the train lines and take the next left. Ryokan Ushio is on the left.

Not far from the youth hostel is *BB House* (☎ 0467-25-5859), which provides accommodation for women only and costs Y5000 per person, including breakfast. It's past the Hase-dera Temple entrance, at the end of the road that runs past the Great Buddha.

Places to Eat

Around the square facing the station is a *McDonald's*, a *Love Burger* and other fast-food places. For real food, the best hunting ground is in Wakamiya-dōri Ave towards Hachiman-gū Shrine, or in the road next to the station that runs parallel with Wakamiya-dōri Ave. There is a large number of budget-to-medium priced places on both of these streets, ranging from noodle shops to Italian restaurants.

Getting There & Away

Trains on the Yokosuka line that are blue with a white stripe operate from Tokyo, Shimbashi and Shinagawa stations – take your pick. The trip takes about 55 minutes and fares are Y930 from Tokyo and Shimbashi, and Y880 from Shinagawa. It is also possible to catch a train from Yokohama on the Yokosuka line. If you're planning to get off at Kita-Kamakura station, it is the stop after Ofuna.

A cheaper but more complicated option begins with a 75-minute ride on the Odakyū line from Shinjuku in Tokyo to Katase-Enoshima station (Y460 by express). When you leave the station, cross the river and turn left. Enoshima station is a 10-minute walk away, and there you can catch the Enoden line to Kamakura (Y170).

It is possible to continue on to Enoshima, either via the Enoden line from Kamakura station or by bus from stop No 9 in front of Kamakura station. The train is the simpler and cheaper option, taking 36 minutes and costing Y170.

ENOSHIMA

Avoid this popular beach on weekends, when it's packed with day-trippers. At the end of the beach is a bridge to **Eno-shima Island**, where the **Enoshima-jinja Shrine** is reached by an 'outdoor escalator'. It houses a *hadaka-benzaiten* – a nude statue of the Indian goddess of beauty. Other sights around the island include the Enoshima Shokubutsu-en (Enoshima Tropical Garden).

Getting There & Away

Buses and trains run frequently between Kamakura and Enoshima (see the Kamakura Getting There & Away section). The Tōkaidō line goes to Ofuna station from Tokyo station, at a cost of Y780. At Ofuna, change to the Shonan monorail and go to Shonan Enoshima station, a trip costing Y260. Alternatively, trains run on the Odakyū line from Shinjuku station to Katase-Enoshima station. The Romance Car takes 70 minutes and costs Y870, while an express takes five minutes longer and costs Y460.

IZU-HANTŌ PENINSULA

The Izu-hantō Peninsula is noted for its abundant hot springs, but there's little of historical interest – it's simply a pleasant day trip or overnight stay. You can get around the peninsula in one long and hurried day or stay overnight at a halfway point, such as Shimoda. If you do this, try to find accommodation at a hot-spring hotel.

A suggested itinerary for circuiting the peninsula is to start at Atami and travel down the east coast to Shimoda; from there you can cut across to Dogashima on the west coast and travel up to Mishima or Numazu, where there are railway stations with direct access to Tokyo. There are frequent and reliable bus services between all the main towns on the peninsula, and some of the towns are also serviced by ferries.

Atami

Atami has more appeal as a naughty hot-spring weekend destination for Japanese couples than it has to Westerners for its sightseeing potential. Its easy access from Tokyo by shinkansen (bullet train) and its fame as a hot-spring resort make it an expensive place to spend the night, so Itō or Shimoda are better for accommodation on the peninsula.

Atami's prime attraction is the **MOA Art Museum**. There's a free shuttle bus from the station, but admission is a hefty Y1500. It has a collection of Japanese and Chinese art that includes a few 'National Treasures' and a good number of 'Important Cultural Properties'. The museum is open Friday to Wednesday from 9.30 am to 4 pm.

Getting There & Away An ordinary Tōkaidō line train from Tokyo station will get you to Atami in 105 minutes for Y1850. The shinkansen takes only 50 minutes but costs Y4000. Ordinary trains leave Tokyo every 40 minutes during the day.

Itō

Itō, a hot-spring resort, is famous as the place where Anjin-san (William Adams), the hero of James Clavell's book *Shogun*, built a ship for the Tokugawa Shogunate. Among the sights around the town are the gourd-shaped **Ippeki-ko Lake**, the **Cycle Sports Centre** and the **Izu Cactus Garden** (ask for Izu Shaboten-kōen), which is 35 minutes by bus from Izu station and charges a prickly Y1550 for admission.

The **Ikeda 20th Century Art Museum**, which has a collection of paintings and sculptures by Matisse, Picasso, Dali and others. The museum, 25 minutes from Itō station, is open daily from 10 am to 4.30 pm. Admission is Y720.

Places to Stay There are a couple of youth hostels with accommodation for around Y2100 in the vicinity of Itō. The *Itō Youth Hostel* (☎ 0557-45-0224) is 15 minutes out of town by bus. The *Tōtaru Youth Hostel* (☎ 0557-45-2591) is 30 minutes out. The *Izu Okawa Youth Hostel* (☎ 0557-23-1063) is easier to get to. It's about five minutes from Izu Okawa station, which is about a third of the way to Shimoda.

Getting There & Away Itō is about 25 minutes from Atami station on the JR Itō line, and the fare is Y310. There is also a JR limited express (tokkyū) service from Tokyo station to Itō, taking 110 minutes and costing Y4000. Direct ordinary trains from Tokyo station are quite a bit cheaper at Y2160 and take about 2 hours, 10 minutes.

Shimoda

If you only have time for one town on the peninsula, make it Shimoda, the most pleasant of the hot-spring resorts and former residence of the American Townsend Harris, the first Western diplomat to live in Japan. It's a peaceful place with a few historical sites as well as the usual touristy stuff.

Things to See Look out for the cable cars in front of the station that lurch their way up **Mt Nesugata-yama** every 10 minutes. The park on the top has good views of Shimoda and Shimoda Bay, and a reasonably priced restaurant. A return cable-car trip, including admission to the park, costs Y820.

About a 25-minute walk from Shimoda station is **Ryōsen-ji Temple**, famous as the site of a treaty signed by Commodore Perry and representatives of the Tokugawa Shogunate. Next door is **Chōraku-ji Temple**, which has a collection of erotic knick-knacks. Look out as well for the pictures depicting the life of Okichi-san, the courtesan who gave up the man she loved to attend to the needs of the barbarian Harris. Admission to this curious little museum is Y200.

To get to the temples, turn right from the square in front of Shimoda station with the bus ranks. Bear left after you cross the bridge and follow the road around in the same direction as you were walking in before. The temples are to your left, on the opposite side of the road, at the T-junction. On the way you will pass **Hōfuku-ji Temple**, which has a museum that commemorates the life of Okichi-san and includes scenes from the various movie adaptations that have been made of her life.

Places to Stay As in the other peninsula resort towns, there is a wealth of accommodation in Shimoda. The *Gensu Youth Hostel* (☎ 05586-2-0035) is 25 minutes by bus from the town and has beds for Y2100. The hostel is opposite a bus stop and a post office.

Staff at the information counter across the square from the station will book accommodation. If you want a cheap room, ask for a minshuku or kokuminshukusha (people's lodge); you should be able to get a room for Y4800 to Y5500 with two meals. If you want to find something yourself, the best hunting ground is the area that fronts onto Shimoda Bay. Turn right as you leave the station square, take the second left and cross the bridge. Follow this road around and bear left when it approaches the bay. The left-hand side of the road is crowded with hotels, ryokan and minshuku for more than a km.

Getting There & Away Shimoda is as far as you can go by train on the Izu-hantō Peninsula; the limited express from Tokyo station takes two hours, 45 minutes and costs Y5560. Alternatively, take an Izu Kyūkō line train from Itō station for Y1340; the trip takes about an hour. There are a few express services each day from Atami station, but the express surcharges make them expensive.

Bus platform No 5 in front of the station is for buses going to Dogashima, while platform No 7 is for those bound for Shuzenji.

Further around the Peninsula

From Shimoda's No 5 bus stop in front of the station, it's a very scenic bus journey to **Dogashima**, on the other side of the peninsula. Along the way is **Cape Matsu-zaki**, recommended for its traditional-style Japanese houses and quiet sandy beach. The bus fare is Y1200 and the journey takes about half an hour.

The unusual rock formations that line the shore are Dogashima's main attraction. There are also boat trips available which allow better views; a 20-minute trip costs Y720, while two-hour tours cost Y1680.

To complete your peninsula circuit, there are a number of bus stops in Dogashima on the road opposite the jetty. The fare to **Shuzenji**, another resort town with a rail link via the Tōkaidō line to Tokyo, from stop No 2 is an outrageous Y1910. A more interesting and not that much more expensive alternative is to catch a ferry to **Numazu**, also on the Tōkaidō line. Boats also go to **Tōi**, where you could stay overnight at the Takasagoya Youth Hostel, continue on to Shuzenji by bus or take another boat to Numazu. Finally, half an hour by rail from Shuzenji is **Mishima**, a town that is short on interesting sights but serviced by the Tōkaidō line. The shinkansen from Mishima to Tokyo station takes 65 minutes and costs Y4310. Ordinary trains take twice as long and cost Y2160.

HAKONE

If the weather cooperates and Mt Fuji is clearly visible, the Hakone region can make a memorable day trip from Tokyo. You can enjoy cable-car rides, visit an open-air museum, poke around smelly volcanic hot-water springs and cruise Ashino-ko Lake. The weather, however, is crucial, for without Mt Fuji hovering in the background, much of what Hakone has to offer is likely to diminish in interest.

An interesting loop through the region takes you from Tokyo to Hakone-Yumoto by train and then toy train to Gōra (Y300); by funicular and cable car up Mt Soun-zan and down to Ashino-ko Lake; by boat around the lake to Moto-Hakone where you can walk a short stretch of the Edo era Tōkaidō Highway; and from there by bus back to Odawara, where you catch the train to Tokyo. (If you're feeling energetic, you can spend 3½ hours walking the old highway back to Hakone-Yumoto, which is on the Tokyo line.)

Hakone Free Pass

The Odakyū line offers a Hakone furii pasu (Hakone free pass) which costs Y4850 for adults and Y2430 for children; it allows you to use any mode of transport within the Hakone region for four days. The fare between Shinjuku and Hakone-Yumoto is also included in the pass, although you will have to pay a Y800 surcharge if you want to take the Romance Car. If you have a Japan rail pass, you'd be advised to buy a free pass in Odawara for Y3500 and Y1750 for children, as this is noninclusive of the fare from Shinjuku. Altogether it's a good deal for a Hakone circuit, as the pass will save you at least Y1000 even on a one-day visit to the region.

Things to See

Between Odawara and Gōra on the toy-train Hakone-Tōzan line is the **Hakone Open-Air Art Museum**. The museum is next to Chōkoku-no-mori station, a little before Gōra station. The museum itself features sculptures by Western artists such as Rodin and Moore in a 30 sq km park. Admission is a hefty Y1300, and the Hakone Free Pass is *not* accepted. The museum is open from 9 am to 5 pm between March and October; during the rest of the year it closes at 4 pm.

The terminus of the Hakone-Tōzan line and the starting point for the funicular and cable-car trip to Togendai on Ashino-ko Lake is **Gōra**. This small town also has a couple of its own attractions, which include **Gōra-kōen Park**, just a short walk beside the funicular tracks up Mt Soun-zan. For Y800 you can take a look at the French Rock Garden. Further up the hill, 10 minutes from Gōra station, is the **Hakone Art Museum**, which has a moss garden and a collection of ceramics from Japan and other Asian nations. Admission is Y500 and it's closed on Thursday.

Take the funicular from Gōra up **Mt Soun-zan**. If you don't have a Hakone Free Pass, you'll need to buy a ticket at the booth to the right of the platform exit for Y280. Mt Soun-zan is the starting point for what the Japanese refer to as a 'ropeway', a 30-minute, four-km cable-car ride to **Togendai**, next to Ashino-ko Lake. On the way, the gondolas pass through **Owakudani**. Get out at this point and take a look at the volcanic hot springs. If the weather is fine, there are great views of Mt Fuji, both from the gondolas and from Owakudani. The journey from Gōra to Togendai costs Y1560; keep the ticket if you pause at Owakudani. The **Owakudani Natural Science Museum** has displays relating to the geography and natural history of Hakone. It's open daily from 9 am to 5 pm, and admission is Y350.

From Owakudani, the cable car continues on to **Ashino-ko Lake**, which is touted as the primary attraction of the Hakone region. Of principal interest is the majestic Mt Fuji rising above the surrounding hills, its snow-clad slopes shimmering on the mirror-like surface of the lake. That is, if the venerable mount is not hidden behind a dirty grey bank of clouds.

From Togendai there are ferry services to Hakone-en, Moto-Hakone and Hakone-machi. At Hakone-en, it is possible to take a cable car (Y600) to the top of **Mt Komaga-take**, where you get good views of the lake and Mt Fuji. You can leave the mountain by the same route or by taking a five-minute funicular descent (Y300) to

Komaga-take-nobori-kuchi. Buses run from there to Odawara for Y910.

Most people take the ferry from Togendai to Moto-Hakone for Y870. **Moto-Hakone** has few places at which you can eat or get an overpriced cup of coffee, and there are a couple of interesting sights within easy walking distance of the jetty. These include **Hakone-jinja Shrine**, which is impossible to miss, with its red torii rising from the lake. The well-maintained shrine is nothing special, but the general effect is quite atmospheric.

Up the hill from the lakeside Moto-Hakone bus stop, is the old **Tōkaidō Highway**, the road that once linked the ancient capital Kyoto with Edo, today the modern capital of Tokyo. You can take a 3½-hour walk along the old road to Hakone-Yumoto station, passing the Amazake-jaya Teahouse, the Old Tōkaidō Road Museum and Soun-ji Temple along the way.

A less arduous walk involves taking **Cryptomeria Ave**, or 'Sugi-namiki', a two-km path between Moto-Hakone and Hakone-machi lined with cryptomeria trees planted more than 360 years ago. The path runs behind the lakeside road used by the buses and other traffic. **Hakone-machi** itself was once the Hakone Checkpoint, operated by the Tokugawa Shogunate from 1619 to 1869 as a means of controlling the movement of everything from people to ideas in and out of Edo. The present-day checkpoint is a recent reproduction of the original.

Buses run from Moto-Hakone back to **Odawara** for Y1000. Odawara is billed in the tourist literature as an 'old castle town', which it is, except that the castle is an uninspiring reconstruction of the original. If you're still interested, it's a 10-minute walk from Odawara station and admission is Y250.

Places to Stay

Hakone's local popularity is reflected in the high price of most accommodation in the area. The *Hakone Soun-zan Youth Hostel* (☎ 0460-2-3827) costs the standard Y2100. The hostel is on the left-hand side of the road that goes off to the right of the cable car. Look for the wooden sign with Japanese writing and the YHA triangle outside the hotel. Alternatively it's Y1000 to pitch a tent at the *Kojiri Campground*, and there are six-person huts available for Y10,000.

If you want the best, the *Fujiya Hotel* (☎ 0460-2-2211) is famous as one of Japan's earliest Western-style hotels and has twin rooms from Y19,100. Prices vary with the season. The hotel is near Miyanoshita station on the

Hakone-Tōzan line; if you ring from the station, someone will give you instructions in English on how to get to the hotel.

Getting There & Away

There are basically three ways of getting to the Hakone region: by the Odakyū express bus service from the Shinjuku bus terminal on the western side of Shinjuku station; by JR from Tokyo station; and by the private Odakyū line from Shinjuku station.

Bus The Odakyū express bus service has the advantage of running directly into the Hakone region, to Ashino-ko Lake and to Hakone-machi for Y1650. The disadvantage is that the bus trip is much less interesting than the combination of Romance Car, toy train (Hakone-Tōzan line), funicular, cable car (ropeway) and ferry. Buses leave from bus stop No 35 in front of the Odakyū department store (Map 6) on the west side of Shinjuku station.

Train Japanese Railway (JR) trains run on the Tōkaidō line between Tokyo station and Odawara. Ordinary trains take 1½ hours, cost Y1420 and run every 15 minutes or so. Shinkansen do the journey in 42 minutes, cost Y3570 and leave Tokyo station every 20 minutes.

Trains also service Odawara from Shinjuku station on the Odakyū line. Quickest and most comfortable is the Romance Car, which takes 85 minutes, costs Y1790 and leaves every half hour. There's also an express service, taking 95 minutes, which at Y750 is by far the cheapest way of reaching Odawara.

At Odawara, it is possible to change to the Hakone-Tōzan line, which takes you to Gōra. Alternatively, if you are already on the Odakyū line, you can continue on to Hakone-Yumoto and change to the Hakone-Tōzan line simply by walking across the platform.

MT FUJI AREA

Mt Fuji, Japan's highest mountain stands 3776 metres high, and when it's capped with snow in winter, it's a picture-postcard perfect volcano cone. Fuji-san, as it's reverently referred to, last blew its top in 1707, when streets in Tokyo were covered in volcanic ash. Unfortunately, despite those wonderful postcard views, Mt Fuji is a notoriously reclusive mountain, often hidden by cloud. The views are usually best in winter and early spring, when a snow cap adds to the spectacle.

Information

Climbing Mt Fuji and *Mt Fuji & Fuji Five Lakes* brochures are available from the Tourist Information Centre (TIC) and provide exhaustive detail on transport to the mountain and how to climb it, complete with climbing schedules worked out to the minute. There is a tourist information office in front of the Kawaguchi-ko station.

Fuji Views

You can get a classic view of Mt Fuji from the shinkansen as it passes the city of Fuji. There are also good views from the Hakone area and from the Nagao Pass on the road from Hakone to Gotemba. The road that encircles the mountain offers good views, particularly near Yamanaka-ko and Sai-ko lakes.

Climbing Mt Fuji

Officially the climbing season on Fuji is July and August, and the Japanese, who love to do things 'right', pack in during those busy months. The climbing may be just as good either side of the official season but transport

Sunrise from Mt Fuji (TW)

View of Mt Fuji (CT)

services to and from the mountain are less frequent then and many of the mountain huts are closed. You can actually climb Mt Fuji at any time of year, but a mid-winter ascent is strictly for experienced mountaineers.

Bear in mind that although this is a popular climb, Mt Fuji is high enough for altitude sickness symptoms to be experienced, and as on any mountain, the weather can be viciously changeable. On the summit it can quickly go from clear but cold to cloudy, wet, windy and freezing cold – not just miserable but downright dangerous. Don't climb Mt Fuji without adequate clothing for cold and wet weather: even on a good day at the height of summer, the temperature on top is likely to be close to freezing.

The mountain is divided into 10 'stations' from base to summit but these days most climbers start from one of the four fifth stations, which you can reach by road. Count on a 4½-hour ascent and about 2½ hours to descend. Once you're on the top, it takes about an hour to make a circuit of the crater.

To time your arrival for the sunrise, also the time that the mountain is least likely to be shrouded in cloud, you can either start up in the afternoon, stay overnight in a mountain hut and continue early in the morning, or climb the whole way at night. You do not want to arrive on the top too long before dawn, as it's likely to be very cold and windy.

Fifth Stations There are four fifth stations around Fuji, and it's quite feasible to climb from one and descend to another. On the northern side of Fuji is the Kawaguchi-ko Fifth Station, at 2305 metres, which is reached from the town of Kawaguchi-ko. This station is particularly popular with climbers starting from Tokyo. The Yoshida route, which starts much lower down, close to the town of Fuji-Yoshida, is the same as the Kawaguchi-ko route for much of the way.

The Subashiri Fifth Station is at 1980 metres, and the route from there meets the Kawaguchi-ko one just after the eighth station. The Gotemba Fifth Station is reached from the town of Gotemba and, at 1440 metres, is much lower than the other fifth stations. From the Gotemba station it takes seven to eight hours to reach the top, as opposed to the 4½ to five hours it takes on the other routes. The Fujinomiya/Mishima Fifth Station, at 2380 metres, is convenient for climbers coming from Nagoya, Kyoto, Osaka and western Japan than for those coming from Tokyo. It meets the Gotemba route right at the top.

Equipment Make sure you have plenty of clothing suitable for cold and wet weather, including a hat and gloves. Bring drinking water and some snack food. If you're going to climb at night, bring a torch (flashlight). Even at night it would be difficult to get seriously lost, as the trails are very clear, but it's easy to put a foot wrong in the dark.

Mountain Huts There are 'lodges' dotted up the mountainside but they're expensive – Y4000 for a mattress on the floor squeezed between countless other climbers – and you don't get much opportunity to sleep anyway, as you have to be up well before dawn to start the final slog to the top. No matter how miserable the nights, don't plan to shelter or rest in the huts without paying. The huts also prepare simple meals for their guests and for passing climbers. Camping on the mountain is not permitted.

Getting There & Away The three routes that are used by climbers from Tokyo are serviced by the two centres of Kawaguchi-ko and Gotemba. To make the Kawaguchi-ko ascent, your best bet is to take the direct bus service from the Shinjuku bus terminal to the Kawaguchi-ko Fifth Station. This takes 2½ hours and costs Y2160. This is by far the fastest and cheapest way of getting from Tokyo to the fifth station. If you take two trains and a bus, the same trip can cost nearly Y6000. The train journey involves taking the Chūō line from Shinjuku to Ōtsuki, where you cross the platform to the Fuji Kyūkō line to Kawaguchi-ko. From here buses run to the fifth station from April to mid-November. The trip takes 55 minutes and costs Y1570 – buses run late during peak season.

From Gotemba station there are bus services both for the Gotemba route (Y930) and the Subashiri route (Y1040). Trains run to Gotemba via the Gotemba line and then the Odakyu line, taking about 105 minutes at Y2150. Alternatively, Tomei buses run from Tokyo station to Tomei Gotemba, about a km from Gotemba, taking around the same amount of time for Y1350.

Fuji Five Lakes

The five lakes arced around the northern side of Mt Fuji are major attractions for Tokyo day-trippers, offering water sports and some good views of Mt Fuji. For visitors to Tokyo, the views of the lakes and Mt Fuji are the area's biggest drawcard. Perhaps the best way to make the most of this is to avail yourself of the area's comprehensive bus network, which includes regular buses from Fuji-Yoshida station. They pass the four smaller lakes and travel around the mountain to Fujinomiya on the south-western side. From Kawaguchi-ko, there are nine to 11 buses daily making the two-hour trip to Mishima on the shinkansen line.

Places to Stay The *Marimo (Yamanaka-ko)* (☎ 0555-62-4210), *Kawaguchi-ko* (☎ 0555-72-1431) and *Fuji Sai-ko* (☎ 0555-82-2616) youth hostels are all youth hostels. The first two cost Y2100 a night, while the Sai-ko is Y2250 or Y2450, depending on the season. The Sai-ko is also about two km off the main road, which can make getting to it a little difficult. The *Fuji-Yoshida Youth Hostel* (☎ 0555-22-0533) in the town of the same name is also Y2100.

There are numerous hotels, ryokan, minshuku and pensions around the Fuji Five Lakes, particularly at Kawaguchi-ko. The tourist information office at the Kawaguchi-ko station can make reservations. The Japanese Inn Group is represented by the *Hotel Ashiwada* (☎ 0555-82-2321), at the western end of Kawaguchi-ko Lake. Rooms are Y4000 per person, or Y5000 with attached bathrooms.

Getting There & Away Fuji-Yoshida and Kawaguchi-ko are the two main travel centres in the Fuji Five Lakes area. Buses operate directly to Kawaguchi-ko from the Shinjuku bus terminal in the Yasuda Seimei second building, beside the main Shinjuku station in Tokyo. The trip takes 105 minutes and there are departures up to 16 times daily at the height of the Fuji climbing season. The fare is Y1520. Some buses continue to Yamanaka-ko and Motosu-ko lakes.

You can also get to the lakes by train, although it takes longer and costs more. JR Chūō line trains go from Shinjuku to Otsuki (one hour and Y2890 by limited express; Y1260 by local train, or futsū). At Otsuki you cross the platform to the Fuji Kyūkō line local train which takes another 50 minutes at a cost of Y1070 to Kawaguchi-ko. The train actually goes to Fuji-Yoshida first, then reverses out for the final short distance to Kawaguchi-ko. On Sunday and holidays from March to November there is a direct local train from Shinjuku which takes two to 2½ hours and costs Y2200.

NIKKŌ

Nikkō is not only one of the most popular day trips from Tokyo, it's also one of Japan's major tourist attractions due to the visual splendour of its shrines and temples. Visitors are advised to pick a weekday for their trip, when the crowds are lighter, but whatever you do, don't avoid it altogether. Nikkō should be included on even the most whirlwind tour of Japan.

There's an excellent tourist information office on the road up to Tōshō-gū Shrine. The office has a wealth of useful pamphlets and maps.

History

Nikkō's history as a sacred site stretches back to the middle of the 8th century, when a Buddhist priest established a hermitage there. In 1617 it was chosen as the site for the mausoleum of Tokugawa Ieyasu, the warlord who took control of all Japan and established the shogunate which ruled for 250 years until the Meiji Restoration ended the feudal era. In 1634, Tokugawa Iemitsu, the grandson of the deceased Ieyasu, commenced work on the shrine that can be seen today. The Tōshō-gū Shrine was built using a huge army of some 15,000 artisans from all over Japan.

The results continue to receive mixed reviews. In contrast with the minimalism that is generally considered the essence of Japanese art, every available space of Ieyasu's shrine and mausoleum is crowded with detail. Animals, mythical and otherwise, jostle for attention from among the glimmering gold-leaf and red lacquerwork. The overall effect is more Chinese than

Japanese but don't let this put you off – Tōshō-gū Shrine, despite continuing accusations of vulgarity, remains a grand experience.

Tickets

Ticketing arrangements in Nikkō are very confusing. Don't let it get to you. Just go and buy a Y750 ticket for Tōshō-gū Shrine and Rinnō-ji Temple. As Futāra-san-jinja Shrine is free, this will get you into Nikkō's three major attractions. Once you're inside Tōshō-gū Shrine you can make up your own mind whether you want to fork out Y430 to see the Sleeping Cat/Tomb of Ieyasu

Shin-kyō Bridge, Nikkō (CT)

and the Roaring Dragon Hall (worthwhile in my opinion). Even if you do, you've still saved Y560 on buying all the tickets separately. The treasure museums at Tōshō-gū Shrine and Rinnō-ji Temple require separate entry fees – both are Y300.

Things to See

Close to the Tōshō-gū Shrine area is the **Shin-kyō Bridge**. The story goes that the monk, Shōdō Shōnin, who first established a hermitage in Nikkō in 782, was carried across the river at this point on the backs of two huge serpents. Today's bridge is a 1907 reconstruction of the mid-17th century original. It costs Y300 to cross the bridge on foot.

The next stop is **Rinnō-ji Temple**, also founded by Shōdō Shōnin of the Buddhist Tendai sect. The **Sambutsu-dō** (Three Buddha Hall) has huge gold-lacquered images, the most impressive of which is the *senjū* (1000 armed Kannon). The central image is Amida Nyorai, flanked by *batō* (a horse-headed Kannon), whose special domain is the animal kingdom.

The **Hōmutsu-den** (Treasure Hall), also on the temple grounds, has a collection of treasures associated with the temple, but admission (Y300) is not included in the two-shrine, one-temple ticket.

A huge stone torii (gate) marks the entrance to **Tōshō-gū Shrine**, while to the left is a five-storeyed pagoda, originally dating from 1650 but reconstructed in 1818. The pagoda is remarkable for its lack of foundations – the interior is said to contain a long suspended pole that swings like a pendulum in order to maintain equilibrium in the event of an earthquake.

The true entrance to the Tōshō-gū Shrine is through the torii at the Omote-mon Gate, protected on either side by Deva kings. Through the entrance to the right is the **Sanjinko** (Three Sacred Storehouses), the upper storey of which is renowned for the imaginative relief carvings of elephants by an artist who had never seen the real thing. To the left of the entrance is the **Sacred Stable**, a suitably plain building housing a carved white horse. The stable's only adornment is an allegorical series of relief carvings depicting the life-cycle of the monkey. They include the famous 'hear no evil, see no evil, speak no evil' threesome that has become emblematic of Nikkō.

Pass through another torii, climb another flight of stairs, and on the left and right are a drum tower and a belfry. To the left of the drum tower is the **Honji-dō Hall**, which has a huge ceiling painting of a dragon in flight known as the Roaring Dragon. The dragon will perform a perfunctory roar for you if you clap your hands beneath it.

Next comes the **Yōmei-mon Gate**, which is covered with a teeming multitude of reliefs of Chinese sages, children, dragons and other mythical creatures. So much effort and skill went into the gate that its creators worried that its perfection might arouse envy in the gods, so the final supporting pillar on the left-hand side was placed upside down as a deliberate error.

Through the Yōmei-mon Gate and to the right is the **Nemuri-neko** (the Sleeping Cat). The Sakashita-mon Gate here opens onto a path that climbs up through towering cedars to **Ieyasu's Tomb**, a relatively simple affair. If you are using the Y750 ticket it will cost an extra Y430 to see the cat and the tomb. To the left of the Yōmei-mon Gate is the **Jinyōsha**, a storage depot for Nikkō's mikoshi (portable shrines), which come into action during the May and October festivals. The Honden (Main Hall) and the Haiden (Hall of Worship) can also be seen in the enclosure.

Nearby is **Futāra-san-jinja Shrine**, which is dedicated to the mountain Nantai, to the mountain's consort Nyotai and to their mountainous progeny Tarō. Also in the vicinity is **Taiyūin-byō**, which enshrines Ieyasu's grandson Iemitsu (1604-51) and is very much a smaller version of Tōshō-gū Shrine. The smaller size gives it a less extravagant air and it has been suggested that it is more aesthetically worthy than its larger neighbour.

Chūzenji-ko Lake

On a quiet day it's a 50-minute bus trip from Nikkō up to Chūzenji-ko Lake along a winding road complete with hairpin bends. There's some beautiful scenery, including the 97-metre **Kegon Waterfall** and the lake, but don't cut short a visit to the shrine area just to fit in Chūzenji-ko Lake. The waterfall features an elevator (Y500) down to a platform where you can observe the full force of the plunging water. Also worth a visit is the third of the **Futāra-san-jinja shrines**, complementing the ones in Tōshō-gū Shrine area and on Mt Nantai.

Buses run from Tōbu Nikkō station to Chūzenji Onsen at 10 to 20-minute intervals from 6.20 am to 7.30 pm and cost Y900. Returning buses depart only once an hour. The cable car at the lake costs Y650 one way.

Places to Stay

Because of Nikkō's importance as a tourist attraction, it is one of the few places in Japan, apart from Tokyo and

Crowds at shrine, Nikkō (CT)

Kyoto, where travellers on a budget actually get some choice as to where to stay. If you're willing to spend Y1000 or so over the standard youth hostel rates, there are some very good accommodation options close to the central shrine and temple area.

The *Nikkō Daiyagawa Youth Hostel* (☎ 0288-54-1974) is the more popular of the town's two hostels. It costs Y2000 per night (Y3000 with two meals) and is just behind the post office. A 10-minute walk away is the *Nikkō Youth Hostel* (☎ 0288-54-1013), which costs Y2650, Y3830 with two meals.

Far and away the most popular of Nikkō's pensions is the *Pension Turtle* (☎ 0288-53-3168), with rooms from Y3700 per person. It's by the river, beyond the shrine area. Also justifiably popular is the *Lodging House St Bois* (☎ 0288-53-0082). This place touts itself as a mountain lodge and has both Western and Japanese-style singles/doubles starting at Y5500/10,000 for rooms without baths. It's across the river, north of the station.

Other pensions around Nikkō are a little more expensive, but feature extra touches such as Italian-trained chefs. Recommended is the *Pension Hillside Terrace* (☎ 0288-54-3235), which charges Y6000 per person or Y7700 for rooms with attached bathrooms. *Humpty Dumpty* (☎ 0288-53-3168) is similarly priced and is near the Lodging House St Bois.

Not far from the Shin-kyō Bridge is the *Nikkō Kanaya Hotel* (☎ 0288-54-0001), where single/twins without bathrooms cost Y6500/7500; the price is very reasonable for a hotel that combines classiness with a great location.

Getting There & Away

The best way to visit Nikkō is via the Tōbu Nikkō line from Asakusa station in Tokyo. The station, which is separate from Asakusa subway station, is in the basement of the Tōbu department store (Map 4), but is well signposted and easy to find from the subway. Limited express trains cost Y2530 and take 115 minutes. These trains require a reservation (on a quiet day you'll probably be able to organise this before boarding the train) and run every 30 minutes or so from 7.30 to 10 am; after 10 am they run hourly. Rapid trains require no reservation, take 15 minutes longer than the limited express and cost Y1270. They run once an hour from 6.20 am to 4.30 pm.

As usual, travelling by JR trains works out to be more time consuming and more expensive; it is only really of interest to those on a Japan Rail Pass. The quickest way to do it would be to take the shinkansen from Ueno to Utsunomiya (Y4510, 50 minutes) and change there for an ordinary train (no other options) for the 45 minute, Y720 journey to Nikkō. The trains from Utsunomiya to Nikkō leave on average about once an hour.

A limited-express service (1½ hours, Y3690) and an ordinary service (110 minutes, Y1850) also run between Ueno and Utsunomiya.

MASHIKO

Mashiko, a centre for country-style pottery, has about 50 potters, some of whom you can see working at their kilns. The town achieved fame when the potter Hamada Shōji settled there and, from 1930, produced his Mashiko pottery. Today he is designated as a 'Living National Treasure' and has been joined in Mashiko by a legion of other potters. The noted English potter Bernard Leach also worked there for several years.

Getting There & Away

It is possible to combine Mashiko with a visit to Nikkō if you set off from Tokyo very early and use the JR route. See the Nikkō Getting There & Away section for travel details to Utsunomiya. From Utsunomiya, buses run regularly during the day to Mashiko, taking one hour and costing Y1000 one way.

Index

Maps

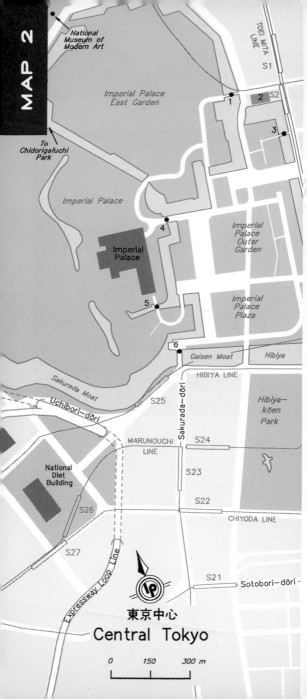

MAP 2

National Museum of
Modern Art

Imperial Palace
East Garden

TOEI MITA
LINE

S1

1
2 S2

3

To
Chidorigafuchi
Park

Imperial Palace

4

Imperial
Palace
Outer
Garden

Imperial
Palace

5

Imperial
Palace
Plaza

6 Gaisen Moat   Hibiya

Sakurada Moat

HIBIYA LINE

Hibiya-
kōen
Park

Uchibori-dōri

S25

MARUNOUCHI
LINE

Sakurada-dōri

S24

National
Diet
Building

S26

S23

S22

CHIYODA LINE

Expressway Loop Line

S27

S21 Sotobori-dōri

東京中心
Central Tokyo

0   150   300 m

MAP 2 - CENTRAL TOKYO

■ PLACES TO STAY

2　Palace Hotel
パレスホテル
7　Tokyo Station Hotel
東京ステーションホテル
10　Hotel Kokusai Kankō
ホテル国際観光
11　Yaesu Terminal Hotel
八重洲ターミナルホテル
18　Business Hotel Heimat
ビジネスホテルハイマート
24　Yaesu Fujiya Hotel
八重洲富士屋ホテル
25　Hotel Seiyo Ginza
ホテル西洋銀座
39　Ginza Capitol Hotel
銀座カピトルホテル
40　Hotel Ginza Dai-ei
ホテル銀座ダイエー
42　Hotel Atamisō
ホテル熱海荘
72　Imperial Hotel
帝国ホテル
79　Ginza Nikkō Hotel
銀座日光ホテル
80　Mitsui Urban Hotel
三井アーバンホテル
81　Ginza Dai-Ichi Hotel
銀座第一ホテル
84　Sun Hotel Shimbashi
サンホテル新橋

▼ PLACES TO EAT

33　Kawa Restaurant
鬼屋
37　Kaiten-zushi Sushi
かいてんずし
38　Chichibu Nishiki Nomiya Saké Pub
ちちぶにしきのみやパーブ
44　Nair's Indian Restaurant
ナイルレストラン
49　Saigon Restaurant
サイゴンレストラン
50　Dondon Restaurant
どんどレストラン
53　Yakitoris
焼き鳥屋
54　Lemon Grass Restaurant
レモングラス
58　New Torigin Restaurant
ニュー鳥ぎん
61　Gandhara Pakistani Restaurant
ガンダーラ
62　Maharaja Indian Restaurant
マハラジャ

SUBWAY STATIONS

S1   Ōtemachi (Chiyoda Line)
大手町（千代田線）

S2   Ōtemachi (TOEI Mita Line)
大手町（都営地下鉄三田線）

S3   Ōtemachi (Tōzai Line)
大手町（東西線）

S4   Nihombashi
日本橋

S5   Edobashi
江戸橋

S6   Tokyo-Otemachi
東京大手町

S7   Nijū-bashi-mae (Chiyoda Line)
二重橋前（千代田線）

S8   Kyobashi
京橋

S9   Takara-cho
宝町

S10   Ginza-Itchome
銀座一丁目

S11   Yūraku-cho
有楽町

S12   Hibiya (TOEI Mita Line)
日比谷（都営地下鉄三田線）

S13   Hibiya (Hibiya & Chiyoda Lines)
日比谷（日比谷線と千代田線）

S14   Ginza (Marunouchi Line)
銀座（丸内線）

S15   Ginza (Hibiya Line)
銀座（日比谷線）

S16   Ginza (Ginza Line)
銀座（銀座線）

S17   Higashi-Ginza
東銀座

S18   Shimbashi (TOEI Asakusa Line)
新橋（都営地下鉄浅草線）

S19   Shimbashi (Ginza Line)
新橋（銀座線）

S20   Uchisaiwaicho
内幸町

S21   Toranomon
虎ノ門

S22   Kasumigaseki (Chiyoda Line)
霞ケ関（千代田線）

S23   Kasumigaseki (Hibiya Line)
霞ケ関（日比谷線）

S24   Kasumigaseki (Marunouchi Line)
霞ケ関（丸内線）

S25   Sakuradamon
桜田門

S26   Kokkaigijido-mae (Marunouchi Line)
国会議事堂前（丸内線）

S27   Kokkaigijido-mae (Chiyoda Line)
国会議事堂前（千代田線）

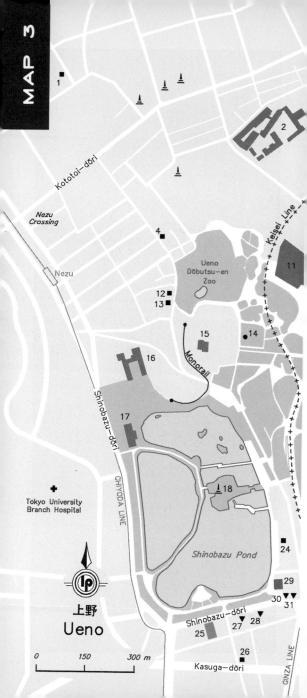

MAP 3

1

2

Kototoi-dōri

Nezu
Crossing

Nezu

4

Ueno
Dōbutsu-en
Zoo

11

Keisei Line

12
13

15

14

16

Monorail

Shinobazu-dōri

17

18

Tokyo University
Branch Hospital

24

29

30
31

上野
Ueno

Shinobazu Pond

CHIYODA LINE

GINZA LINE

25

Shinobazu-dōri
27   28

26

Kasuga-dōri

0   150   300 m

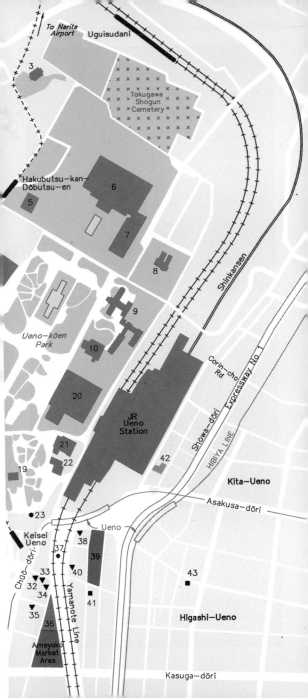

To Narita Airport

Uguisudani

3

Tokugawa Shogun Cemetery

Hakubutsu–kan–
Dōbutsu–en

5

6

7

8

9

Shinkansen

Ueno–kōen Park

10

Corin–chō Rd

20

JR Ueno Station

Shōwa–dōri

HIBIYA LINE

Expressway No 1

21

22

42

Kita–Ueno

19

Asakusa–dōri

23

Ueno

Keisei Ueno

Chūō–dōri

38

37

39

40

43

33

32

34

41

Yamanote Line

35

Higashi–Ueno

36

Ameyoko Market Area

Kasuga–dōri

MAP 3 - UENO

■ PLACES TO STAY

1 Sawanoya Ryokan
澤の屋旅館
4 Ryokan Katsutaro
旅館勝太郎
12 Hotel Ohgasio
鷗外荘
13 Suigetsu Hotel
水月ホテル
24 Kinuya Hotel
キヌヤホテル
25 Hotel Parkside
ホテルパークサイド
26 Hotel Pine Hill Ueno
ホテルパインヒル上野
41 Ueno Capsule Kimeya Hotel
上野カプセルきめやホテル
42 Hotel New Ueno
ホテルニューウエノ
43 Ueno Terminal Hotel
上野ターミナルホテル

▼ PLACES TO EAT

27 Yoshibei Restaurant
吉平
28 Menja Restaurant
麺じゃ
30 Kameya Restaurant
カめや
31 McDonald's
マクドナルド
32 Kappazushi Restaurant
かっぱ寿司
33 Spaghetti House
ママスパーゲテイ
34 Maharaja Restaurant
マハラジャ
35 Samrat Indian Restaurant
サムラート
38 Irohazushi Restaurant
いろはずし
40 Uroya Restaurant
うろや

OTHER

2 Tokyo University of Fine Arts
東京芸大
3 Kanei-ji Temple
寛永寺
5 Gallery of Hōryū-ji Treasures
法隆寺宝物館
6 Tokyo National Museum
東京国立博物館

Shinobazu Pond, Ueno (TW)

MAP 4

SHITAMACHI
WALKING TOUR

1

2

Kappabashi–dōri

Shitamachi

13 ▼

14

Kokusai–dōri

18 ■

15

19 ▼

16

17 ✉

Tawaramachi

GINZA LINE

浅草
Asakusa

0   100   200 m

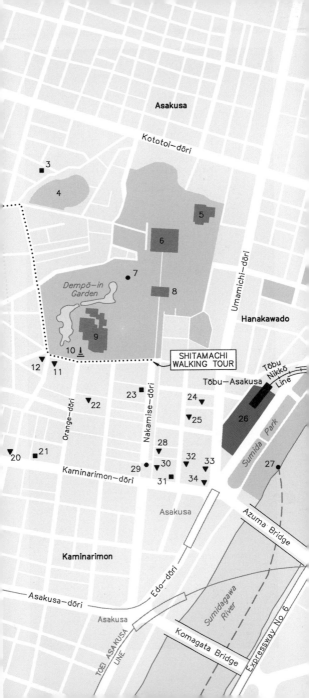

Asakusa

Kototoi-dōri

3

4

5

6

7

8

Dempō-in
Garden

Umamichi-dōri

Hanakawado

9

10

SHITAMACHI
WALKING TOUR

12 11

Tōbu-Asakusa

Tōbu
Nikkō
Line

22

23

24

26

Sumida Park

25

Orange-dōri

Nakamise-dōri

28

20   21

29   30

Kaminarimon-dōri

31

32   33

34

27

Asakusa

Azuma Bridge

Kaminarimon

Edo-dōri

Asakusa-dōri

Asakusa

Sumidagawa
River

TOEI ASAKUSA LINE

Komagata Bridge

Expressway No. 6

MAP 4 - ASAKUSA

■ PLACES TO STAY

2 Asakusa View Hotel
   浅草ビューホテル
3 Sukeroku-no-yado Sadachiyo Bekkan
   助六の宿貞千代別館
18 Hotel Pine Hill Asakusa
   ホテルパィーンヒル浅草
21 Hotel Top Asakusa
   ホテルトップ浅草
23 Ryokan Mikawaya Bekkan
   三河屋別館
31 Asakusa Plaza Hotel
   浅草プラザホテル

▼ PLACES TO EAT

11 Rāmen Restaurant
   ラーメン レストラン
12 Edokko Restaurant
   江戸ッ子
13 Big Boy Restaurant
19 Tendon Restaurant
   天丼レストラン
20 Naowariya Restaurant
   尾張屋
22 Restaurant Bell
   レストランベル
24 McDonald's
   マクドナルド
25 Tatsumiya Restaurant
   東南屋
28 Tonsu Restaurant
   とんスレストラン
30 Real Italian Gelato
   イタリィャンジェラト
32 Ramen House Asakusa
   ラーメンハウス浅草
33 Kentucky Fried Chicken
   ケンターキフライドチキン
34 Kamiya Bar
   神谷バー

   OTHER

1 Banryo-ji Temple
   万隆寺
4 Hanayashiki Amusement Park
   花やしき遊園地
5 Asakusa-jinja Shrine
   浅草神社
6 Sensō-ji Temple
   浅草寺
7 Five Storeyed Pagoda
   五重塔

Monk collecting alms, Asakusa (CT)

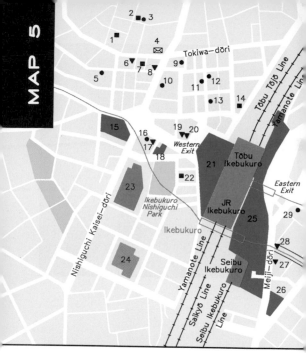

■ PLACES TO STAY

1	Kimi Ryokan	貴美旅館
2	Hotel Castel (love hotel)	ホテルカセル
5	Ikebukuro Plaza (capsule hotel)	池袋プラザ
7	Hotel Star Plaza Ikebukuro	ホテルスタープラザ池袋
14	Hotel Sun City Ikebukuro	ホテルサンシテイ池袋
22	Business Hotel Ikebukuro	ビジネスホテル池袋
24	Hotel Metropolitan	ホテルメトロポリタン
30	Hotel Sun Route Ikebukuro	ホテルサンルート池袋
36	Plaza Inn Ikebukuro	プラザイン池袋
37	Hotel Grand Business	ホテルグランドビジネス
41	Capsule Kimeya Hotel	カプセルきめやホテル
43	Prince Hotel	プリンスホテル

▼ PLACES TO EAT

6	Sushi Kazo Restaurant	寿し和
8	Fushin Restaurant	福しん
9	Toneria Izakaya	となりや
17	Pekintei Restaurant	北京亭
19	Spaghetteria Ricco Tomieno	スパゲテリヤリチイオトミェノ
20	McDonald's	マクドナルド
27	Taiyuzushi Restaurant	大漁寿司
34	Shakey's Pizza	シューキーズ

池袋
Ikebukuro

35	Komazushi Restaurant	こま寿司
38	München Beer Hall	ミュンヘン
39	Jack & Betty Club	
	OTHER	
3	Kimi Information Service	
4	Post Office	郵便局
10	Cinema Rosa	ロサ会館
11	Winners Bar	
12	Doutor Coffee	どとーる
13	Reggae Bar Kingston	
15	Marui Department Store	丸井
16	Horindo Bookshop	芳林堂書店
18	Marui Sports	丸井スポーツ館
21	Tōbu Department Store	東武百貨店
23	Tokyo Metropolitan Art Space	東京芸術劇場
25	Seibu Department Store	西武百貨店
26	Wave Record Shop	
28	Café Presto	
29	Wise Owl Bookshop	サンシャインアルパ店
31	Mitsukoshi Department Store	三越百貨店
32	Pronto Coffee	プロント
33	Bic Camera	ビックカメラ
40	Tōkyū Hands Store	東急ハンズ
42	Toyota Amlux	トヨタアムラックス

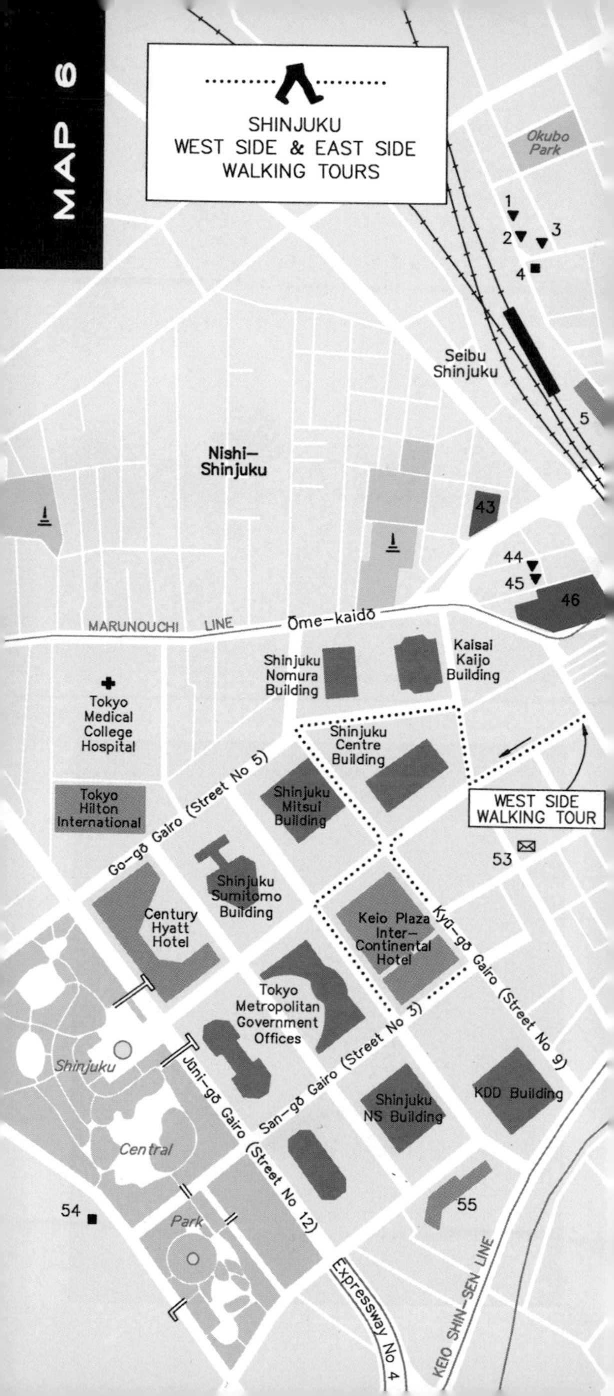

MAP 6

SHINJUKU
WEST SIDE & EAST SIDE
WALKING TOURS

Okubo Park

1
2
3
4

Seibu
Shinjuku

5

Nishi–
Shinjuku

43

44
45
46

MARUNOUCHI LINE   Ōme-kaidō

Tokyo Medical
College Hospital

Shinjuku
Nomura Building

Kaisai
Kaijo
Building

Shinjuku Centre
Building

Tokyo Hilton
International

Shinjuku
Mitsui
Building

WEST SIDE
WALKING TOUR

53

Shinjuku
Sumitomo
Building

Century
Hyatt
Hotel

Keio Plaza
Inter-
Continental
Hotel

Tokyo
Metropolitan
Government
Offices

Shinjuku

Kyū-gō Gairo (Street No 9)

Go-gō Gairo (Street No 5)

Jūni-gō Gairo

San-gō Gairo (Street No 3)

Shinjuku
NS Building

KDD Building

Central

54

Park

55

Expressway No 4

KEIO SHIN-SEN LINE

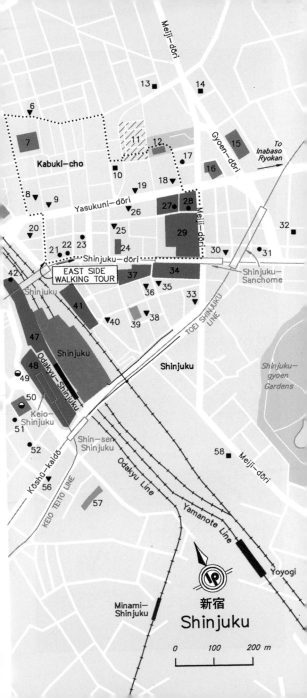

MAP 6 - SHINJUKU

■ PLACES TO STAY

4 Green Plaza Shinjuku (capsule hotel)
グリーンプラザ新宿
5 Shinjuku Prince Hotel
新宿プリンスホテル
10 Shinjuku-ku Capsule Hotel
新宿区カプセルホテル
13 Shinjuku Palace Hotel
新宿パレスホテル
14 Hotel Sun Lite
ホテルサンライト
32 Winning Inn Shinjuku (capsule hotel)
ウイニングイン新宿
39 Central Hotel
セントラルホテル
43 Star Hotel Tokyo
スターホテル東京
54 Shinjuku New City Hotel
新宿ニューシティホテル
55 Shinjuku Washington Hotel
新宿ワシントンホテル
57 Hotel Sun Route Tokyo
ホテルサンルート東京
58 Shinjuku Park Hotel
新宿パークホテル

▼ PLACES TO EAT

1 Negishi Restaurant
なぎし
2 Pekin Chinese Restaurant
ペキン中国料理
3 Tainan Taami Taiwanese Restaurant
台南担仔麺
6 Tokyo Kaisen Ichiba
東京海鮮市場
8 Ban Thai Restaurant
バンタイ
9 Tōkaien Korean Restaurant
東海苑
18 Tokyo Dai Hanten Chinese Restaurant
東京大飯店
19 Hofbräuhaus Beer Hall
ホフブロイハウス
20 Ibuki Restaurant
いぶき
25 El Borracho Mexican Restaurant
エルボラチョ
26 Irohanihoheto Restaurant
いろはにしほへと
30 Istanbul Turkish Restaurant
イスタンブル
33 Daikokuya Restaurant
大黒屋
35 Tsunahachi Restaurant
つな八
36 Funabashiya Restaurant
ふなばし屋

HARAJUKU
WALKING TOUR

Yamanote Line

Takeshita—dōri

Harajuku

Harajuku

To
Meiji—jingū
Shrine

Meiji—jingū—mae

To
Yoyogi
Park

Meiji—dōri

Shibuya River

Promenade

Kyū Shibuya River

To
Shibuya

原宿/青山
Harajuku
& Aoyama

0   100   200 m

1   Keystone Korner Tokyo
2   McDonald's
3   Octopus Army
4   Tōgō-jinja Shrine
5   Shūtarō Restaurant
6   Ryunoko Restaurant
7   Ghee Restaurant
8   AKA Reggae Bar
9   Stage Y2 Coffee Shop
10   El Pollo Loco
11   Ota Memorial Art Museum
12   Laforet
13   Suehiro Restaurant
14   Studio V Coffee Shop
15   Chicago Thrift Shop
16   Lotteria
17   Body Shop
18   Time's Café
19   Café de Rope
20   Oh God/Zest

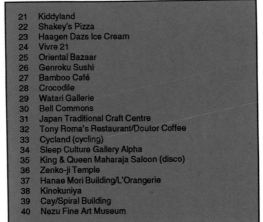

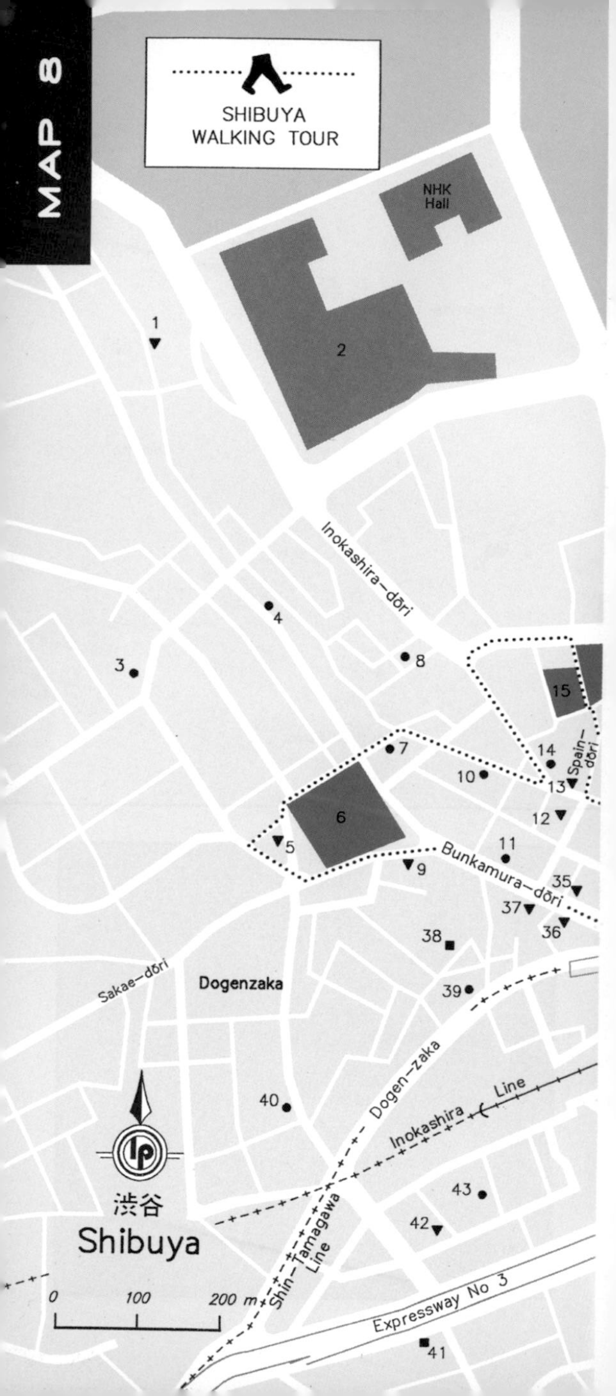
MAP 8
SHIBUYA
WALKING TOUR
NHK
Hall
1
2
Inokashira-dōri
4
8
3
15
7
14
Spain-dōri
10
13
6
12
5
11
9
Bunkamura-dōri
35
37
36
38
Sakae-dōri
Dogenzaka
39
Dogen-zaka
Line
40
Inokashira
43
渋谷
Shibuya
42
Shin-Tamagawa Line
0
100
200 m
Expressway No 3
41

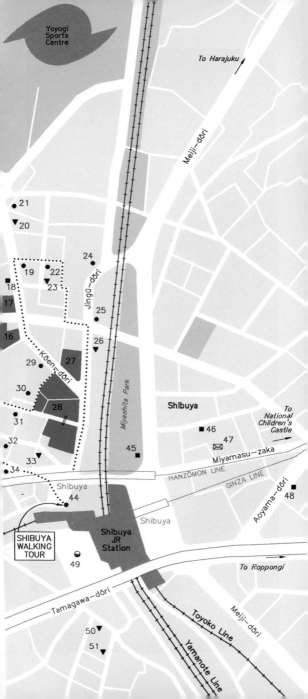

MAP 8 - SHIBUYA

■ PLACES TO STAY

18	Shibuya Tōbu Hotel
38	Hotel Ivy Flat
41	Hotel Sun Route Shibuya
45	Shibuya Tōkyū Inn
46	Shibuya Business Hotel
48	Aoyama Shanpia Hotel

▼ PLACES TO EAT

1	Sunda Restaurant
5	Chef's Gallery Restaurant
9	Bougainvillea Restaurant
12	Samrat Indian Restaurant
13	Victoria Station Restaurant
20	Siam Thai Restaurant
23	Restaurant Building
26	Suehiro Restaurant
33	Chicago Dog
35	Only Malaysia
36	Tamakyu Restaurant
37	Warung I
42	Tainan Taami
50	Ninnikuya Garlic Restaurant
51	Kantipur Restaurant

OTHER

2	NHK Broadcasting Centre & Tenji Plaza
3	Kanze Nō-gakudō Theatre
4	Tsutsuma Factory
6	Tōkyū Department Store
7	The Cave/Bistro de Hanna
8	Tower Records
10	Club Quattro
11	One Oh Nine Building
14	Octopus Army
15	Parco Part III
16	Parco Part I
17	Parco Part II
19	Tobacco & Salt Museum
21	Eggman
22	Club Circuit
24	Tepco Electric Energy Museum
25	Bic Camera
27	Marui Department Store
28	Seibu Department Store
29	Seibu Seed
30	Loft
31	Hub Bar
32	Shot Bar
34	109 Building
39	Aspen Glow
40	Dr Jeekhan's
43	La Mama
44	Hachikō Statue
47	Shibuya Post Office
49	South Exit Bus Station

Top: Wall mural, Shibuya (CT)
Bottom: Hanging out, Shibuya (CT)

MAP 9

New Otani Hotel

Akasaka Prince Hotel

Benkei Moat

Sotobori–dōri

Nagatchō

Akasaka Tōkyū Hotel

1

2

Akasaka–Mitsuke

Aoyama–dōri

HANZŌMON LINE

GINZA LINE

Hitotsugi–dōri

3

4

5

6

7

8

9

10

11

12

To Aoyama–Itchome Station

15

17

18

16

14

20

19

21

22

Akasaka

Akasaka

29

30

31

32

33

To Harajuku

lp

赤坂

Akasaka

0   100   200 m

To Roppongi

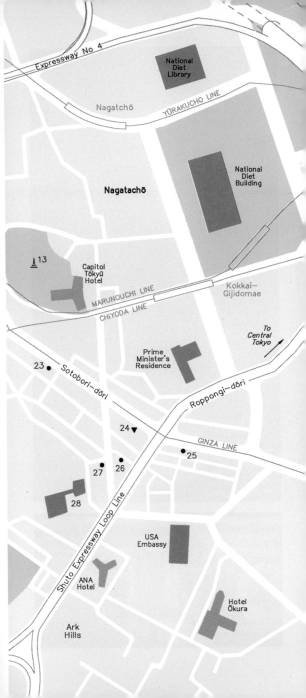

Expressway No 4

National Diet Library

Nagatchō

YŪRAKUCHO LINE

Nagatachō

National Diet Building

⊥ 13

Capitol Tōkyū Hotel

MARUNOUCHI LINE

CHIYODA LINE

Kokkai–Gijidomae

To Central Tokyo

23 ●

Sotobori–dōri

Prime Minister's Residence

Roppongi–dōri

24 ▼

GINZA LINE

● 25

27 ● ● 26

28

USA Embassy

Shuto Expressway Loop Line

ANA Hotel

Hotel Ōkura

Ark Hills

MAP 9 - AKASAKA

■ PLACES TO STAY

14 Capsule Hotel Fontaine Akasaka
31 Capsule Inn Akasaka
32 Hotel Yōkō Akasaka
33 Marroad Inn Akasaka

▼ PLACES TO EAT

3   Shakey's Pizza
4   Chapter One Restaurant
5   Subway Sandwiches
7   Mughal Restaurant
8   Tate Vin Restaurant
9   Pizzeria Marumo
10 Trattoria Marumo
11 Moti Indian Restaurant
12 Tokyo Joe's
15 Suehiro Restaurant
17 Sushi-sei Restaurant
21 Kentucky Fried Chicken
22 Moti Restaurant
24 Tony Roma's
29 Aozai Restaurant
30 Yakitori Luis

OTHER

1   Suntory Museum of Art
2   Tōkyū Plaza
6   Rondo Club
13 Hie-jinja Shrine
16 Victoria Station
18 Goose Bar
19 Anna Miller's
20 Henry Africa
23 Akasaka Sakuradō (dolls)
25 Inachu Lacquerware
26 Rock n' Roll Alba
27 Doutor Coffee
28 Laforet Museum/Akasaka Twin Tower

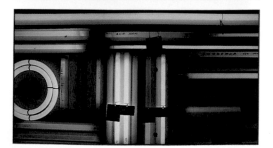

Top: Sensō-ji Temple, Akasaka (CT)
Bottom: Square Building, Roppongi (CT)
Opposite: Lighting store, Akihabara (RI'A)

MAP 10

To Akasaka &
Asia Centre of Japan

Gaien–higashi–dōri

Roppongi

Expressway No 3

Roppongi

六本木
Roppongi

0   50   100 m

To Pentax Forum

OTHER

3   Hotel Ibis
5   Victoria Station
6   Haiyū-za Building
8   Suntory Shot Bar
10 Pronto Coffee Shop
11 Square Building (Birdland & Java Jive Nightclubs)
15 Motown House
17 Lexington Queen Disco
18 Maggie's Revenge
19 Gaijin Zone
21 Charleston Bar
25 Jack & Betty Club
26 Pips Disco
28 Gas Panic
29 Déjà Vu Bar
30 Bogey's Bar
31 Henry Africa Bar
33 Zipang
34 Roy Building
39 Kento's Oldies but Goodies
40 Droopy Drawers
44 Serendip Bookshop
46 Meidiya International Supermarket
48 Wave Building

MAP 11

Lines and symbol colors

GINZA LINE
MARUNOUCHI LINE
HIBIYA LINE

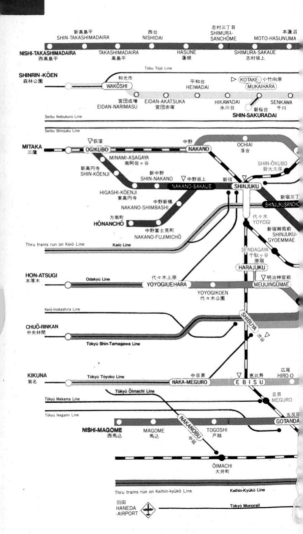

新高島平 SHIN-TAKASHIMADAIRA
西台 NISHIDAI
志村三丁目 SHIMURA-SANCHŌME
本蓮沼 MOTO-HASUNUMA

NISHI-TAKASHIMADAIRA 西高島平
TAKASHIMADAIRA 高島平
HASUNE 蓮根
SHIMURA-SAKAUE 志村坂上

SHINRIN-KŌEN 森林公園

Tobu Tōjō Line

和光市 WAKŌSHI
平和台 HEIWADAI
▷ (KOTAKE-)小竹向原 (MUKAIHARA)

宮団成増 EIDAN-NARIMASU
EIDAN-AKATSUKA 宮団赤塚
HIKAWADAI 永川台
新桜台 SENKAWA 千川

Seibu Ikebukuro Line

SHIN-SAKURADAI

Seibu Shinjuku Line

MITAKA 三鷹
▽荻窪 OGIKUBO
中野 NAKANO
OCHIAI 落合

MINAMI-ASAGAYA 南阿佐谷
SHIN-ŌKUBO 新大久保

新高円寺 SHIN-KŌENJI
新中野 SHIN-NAKANO ▽中野坂上
新宿 SHINJUKU

NAKANO-SAKAUE

HIGASHI-KŌENJI 東高円寺
新宿三丁目 SHINJUKUSANCHŌME

NAKANO-SHIMBASHI 中野新橋

方南町 HŌNANCHŌ
中野富士見町 NAKANO-FUJIMICHŌ
代々木 YOYOGI
新宿御苑前 SHINJUKU-GYOEMMAE

Thru trains run on Keiō Line
Keiō Line

SENDAGAYA 千駄谷
原宿 HARAJUKU

HON-ATSUGI 本厚木
Odakyū Line
代々木上原 YOYOGIUEHARA
明治神宮前 MEIJIINGŪMAE

YOYOGIKOEN 代々木公園

Keiō-Inokashira Line

CHUŌ-RINKAN 中央林間
SHIBUYA 渋谷

Tōkyū Shin-Tamagawa Line

KIKUNA 菊名
Tōkyū Tōyoko Line
中目黒 NAKA-MEGURO
広尾 HIRO-O
▽恵比寿 EBISU

Tōkyū Ōimachi Line
目黒 MEGURO

Tōkyū Mekama Line

Tōkyū Ikegami Line
五反田 GOTANDA

NISHI-MAGOME 西馬込
MAGOME 馬込
NAKANOBU 中延
TOGOSHI 戸越

ŌIMACHI 大井町

Thru trains run on Keihin-kyūkō Line
Keihin-Kyūkō Line

羽田 HANEDA-AIRPORT
Tōkyō Monorail